# LIZZIE BORDEN
## The Legend,
## The Truth,
## The Final Chapter

# LIZZIE BORDEN

*The Legend,*
*The Truth,*
*The Final Chapter*

Arnold R. Brown

Rutledge Hill Press
*Nashville, Tennessee*

*For Robert W. Brown (1918–1989)*
*We miss you, Bob*

Unless noted otherwise, photographs are courtesy of the Fall River Historical Society, Fall River, Massachusetts.

Published in Nashville, Tennessee, by Rutledge Hill Press, 513 Third Avenue South, Nashville, Tennessee 37210

Typography by Bailey Typography, Inc., Nashville, Tennessee.

Library of Congress Cataloging-in-Publication Data

Brown, Arnold R., 1925-
    Lizzie Borden : the legend, the truth, the final chapter / Arnold
R. Brown.
        p.    cm.
    Includes bibliographical references and index.
    ISBN 1-55853-099-1
    1. Murder—Massachusetts—Fall River—Case studies.  2. Borden,
Lizzie, 1860-1927.   I. Title.
HV6534.A2B673   1991
364.1'523'092—dc20
    [B]                                                                91-19250
                                                                            CIP
I. Title.

Printed in the United States of America
1 2 3 4 5 6 7 8 — 97 95 94 93 92 91

# Contents

# *Acknowledgments*

There were no witnesses to the Borden murders; the murderer is dead; there is no one alive who can witness to what did happen or what might have happened. Many people, each in his or her season, recorded their testimony, their observations, their thoughts, their denials or their suspicions. These are preserved for us without any possibility of alteration or embellishment. Finding them demands extensive research—far beyond the capacity or the capability of one person working alone. The determination of what factually happened is hidden in recorded history. This account is based on the reported facts. The following persons or institutions provided pages.

Special acknowledgment is reserved for Mrs. Florence Cook Brigham, Curator Emeritus of the Fall River Historical Society Museum. Mrs. Brigham answered the multitude of questions asked of her with provable, factual answers. She offered no subjective suggestions or opinions, and she, of the world's population, is the most qualified expert in both the "facts" and "maybes" of the Borden murders. Through the combined efforts of Mrs. Brigham and Curator Michael Martins, I was able to determine facts in the case that make a mockery of the legend.

The overwhelming majority of newspaper quotations and articles referenced in this account were gathered from the files of the Fall River Public Library. Anne-Marie Klegraefe, of their Information Services, provided outstanding assistance and dug longer, deeper, and more thoroughly than the accepted standards required by her profession. She was assisted in her splendid effort by Midge Cornell and Paula Costa.

All requests made of Charles S. Longley, Curator of Micro-texts and Newspapers, and Jamie McClone, Staff officer for Special Projects, of the Boston Public Library, were filled promptly and professionally. Between them, they found and provided all that was asked of them. Their suggestions and added materials were especially helpful.

Historically, "original" material in the Borden case has, with amazing ease, vanished from secured archives and locked files. Mary Anne McGuire of the New Bedford Free Public Library went far afield to secure privately held copies of material long gone from their shelves. Her efforts are appreciated.

Priceless material not previously referenced was found in both the Taunton (Massachusetts) Public Library and the Providence (Rhode Island) Public Library. Each is thanked for its very existence.

Requests for information in city or state public records met with mixed results. Those who were helpful are:

Charlotte L. Kitchen, Assistant City Clerk, who supervised the extensive file search conducted in Fall River's Vital Statistics Department;

Althea May Manchester, Town Clerk, Westport, Massachusetts;

Al Florence, Administrative Assistant, Bristol County Registry of Deeds;

Gary C. Phillips, Director of Program Evaluation and Development, Commonwealth of Massachusetts, Department of Mental Health; and

The Honorable Robert L. Steadman, Chief Justice, Commonwealth of Massachusetts, Superior Court.

Researchers in the greater Fall River area who accepted assignments, dug tenaciously, and offered contributions are: Christine Cabral of Westport, Mary Nasser Place of North Dartmouth, Norma Bliss Orsi and the late Dr. Jordan D. Fiore of Taunton, Jean Judge and Bernie Sullivan of the Fall River *Herald-News*, Sandra Ward of the New Bedford *Standard-Times*, and Richard P. Gulla of The Boston *Globe*.

Harriet D. Erwin of East Taunton was my first researcher. Her independent determination of facts that both reinforced and confirmed those written ten years before by Henry Hawthorne was the genesis of the fact-finding this book demanded. Without knowing the reason for my quest, she did a masterful job of filling in blank spaces that led to discovery.

Mrs. Marion Sherman of Westport, Massachusetts, was a special aide and friend. She dug in as enthusiastically and as earnestly as a teenager and she added a generous share of both insight and support. In September of 1990, at the age of ninety-five, she was promoted to Glory. She is remembered.

Friends and family contributed untold encouragement and direction. Thank you, Barbara and Bob, Sherri and Ken, Paula, Dottie and Gordon. My long-suffering wife, Ann, and my friend Robert L. Collins (who physically suffered through the ordeal but still speaks to me), earned, deserve, and have my undying gratitude.

*Miss Lizzie Borden*

# Introduction

Between nine and eleven o'clock on the morning of Thursday, August 4, 1892, in Fall River, Massachusetts, Andrew Jackson Borden, age seventy, and Abby Durfee Borden, age sixty-five, second wife of Andrew, were murdered, both struck about the head, neck, and shoulders with multiple hatchet blows. The when, the where, and the how of this carnage are general knowledge; the by whom and the why have, for nearly a century, been relegated to subjective speculation and legend. This account is the objective, definitive answer to the two unanswered questions of who and why.

Miss Lizzie Andrew Borden, age thirty-two, was Andrew Borden's younger surviving daughter. An inquest was held August 9–11, 1892, and on August 12, Lizzie was arrested for the murder of Andrew, arraigned, and ordered held in the county jail in Taunton, Massachusetts. At a preliminary hearing held August 25–September 1, 1892, it was decided that there was "probable cause" and that Lizzie should be bound over to the grand jury. A grand jury hearing was held November 15 through December 1, and on December 2 Lizzie Andrew Borden was indicted on three counts of murder: first, for the murder of Abby Borden; second, for the murder of Andrew Borden; and third, in a most unusual action, for the murders of both Abby and Andrew Borden. A trial was held in New Bedford, Massachusetts, from June 5 to 20, 1893. After only a few minutes of deliberation, the jury found Lizzie not guilty on all charges.

Lizzie lived, she stood trial for the double murder, and she died a natural death. She is known only in the legend that she initiated and that grew and expanded until it ousted truth.

The legend was conceived the instant the Borden murders were made public, and it grew insidiously strong, nurtured by the corruption of absolute power—the complete corruption of the duly elected and appointed public officials.

Lizzie Borden, the legend, is forever immortalized in the child's verse that conveys inaccurate information and has been teaching its message through the decades.

<blockquote>Lizzie Borden took an axe</blockquote>

The murder weapon was *not* an axe; it was a simple hatchet.

<blockquote>And gave her mother forty whacks.</blockquote>

The woman murdered was *not* Lizzie's mother; she was her stepmother. The number of "whacks" delivered was *not* forty; it was half that.

<blockquote>And when she saw what she had done,</blockquote>

The interval between the two murders was estimated as an hour and a half.

<blockquote>She gave her father forty-one.</blockquote>

The man murdered was indeed Lizzie's father, but he was *not* whacked forty-one times; it was ten.

In the almost 100 years since the deaths of Abby and Andrew Borden, no one other than Lizzie has ever been charged with the crime. And yet Lizzie was officially declared without guilt. The popular verse summarizes what is "common knowledge": Lizzie murdered Abby and Andrew Borden; she paid off her maid, her doctor, and the police; and her trial was fixed. Everyone "knew" she was guilty.

But if common knowledge is wrong and Lizzie really was innocent, who was guilty? Many murderers have been suggested, but the majority of experts who know the crime have insisted, without reservation and in spite of the superior court verdict to the contrary, that Lizzie, and she alone, murdered her stepmother and her father. They cite legendary "facts" as proof, forgetting that the legend has two branches: one may prove she did it; the other, just as effectively, proves she did not.

On the day Miss Lizzie was arraigned, those in charge closed the investigation into the crime, and it remained closed through the months of her hearings and her trials. The final trial cleared her. The case was never reopened.

In what follows, you have the true, factual report of an historic event—the happenings, the actions, the circumstances, and the facts known to only a select few and voiced by no one until now. This is the factual story of the murders of Andrew J. Borden and his wife Abby. Entwined in this story is the legend of Lizzie Borden.

Like Lizzie, I was born and bred in Fall River. She died there eight days before my second birthday, and the day she died, a colossal and heartfelt collective sigh of relief arose from the city. As a teenager, I "knew" lots of things about Lizzie Borden. I "knew" she was guilty. No one cared that she had not been convicted. She did it; she was lucky; she had money; and she got away with it. And that, dear friends, was that!

After a lifetime in a job that took me all over the world, I retired, along with millions before and after me, to Florida. One day, in a casual conversation with Lewis Peterson, another displaced native of Fall River, the subject of Lizzie Borden surfaced. For a number of years, Pete had been part of the constabulary of Old Cape Cod and he has many a fascinating yarn to spin about Massachusetts politics, payoffs, and unsolved crimes. When Lizzie's name came up, just after his commentary on the Chappaquiddick Bridge incident, he smiled and said, "*That* one is no mystery either. My father-in-law knew the killer."

"You mean Lizzie?" I asked, smartly.

"Hell, no. I mean the guy who killed them!" A positively knowing smile accompanied his answer.

The story he then told me was unquestionably fascinating. It was totally beyond belief, of course, to someone as steeped in the legend as I was, but nonetheless fascinating. Pete explained that when his father-in-law, Henry Hawthorne, was eighty-nine years old in 1978, he knew death was near. Henry had a story to tell, and he wrote down what he wanted to say. Pete promised me a look at what Henry had written.

When the materials arrived, my first reading invoked smiles. What I had was a collection of disconnected ramblings with events choreographed backwards, with simple timing wrong, and with major characters totally ignored or, at best, moved from their traditional locations.

But there was something compelling in what Henry Hawthorne wrote, something that focused more sharply with each reading. Henry introduced names never before mentioned, people with motivations that were new and believable, motives that offered some semblance of sense to what has always been a senseless crime, and finally a motive that surviving members of the family would generate all necessary pressures to keep hidden.

If what Henry Hawthorne offered as fact was, indeed, truth, it should stand up to rigorous probing, checking, and historical verification. My investigation into his claims produced this account.

I spent two *full* years researching and checking the facts and records surrounding the legend of Lizzie Borden and the story told by Henry Hawthorne. I cannot disprove him. Moreover, his account fits the facts of the case better than any other theory. In the process I found out how thoroughly the Lizzie Borden legal proceedings were manipulated. Although she was not guilty of the murders, the judicial system of Massachusetts prostituted itself to make sure she was declared not guilty. I was also able to use valuable primary source material unavailable to earlier students of the case, which, if anything, contributed to a verification of Henry Hawthorne's account.

So who killed Andrew and Abby Borden? It was no one who has been mentioned in any of the many studies into the legend surrounding the murders—not Lizzie's sister Emma, not Uncle John Morse, not the maid Bridget, not Lizzie's made-up boyfriend, not Dr. Seabury Bowen, and certainly not Lizzie herself. It was someone whose identity was kept secret by the legend. The purpose of the legend created by Lizzie and surviving members of the Borden family was to hide the murderer's identity. The purpose of Lizzie's allowing herself to be charged with murder and then going to elaborate lengths and tremendous cost to prove that she did not kill Andrew and Abby Borden was to hide the murderer's identity.

Her plan was successful—until by a remarkable coincidence, it was discovered by Henry Hawthorne's mother-in-law.

Here, then, is the story of Lizzie Borden—the legend and the truth, the final chapter in the story of who killed Andrew and Abby Borden.

# Overture

# Summer 1911

As difficult as it was to admit, Ellan Eagan realized she was getting old. Times were changing, and anytime she looked at her daughter and listened to the things the girl said—right out loud in front of anybody—she knew that the world she had known when she was young no longer existed.

Her daughter, Little Mary, was already at marrying age, and this mere slip of a lass was talking about who should be elected president of the United States and saying that women should be able to vote just like men. It was ridiculous. That was men's business, but Little Mary was acting like it was hers.

Ellan could remember herself at her daughter's age, when the whole world was rolling along at a pace she found comfortable. Life was different now. Electricity was in almost every home, and if Mr. Lincoln could take credit for freeing the slaves, then Mr. Edison should get credit for freeing the housewife. Why, not having oil lamps to clean and trim and keep filled was enough to make her thankful. Every day she heard talk about new things that electricity would soon be doing.

Horseless carriages (most people called them automobiles, although she never understood why) were no longer rare, and just a week ago there was an airplane at the state fair in Providence. It flew over to Fall River and up and down above the Taunton River. She wouldn't even try to guess how it stayed up in the air.

Fall River had changed along with the times. Just this

19

week the city sponsored a Cotton Centennial Celebration that was more grand than anything she had ever seen. Cotton was still the boss in Fall River, even if it wasn't quite king any more. She missed the old times when the cotton mills were the only thing that mattered, and she found herself thinking about those days much too often lately.

"Old age," she chuckled to herself.

Ellan's whole family had come to the parade together. Even Little Mary's beau—Henry Hawthorne—was there. It was all so grand until she saw the horsecars, two of them, like those that had disappeared from the streets twenty years earlier when, almost overnight, the electric streetcars replaced them. The instant she saw the first horsecar, she shivered with the strangest chill. Then, as they passed where she was standing, suddenly Ellan gave a small cry of alarm, and—for only the second time in her life that she could remember—she fainted.

When she regained consciousness, she tried to convince her family that nothing was wrong. In fact, nothing was, at least nothing she could explain. It had been years since she had thought about her "devil," not that she didn't talk about the day of the Borden murders. Why, hardly a week went by without someone talking about it.

That shameless younger daughter Lizzie (who most folks claimed must have done the killing) flaunted herself about the city as if she owned it (some of the same folks claimed she *did*!). Over and over again, Ellan had volunteered her story about seeing the maid outside the house washing the windows, being sick in Dr. Kelly's yard, talking with the police, receiving the nice letter saying she might be called as a trial witness (she had given special thanks to the Virgin when she was not called), and having the newspaper article that had her name in it.

Ellan had been surprised at her reactions when the horses passed by in the parade. It was the odor that had stunned her, and when the first horsecar passed, she had had an imaginary glimpse of the man in the long coat, an imagined stare into his burning eyes, and a lingering, chilling whiff of that forgotten smell—whatever it was—that she had so successfully banished from her senses all those many years. She knew what horses smelled like, and this odor was nothing related to any of the hundreds of horses with which she had had contact. She was honestly frightened.

Something she wanted no part of was haunting her.

# Thursday, August 4, 1892

I t was hot, and Ellan Eagen was sweating. "Ladies don't sweat," she admonished herself, as her mother had admonished her so many, many times. "Ladies don't do lots of things," she mused, "especially if it's pleasurable, takes time from the chores, or costs money!"

She was feeling sorry for herself this morning. If it wasn't six things over here that needed doing, it was half a dozen things over there. "Sometimes I could just . . . just . . . spit! There, I said it!" She felt better.

Her stride was firm and determined. There was no time to mince along as a lady should. Get downstreet, buy what she needed, get back to fix dinner, then wade into the ironing. "Spit, spit, spit!"

Even Second Street looked shabby this morning. No doubt about it, the neighborhood was going downhill. She laughed at her joke because Second Street was a steep downgrade in this stretch, all the way to City Hall. *Must be why they say going downstreet instead of going downtown*, she thought, then realized she was smiling at her little joke and allowed a tiny giggle to escape. She felt her face redden and quickly looked around to see if anyone had caught her embarrassing show of silliness. *I'm acting like a greenhorn washerwoman on payday*, she thought. Then her eyes darted into the yard between two houses, and she saw something that made her gasp and miss a step.

"Speak of the Devil and he'll appear," she said as she remembered the old caution. Quickly she crossed herself and kissed her thumb. She was passing the Borden house, and they, indeed, had a greenhorn maid who, at that very moment, was not more than twenty feet away. "Hope she *did* see me!" Ellan whispered to herself as she continued on her way. "Imagine being so dumb as to be outside washing windows in this heat. Landagoshen!"

*It must be nice being the Bordens*, Ellan thought. *Live in a nice home, more money than anybody could ever count, a servant girl to do all the real work, go to the ocean and breathe air without all this soot in it. It must be real, real nice. I'll bet them girls don't have to hurry to get to Sargent's before them Portuguese buy up all the bargains!*

Between Frenchmen and Portuguese, Ellan couldn't tell which was worse. No one could understand anything they said, but who would possibly want to anyhow? Imagine if someday one of her children brought one of them in the house. "Blessed Mary," she begged in quiet supplication, "please don't you ever let nothin' like that ever happen!"

At Sargent's Ellan found exactly what she wanted in yard goods, and the bolt had enough on it for two dresses! Buying the whole bolt was certainly an extravagance that would pinch for the rest of the month, but Mr. Sargent himself told her she could have the whole bolt for just seven cents a yard rather than the eight cents it was marked. Sometimes you just had to stand up and do things like make believe you were a Borden instead of an Eagan! She was proud of herself, even though she was sure her mother would not have approved.

The only thing wrong with going down Second Street was having to go up it on the way home. Some folks took the horse car on Main Street for the second half of the trip, but that cost a nickel and you could buy a good loaf of baker's bread for a nickel, even though no self-respecting housewife would pay a nickel for a loaf of bread. That would be a display of laziness. Those who could afford the nickel generally could afford a maid or, at the very least, a girl to come in and do things like baking. It was not considered laziness if you could afford to pay someone else to do your work. That was status.

The nickel didn't matter to Ellan. She would have walked even if she had a hundred nickels. The horse cars were being replaced by "electrics," and no power on earth could make her ride in one of them. "Enough noise for ten steam tractors, all clankin' and squallin'-like and sparks flyin' over the top and sometimes from underneath, and the smell of what some folks said was what electricity smelled like. No thank you! Those electrics are right out of hell." And Ellan would have no part of them.

As she headed home, Ellan realized it was hotter than she remembered it, but she didn't care. She was lightheaded and pleased with herself, and the world was almost beautiful again. Although it was too hot to hurry, she did step a bit quicker, for she felt kind of sick.

As she neared the Borden House on her way up the hill, she wondered if that silly girl was still washing the windows. Never in a million years would she even think about washing windows in this hot weather! She had thought about a green-horn maid on her way downstreet, and one had appeared. She knew the maid would appear again because her mother had taught her to be careful about how she spoke about people because once you spoke of the Devil, he was sure to appear.

No, the maid was not in sight, but Ellan saw a man in the Borden yard, just standing there. She started to do the ladylike thing and avert her eyes when, for the first time in her life, she found herself staring at a stranger. There was something about this man that was wrong! He was about halfway between the gate and the back stoop, and he was facing her. He turned as if to go back. His left side and his back were all that she could see now. His clothes were dirty and coarse, but what had caught her eye was that he was wearing an overcoat—and on one of the hottest days of the year! At first Ellan thought his coat was burlap, then she realized he had a burlap bag over his shoulder and partially tucked under his arm. The overcoat, she could see, was a long duster-type like nothing she had ever seen. She felt funny, sort of scared. He stopped and turned his face toward her. His eyes looked into hers.

She sucked in her breath, gasping. Feeling faint, she shivered and almost cried out in terror. *Speak of the Devil and he will appear* roared in her ears. *I am seeing the Devil!*

When he took a step toward her, she ran. She had to get away, and somehow she did, feeling the fire from his eyes burning right through her. Even though she was confused and filled with terror, she knew something else was wrong, too. As she sped away, her senses finally told her what it was. It was his odor—one that she had never smelled before. It was not sour, not sweet, not a manure smell, not sweat . . . not anything she could even imagine! Intent on getting help, she ducked into the first yard she came to, gasping and sobbing. Then she was sick.

When her wits returned, Ellan was on the ground under a shade-giving elm tree on cool, comforting grass. She wasn't sure whether she had fainted, but she realized she must have done so. Even if she had fainted, she had no idea how long she had been there.

Suddenly she remembered what had frightened her and looked all around. There was nothing but the usual traffic. There was no man in a long overcoat, no "devil," and no one was paying the slightest attention to her.

Her fright vanished as quickly as it had come. Instead, she felt outrage directed inward. She told herself she had acted like a big, silly goose. "Mother," she whispered to the heavens, "I think you was a mean old thing to tell me such a scary thing."

Looking around again, she saw nothing, gathered her packages together, and hugged her bargain bolt of cloth close to be sure everything was real. Looking up and down the street one more time, she headed home with a firm, determined stride. She had dinner to prepare and ironing to do, and she had no time for the vapors. She had heard the clock at city hall chiming. *It must be getting after eleven o'clock,* she thought.

She was late.

# Part One

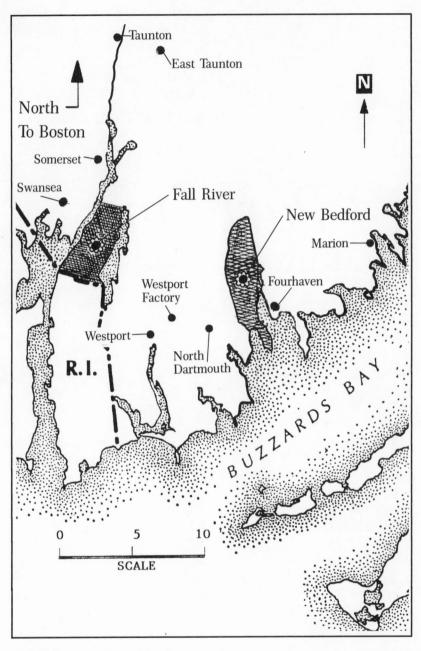

Taunton

East Taunton

North
To Boston

Somerset

Swansea

Fall River

New Bedford

Marion

Westport
Factory

Fourhaven

Westport

North
Dartmouth

R.I.

BUZZARDS BAY

0          5          10

SCALE

*Fall River and surrounding area*

# *Chapter 1*

F all River, Massachusetts, fifty miles south of Boston, is situated on Mount Hope Bay, a near neighbor to Rhode Island. Flowing into the bay and important to the life of the city is the Taunton River. Fall River was settled in 1656 on a site blessed with a sheltered deep-water harbor with an open access to the sea. In their wild cascade to the sea, the pure water streams of Fall River provided power that was harnessed to turn wheels.

The Quequechan River was of particular importance in the early history of Fall River since it drops 125 feet in less than half a mile. Today it is relegated to flowing through conduits beneath the city. Its Pocasset Indian name means "swift" or "falling water." Fall River was first called Pocasset, later Troy; in the early 1800s it was given its present name in honor of the Quequechan.

At one time Fall River was one of the leading textile-manufacturing cities in the United States, and it created wealth for those who practiced the protestant ethic and were sanctified with good-old-Yankee acumen. Not all the early families of the area embraced land and industry. Some looked to the sea for their fortunes, and shipbuilding and fishing industries grew up there. The shipowners of New England and Fall River developed a three-corner trade route between New England, Africa, and the southern states. New England-manufactured rum was carried to Africa to exchange with the native chiefs for their spoils of war: African men and women. These were transported as cargo to the southern United States to exchange for molasses and, on a space-available basis, cotton. The molasses brought to New England could be distilled into the rum necessary for the first run of the triangle. Cotton was also necessary for textile manufacturing.

Bordens were among the earliest settlers of Fall River. A member of the Borden clan was present with the group that joined Anne Hutchinson when she was ousted from the Massachusetts Bay Colony for heresy in the early 1600s. By the early 1700s, third generation Bordens owned everything on both sides of the Taunton River in the Fall River area. All that was done to acquire this land was unquestionably legal because, by royal decree, the Indian claim of eminent domain was simply not valid. Thus the Borden forebears were given all "legal" rights of ownership.

Mother England allowed farming and lumbering in Massachusetts, but not manufacturing because the primary purpose of the colonies was to supply cheap raw materials to the established, home-based industries. This system produced little profit and even less promise for a prosperous future for the colonists, and so they revolted against it. Not the least of these rebels were the Bordens.

Just above the eastern shore of the estuary that was the Taunton River, and on the banks of the Quequechan River a fifth generation Borden built a home, a sawmill, and a gristmill. History credits this Borden with being among the first in the area to use the river's rapidly falling waters to provide power.

In the Battle of Fall River, a redcoat landing party, supported by naval cannon, invaded the city in 1778. It came ashore close to the mouth of the Quequechan and fought its way up the hill to what is now City Hall Square, where it was stopped by a renegade group of Tories under the leadership of Colonel Joseph Durfee. As the thoroughly defeated invaders made their cowardly, hasty retreat back to their ships (or as His Majesty's victorious troops had completely razed and laid waste everything in the immediate area and withdrew to other battle areas of more importance, depending on which country's history books you read), they burned the Borden mills and home and left behind two dead and several wounded. The Battle of Fall River did not rank with Bunker

Hill, but it is still considered an important event in Fall River's history.

Phoenixlike, the Durfees and later the Bordens became mill owners once again. Colonel Durfee is credited with the first successful local venture into textiles. The Borden fortune in both cash and land came early, developed and maintained by "nerve, grit, and cheek," which were evidently Borden characteristics. These characteristics were the subject of a letter written by one member of the Borden clan to another after watching Lizzie's deportment during the ordeal. On August 17, 1892, on a slow news day between the initial inquest into the murder of Andrew and Abbey Borden and the preliminary hearing of Lizzie Borden, the Fall River *Daily Globe* reprinted the letter:

> By blood! If she [Lizzie] did it, the old Borden nerve, grit and cheek are not degenerated.
>
> No woman except a Borden could have done it, and yet it seems impossible that a woman could do it.
>
> I have watched her indomitable nerve and bearing with admiration, and I recalled that Aunt Nannie Borden, who ran out when the bullets were flying and kicked a wounded British redcoat and then tore up her skirts for wadding; and I remember that my poor old grandmother, when a constable seized her broadcloth cloak for grandfather's rum bill, when he read his warrant and said: "I seize this cloak," she took him by the throat and said: "God! and I seize you."
>
> And he was glad to drop the cloak and git.
>
> So if this girl has done this thing it is the old Borden nerve and grit that has carried her through, and I predict that she will not wilt. No, by blood!

Immigrant workers provided the labor for the textile mills and other industry in Fall River. Commerce and industry flourished, and life was good—at least for those in charge. The minimum workday was fourteen hours (just ten on Saturday), and the minimum hiring age was seven (if the child was trainable). The various ethnic groups and nationalities in Fall River hated each other, and those who owned the industry perpetuated that natural hatred because it ensured competition for cheap labor. French Canadians (19 percent of the population) settled in the east end of the city while the Portuguese (3 percent) were in the south end. There was no west side to the city because of the Taunton River and the mills.

The north side of the city was the most important because it was the site of *The Hill.* The north end of the city was divided into the portion below The Hill and The Hill proper. The Hill was actually the uppermost reaches of a mesalike bluff that rose, first gradually and then rapidly, from the east bank of the Taunton River. In the nineteenth century, The Hill was as close to a walled city within Fall River as a democracy would allow. The "peasants" were allowed to walk through the area, but tacit agreement said who could live there and, perhaps of more importance, just *where* an approved member could locate according to his rank in relation to the hierarchy who were already there.

By 1892 the autocratic system that had prevailed in Fall River was beginning to distintegrate. This disintegration began slowly, but gained speed through the turn of the century, pausing for World War I just long enough to give the impression that the autocracy had some life yet to it, before being dashed to ashes by the Great Depression. Today the city is comparatively classless.

Indirectly, this distintegration of The Hill was fostered by the Roman Catholic Church. In the early nineteenth century, Irish immigrants began to arrive in New England. All who came found relatively well-paying jobs, and all managed to find someone who could write back home to report this magnificent news. Slight embellishments were allowed. Because of the wildfire growth at the time, when newcomers arrived, lured by the glowing reports they had read in letters, the letters read seemed to have been understated. The New World offered the good life and a chance for everything lacking at home. By the 1840s there was hardly a family in Ireland without a member in New England. Then the Potato Famine hit, and a true flight for life began from Ireland.

Of all the groups arriving in Massachusetts, the Irish were most deeply immersed in the Roman Catholic Church and the ones most readily drawn to its priesthood. This group was the least feared by The Hill because each household had one or more trusted Maggie, Bridget, or Birdie in the kitchen, and they were such lovely, harmless girls. The Hill forgot that these girls had brothers who could become fathers, monsignors, bishops, and even cardinals. In Rome the Church was Italian; in Massachusetts it was Irish. The male Irish who did not choose the Church became saloon keepers, and their sons became politicians. *This* led to The Hill's downfall.

One of the basic tenets of the Church was to obey the priest. If what God's ambassador said to do was right and you did it, you were blessed; but if what he said was wrong and you did it, that was his worry. You would still be blessed because you did what he said. When election time rolled around, members of the Roman Catholic Church voted their convictions exactly as they were told to vote them, for they were told what their convictions should be. They formed, shaped, and soon assumed control of a most colorful political coalition.

Too late for a counteroffensive, The Hill found it had a problem. The newly elected officials passed legislation which, if enforced, would raise costs and lower profits. The new laws attempted to limit the number of hours a worker under ten could work; they forced costly safety measures; and—least acceptable of all to those on The Hill—they gave labor the right to redress grievances before a committee that, although it had undefined powers of correction, could make waves. In addition, these new local governments found a need to raise revenue for public projects (like roads, sewers, and water and school systems), and they discovered that The Hill (and other similar locations in Massachusetts) had been virtually tax-exempt. Taxation hit with a vengeance.

Of economic necessity, some mill owners began looking for greener pastures. The Carolinas and the rest of the South offered cheap labor and lower transportation costs for the raw material. Eventually the entire textile industry moved south.

Except for The Hill itself, the English (11 percent of the population) and the Irish (7 percent) were allowed their choice of what was left in Fall River. The English were most welcome in an imaginary buffer zone around The Hill. Most of them settled there.

Negroes were not unwelcome in Fall River. "Everyone

knew" they were not suited to indoor mill jobs. The city is proud of its part as a busy station in the underground railroad prior to and during the Civil War. Overnight shelter was given freely to fleeing slaves on their journey north to Canada. However, the eventually emancipated slaves were not encouraged to settle in the city.

In 1892 Fall River had three newspapers (five, actually, but one was printed in French and another in Portuguese). The *News* and the *Herald* both served The Hill and were dedicated to reporting stock prices, social events, and little else. They were both owned by a publishing company that was partially owned by Frank Almy, who was one of the pallbearers at the Bordens' funeral and who had been Andrew Borden's partner years earlier in an undertaking business. Both these papers were understandably friendly to Lizzie.

The interesting newspaper of the time was the Fall River *Daily Globe*. The antithesis of the other two in every regard, it was the only morning paper, and its management was staunchly Democrat, advocating ambitious and progressive policies. The fundamental aim of the *Globe* was to increase its already respectable circulation by any means available, respectable or otherwise. Lizzie's attorneys labeled this newspaper "sensational" and ignored anything it published with which they did not agree. Neither the *News* nor the *Herald* reported any of the testimony because they would not touch the Borden case in anything approaching a straightforward manner after Miss Lizzie—one of their own—had been accused of the crime. Each suggested the police would better have spent their time hunting for the Portuguese who must have done the dastardly deed.

The Fall River *Globe* did one thing well, however. It reported rumors, hunches, wild guesses, police leads, and even gossip. Most of that had the same value as rumors, hunches, and wild guesses today. But when one realizes that what *was* introduced as evidence was not convincing enough for a conviction, one begins to review what was *not* introduced as evidence.

Andrew Borden could have purchased and lived in almost any house he wanted in Fall River. The house he wanted and bought in 1872 was a modest one—especially compared to those on The Hill—at 92 Second Street. In most New England cities, the first street one block away but parallel to the main street is named First Street. Fall River is an exception. The first street east of Main Street is Second Street, and 92 Second Street was within sight, sound, and smell of most of Andrew's downtown holdings.

The house still stands today. Its number is now 230, and except for a window air-conditioning unit that seems somehow out of place, it looks almost exactly as it did in 1892, although the barn and fences are long gone. It still has the firm, steady, practical look that would have attracted its famous owner. It has been called "flimsy" and a "cracker box," but it is anything but that. One look at its solid granite foundation fitted with the care known only in a long-forgotten craft should be proof enough.

When Lizzie was tried before the superior court, William H. Moody, who shared the district attorney's role with Hosea M. Knowlton, did an excellent job of describing the house and the area.

> The house occupied by this family was a common type of house in this community and in this state, a house with the end to the street and the front door upon the end. It was a rectangular house. It was situated upon Second Street, in Fall River, which is one of the most frequented streets outside of the main business streets in the city, and is within, as probably most of you know, a very short distance of the City Hall. It may fairly be called a thoroughfare, as well for foot passengers as for carriages. It is a street used partly for residences and partly for business purposes.
>
> Second Street runs substantially north and south. It is a street which ascends toward the south. The higher part is south; the lower part is north; and upon the east side of Second Street this house is situated.
>
> At the south of the house is the residence of Dr. Kelly, and also very near the house. To the north of the house, and also near it, is the residence occupied by Mrs. Churchill; and diagonally in the rear of the house is the residence occupied by Dr. Chagnon.
>
> The house is separated from the sidewalk by a wooden

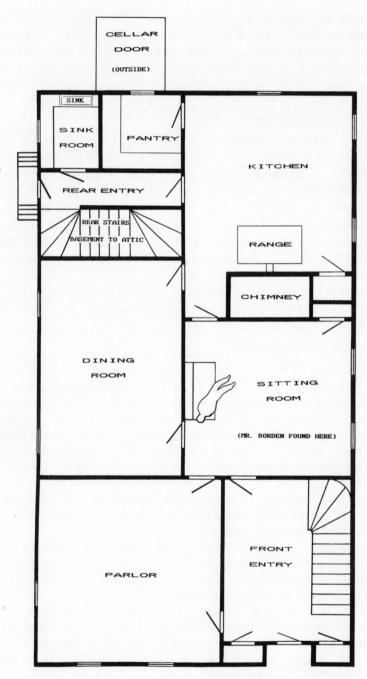

*First floor plan of Borden house* [COURTESY ANNA BROWN, BASED ON TRIAL EXHIBITS]

fence, a picket fence, with two gates; and in the rear of the yard, in which is situated a barn, there is a high board fence, on the top and bottom of which there was at that time, and is now, a line of barbed wire.

There are three exterior doors, three entrances to these premises, and only three, excepting of course the windows. There is the front door, leading directly from the sidewalk up a pair of stairs into the hall. There is a side door upon the north side, facing Mrs. Churchill's house, leading into a small entryway which leads into the kitchen. There is a third door in the rear of the house, which leads down to the cellar.

As you enter the front door you enter a hall from which lead two doors: a door into a parlor, which is the front room in the house, a door leading into the sitting room and a stairway leading upstairs. Let us, in the first place, go upstairs and see the arrangement there. It will aid us in considering this arrangement to remember that this house was originally a double tenement house, and with the slight exception that I shall refer to later on, the arrangement as it is upstairs is as it is upon the first story.

As you turn and go upstairs from the front entry, you come into a hallway. From that hallway lead three doors: first, a door which leads into a large closet, used at this time for the keeping of dresses, and which is almost large enough to be a small bedroom; another door, which leads into the guest chamber, which is directly over the parlor below and corresponds to it in every respect. The guest chamber is the chamber in which you will subsequently hear that Mrs. Borden was found dead. It is a matter which is to be carefully considered, that, as you turn upon the journey upstairs, as the stairs wind about and begin to face into the hall towards the north, you can look directly into the door of the guest chamber. The other door which leads from this hall is a door which leads into a bedroom and leads towards the rear of the house. Following, then, my direction, gentlemen, as you come up the stairs, turn to your left. As you approach the entry, in front of you is the door leading into the guest chamber and to your right is a door leading into a chamber which at that time was occupied by the prisoner. Between the guest chamber and the bedroom of the prisoner there was a door. I may as well dispose of it now for good. It was a door which always, including the day of this homicide, was kept locked upon both sides, and upon the side towards the prisoner's room there was against the door a desk which she used. In other words, it was not a practicable opening.

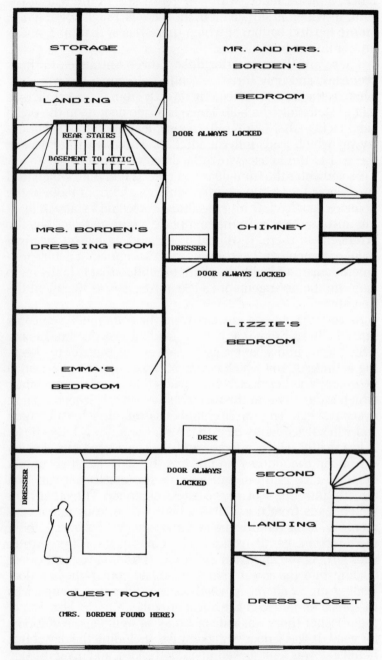

*Second floor plan of Borden house* [Courtesy Anna Brown, based on the trial exhibits]

When you have got up into this part of the house, gentlemen, you can go nowhere except into this clothes closet, into this guest chamber, and into the room occupied by the prisoner. It is important to remember that. All access to the other part of the house is cut off, not by the natural construction of the house but by the way in which the house was kept. Follow me, if you please, then, into the prisoner's bedroom. As you enter her bedroom a door leads to the left into a room that has no other entrance than that door. That is the room that was occupied by Miss Emma when she was at home. The only access to it was through the prisoner's room. There is another door at the rear of the prisoner's room, and directly opposite the door of entrance which leads into the room occupied by Mr. and Mrs. Borden, which is over the kitchen. The prisoner's room was exactly over the sitting room.

That door leading into that room was kept always locked upon both sides. It was locked upon the front toward the prisoner's room by a hook. It was locked in the rear toward Mr. and Mrs. Borden's room by a bolt, and I may as well say here as at any time that the proof that that door was locked upon both sides upon this morning, from the morning down to the time of the arrival of those who came alarmed by this homicide, will be ample and complete. But as we go further, passing to the rear into Mr. and Mrs. Borden's room, we find a door, and only a single door, leading out into the entryway which is over the entryway leading into the kitchen. That door, it will be clearly, amply and satisfactorily proved, was locked all through this day up to and beyond the time of the homicide.

Now then, gentlemen, if I have made myself clear upon this description, which is wearisome, I know, but it is one of the wearisome duties that we must undertake in this cause, I have made it clear to you that as you go up the hallway you get access to but four rooms, the hallway itself, if you call that a room, the closet, the guest chamber in which Mrs. Borden was found, the room of the prisoner, and the room leading out of that, the blind room, so to speak, that was occupied by Miss Emma when she was at home, and there is no other access whatever to the rear of the house.

Now gentlemen, let me, at the expense of tediousness, go below. As you enter the hallway below it is exactly as above except, of course, there is no clothes closet as there is above. There are two small closets, very small ones, as you will see.

To your left as you enter is the door that leads into the parlor under the room where Mrs. Borden was found dead. Going straight ahead you enter into the sitting room directly under and corresponding to the prisoner's bedroom.

Now you come to a difference of construction in the two stories. You turn to the left from the sitting room as you enter and you enter the dining room which is upon the north side of the house and is directly under Miss Emma's room and a large room which was used as a closet by Mrs. Borden and which joined the bedroom, another blind room. That difference is caused by the lack of a partition between the two areas as is in place on the second story. The dining room has a door of exit which goes into the kitchen. The effect of that partition is that while there is free communication two ways from the kitchen to the front part of the house downstairs, upstairs this partition reduces those ways of communication to one, and that one, you will recall, always and upon the day of the homicide, was barred by two doors, locked.

Mr. Morse [brother of Andrew Borden's first wife] returned upon a Wednesday night. It is important to show who occupied the house on Wednesday night. Let us first go to the front part of the house. The prisoner came in the last one that night and locked the front door. Upon that front door were three fastenings, a spring latch, a bolt, and a lock which operated by key. Those three fastenings were closed, by the way, when she came in, the last person that night by the front way of the house. The door leading into the cellar, the other exterior door, had been closed since Tuesday, the washing day, and by complete and ample evidence will be proved to you to have been closed all through Wednesday night and on Thursday morning including up to and beyond the time of these homicides.

Bridget [the Bordens' live-in maid] came in through the back door that night, found the back door locked when she came, unlocked it, locked it as she went in, went upstairs and went to bed. So, when Bridget and the prisoner had come in at their respective doors, every exterior approach to this house was closed.

Now in the front part of the house that night, the prisoner slept in one room. Mr. Morse slept in the guest chamber. There was no other room in that part of the house except Miss Emma's room, which led out, as you will remember, of Miss Lizzie's room. Mr. and Mrs. Borden slept in their room over the kitchen, and Bridget slept in some room above, in the third story of the house.

# Chapter 2

Five people lived in the house at 92 Second Street in Fall River: Emma Borden, Bridget Sullivan, Abby Borden, Andrew Borden, and Lizzie Borden. On August 4, 1892, Emma Borden was not in Fall River. Emma was a forty-two-year-old spinster who, in keeping with the mores of the age, lived at home and, as far as can be determined, had never in her adult life been away from home for as long as overnight. At the time of the murders, however, she had been away for two weeks visiting friends at a seaside cottage in Fairhaven, Massachusetts. A striking coincidence if there ever was one. It is, however, only the first of many.

On the afternoon before the murder, Uncle John Morse arrived at the Borden house and stayed overnight. He had been a guest at the house seventeen years earlier for almost a full year, but between that time and August 4, 1992, he had stayed overnight a total of only four times. He arrived and was in residence on the eve of the day the Bordens were murdered. Another coincidence.

Emma Borden's absence and Uncle John Morse's presence are not indications of a plan for murder. There was no premeditated murder; but an event had been planned that, intended or not intended, culminated in two murders.

*Emma Lenora Borden*

Emma Lenora Borden was born on March 1, 1851, of Sarah A. and Andrew J. Borden. She was twelve years old when her mother died. We know nothing of her schooling, her activities in the community, her suitors, or the implied total lack of them. Her physical description is given as "slight," nothing more. Photographs of her are rare, and the one courtroom sketch in which she appears shows her with her hand covering her face. Unlike her sister, she was never known to express dissatisfaction with her lot in life, her "humble" home, or her lack of the material things seemingly so important to Lizzie and so easily obtainable for those with Andrew Borden's wealth. We do know that she did not like her stepmother, Abby.

While the murders were taking place, Emma was vacationing with the Brownells (friends and distant relatives) at a seaside cottage in Fairhaven, about fifteen miles from Fall River. She had been at the cottage for two weeks prior to the crime and was notified of the murders by a telegram sent to her by the Borden family physician, Dr. Seabury W. Bowen. She arrived home in the early evening of the murder day.

Those who were at the Brownell cottage with Emma were questioned mercilessly by the police and interviewed to the point of harassment by newspaper reporters. The Brownells were unanimous and unequivocal in their confirmation of Emma's presence in Fairhaven at the time of the murders. In spite of this fully substantiated testimony, some accounts of the Borden murders insist that Emma was guilty of the crime.

In his 1937 publication, *Trial of Lizzie Borden*, Edmund Pearson stated, "To exonerate Miss Lizzie, who was actually present in the house, and throw blame upon her sister, in Fairhaven, is intellectual bankruptcy" (page 88). Mr. Pearson had spent years researching the case and, since Emma had been dead for twelve years when he made this statement, he had no hope for a Borden payoff. It is a safe conclusion that Emma Borden was in Fairhaven when her stepmother and her father were murdered.

The attraction Emma has had for those who "prove" her guilt is a most natural one: she is an unknown. The Emma-did-it theory states that she must have had some substance so important that she went to extraordinary lengths to hide it. This feeling is fueled by the little that is known because she is the antithesis of her almost ten-years-younger sister to whom she was always subservient. Whenever Emma had any power or position, she freely relinquished it to Lizzie and acquiesced to Lizzie's every whim and demand.

Because her father's often-mentioned-but-never-seen will was never probated and because her father's wife predeceased him, when Lizzie was arrested for the murder of both, Emma Borden became the sole legal heir to the Borden fortune and had full control over it. The irony in this situation is generally overlooked. The daughter with no expressed desire for her father's money now had it all, while the daughter with an overt hunger for it was ordering meals from a jailhouse menu. All trial expenses and payoffs—real, rumored, or imagined—were Emma's to govern with a yea or nay. Admittedly, she had constant, diligent, and effective professional assistance from her most capable legal advisor, Andrew Jennings. Just how many decisions were deferred to him is not known, but between them they did everything right.

When Lizzie was declared not guilty, the estate was split down the middle, and Lizzie was presented with her hard-earned birthright with no opposition from her sister. This was used by the "Emma-did-it" crowd to prove Emma's fear of exposure and thus her guilt. There is no acceptable logic in this premise because once tried, Lizzie was protected from further accusation. If Emma had killed her father and step-mother, Lizzie would have known it and could have taken all the estate if she had only betrayed her sister.

Emma Borden was a friend to her sister and a supporter of her sister's cause with no sinister or hidden motives or over-tones. It was more than ten years after the trial before she declared some independence and separated herself from Lizzie. By then the actual murderer had been dead for almost two years.

We will accept Emma for what she appeared to be. Like Lizzie, she knew who he was.

*Bridget Sullivan*

Bridget Sullivan, the Bordens' live-in maid from 1889 to 1892, had emigrated from Ireland more than six years before the murder and had worked for three other families before coming to the Borden household. One of thirteen children, she was "about twenty-five years old" but had no clue as to

*Bridget Sullivan*

her birthdate. Her character was without blemish. She was loyal to her employer (whom she considered to be Mrs. Borden), and she was devoutly Roman Catholic.

Bridget testified extensively at all of Lizzie's hearings and at the trial, with a total time on the stand far in excess of that of any other witness. Most of the intimate facts known about the Borden household come from Bridget's testimony. For the most part, she was concise and straightforward, with almost no memory losses or obvious evasions. Her testimony was neither helpful to Lizzie nor harmful. She was never trapped in provable lies or omissions, and she seems to have told the truth and the whole truth as she knew it.

Bridget's duties included washing, ironing, cooking, and a "little sweeping and scrubbing." She did not take care of any beds, bedrooms, or bedroom toilet accessories other than her own. She had no duties whatsoever that required her physical presence in any of the rooms on the second floor of the house. She even professed an ignorance of their basic layout and furnishings. She confirmed that Emma had been away from the house about two weeks and had not been back at all during that time.

The legend insists that Bridget was paid off with a huge

sum, returned to Ireland after the trial, and lived there in posh luxury for the remainder of her life. This is demonstrably hogwash, for she actually spent her later years on a Montana farm in abject poverty. Like Emma, Bridget was exactly what she seemed to be.

Bridget's major crime was being an Irish immigrant in a community that had about the same respect for its Irish immigrants as the deep South had during the same era for its "coloreds." Her lowly status branded her guilty of *something*, and when murder could not be proved (and was, in fact, ruled out by Lizzie's own testimony at the inquest), then she must have been, at the very least, a blackmailer. After all, she *was* Irish!

Again, as with Emma, some accounts "prove" Bridget was the murderer of both Bordens. Accusing her of the crime makes a bit more sense than accusing the absent Emma because, while Bridget's opportunity to kill Mrs. Borden was not nearly as good as Lizzie's, her opportunity to kill Andrew Borden was perfect.

By everyone's testimony (including her own), Bridget was outside the house gossiping or washing windows at the time Abby Borden was slaughtered. But she most certainly was *inside* the house when the butchering of Andrew Borden took place. Moreover, she was the only one mentioned in any of the hearings who *was* inside the house at that time because the name of the murderer was not once mentioned in any of the legal proceedings. Making a case against Bridget Sullivan is easier than making one against Emma.

However, the facts are that Bridget was not inside the house when Abby Borden was murdered, and she was in her room, two floors away in an almost diagonally opposite corner of the house, when Andrew Borden was dealt his fate. In spite of rumors of a payoff, Bridget Sullivan had no knowledge of who *was* in the house at either time. She did, however, steadfastly insist that something evil was in or stalking the house, and she absolutely refused to sleep in it the night after the murders. The next day (Friday) she was forced to return, and she did spend the night there. On Saturday she removed her precious lares and penates and never set foot in the house again after dark.

*Abby Durfee (nee) Gray Borden*

Andrew Borden's first wife, Sarah A. Morse (mother of Emma and Lizzie and the sister of Uncle John), died in March of 1863 of uterine congestion and "disease of the spine." Her death was viewed with suspicion by those who considered all Borden actions strange, and it provided speculation for the gossipmongers of The Hill.

Approximately two years after Sarah's death, Andrew married a resigned spinster named Abbie Durfee Gray (both spellings, *Abby* and *Abbie*, have been reported as correct). Abby was about thirty-seven when she married the forty-two-year-old Andrew. The "Durfee" in Abby's name links her to the other first family in the area and cloaks Abby with respectability. The fact that she was a Durfee, however, gave her no more social position than Andrew's being a Borden afforded him. Abby's father, Oliver Gray, was a pushcart peddler that, while it was an honorable means of supporting a family in those days, was not quite the noble background required of The Hill for unrestricted membership. This would have meant nothing to Andrew, for his father had been a fishmonger whose place of business was also a pushcart. When Abby was married, she was described as being "short." When she died, the coroner reported her weight as between 210 and 220 pounds.

To Abby, Andrew's proposal of marriage must have seemed a fantastic stroke of good fortune. She was old (by the standards of the era), unattractive and undesirable (by the standards of the community), and church-mouse poor (by any standard). One can only imagine her joy at being asked to be the bride of the most eligible widower in town.

To Andrew, the marriage was strictly a convenient means of securing a housekeeper and a nursemaid who would work for far less than minimum wage. For reasons never questioned, there were no offspring from this union. There is no reason not to believe that, in their separate ways, each found in the marriage exactly what he or she was seeking.

That there are no records of child abuse or neglect by Abby toward her stepdaughters, means nothing at all because, in that era, short of killing a child as a discipline, anything was

*Mrs. Abby Durfee Gray Borden*

allowed if its intent was to produce character or "godliness." In my research, many dear people offered their remembrances of stories they had heard in their youth. One dealt directly with Abby Borden's demeanor toward Lizzie. Mrs. Marion D. Sherman of Westport, Massachusetts, said,

> My mother, who passed away several years ago at the age of 104, was a friend of Lizzie Borden. Lizzie was her Sunday school teacher and my mother used to go to the Borden house every Sunday morning and they would walk to church together. My mother told me she arrived early and went into the hall and waited on the haircloth sofa where one of the murders took place. Once in a while Bridget would bring a little milk and a cookie, but there apparently was no surplus of food (or anything else) in the house.
>
> My mother told me Lizzie was treated mean by her stepmother. Her clothes were shabby and her gloves (Mother's words) were more "mends" than gloves.
>
> By the way, when anyone asked my mother whether she considered Lizzie guilty or innocent, the reply was, "She is dead and buried, so let her rest in peace."

Try as we might, it is hard to remember Lizzie's gloves as being "more mends" than gloves without thinking of Abby as being penurious toward Lizzie.

This is not meant to denigrate or condemn Abby. She was merely following the dictates and policies established by the gentleman of the house, who had "habits of economy."

Abby's closest (and only reported) friend was her half sister Sarah Whitehead, who was thirty-five years younger. Their relationship was more mother-daughter than sister-sister, and Sarah undoubtedly filled Abby's maternal void by returning the love that Abby could have shown her stepdaughters had they accepted her as a mother. Sarah grieved at her half sister's death as a loving daughter would grieve for her mother. Emma and Lizzie did not.

Although two persons were murdered on August 4, 1892, it was Andrew's death that made the murders newsworthy. The death of Abby Borden was of little consequence to anyone outside a five-mile radius of the Borden household. Some who believe that Lizzie was the murderer say that she killed Abby because of her hatred of her stepmother and then killed her father because she loved him and wanted to spare him the grief she knew his wife's death would cause him. Admittedly, this convoluted logic produces a motive where one is difficult to find, but the substitution is equally difficult to accept.

### Andrew Jackson Borden

At the time of the Borden murders, Fall River's population was more than 75,000, with more than 125 families named Borden. Andrew Borden was eight generations removed from the first founding father, but just five generations removed from the registered owner of all lands now known as Fall River (on the east side of the Taunton River) and Somerset and Swansea (on the west side of the Taunton River).

Along the way, most of these holdings slipped away from direct control by Andrew's branch of the family, and by the time he was in line for his share nothing was left. Early in his life, Andrew developed an obsession to rectify this situation and restore his birthright. He devoted his entire life to doing just that and, by any standard, was overwhelmingly successful. While the Bordens never again became the power

*Andrew Jackson Borden*

they once were, the Borden name could still command awe and respect from the common folk.

Andrew made money any and every way he could, and once he made it, he made it grow. Money saved could be reinvested to make more money, but money spent was lost forever. Thrift may be a virtue, but Andrew Borden made it a vice. The accumulation of wealth is not a sin, but Andrew's methods were worse than sinful.

Andrew's initial fortune was made from his partnership in an undertaking business, and his reputation in that profession was widely cited as an example of the need for extensive reform. His favorite ploy was overselling, convincing the grieving spouse or surviving family that the departed loved one should have a sendoff more grand than their economic situation could possibly handle. He then offered to hold his charges as a simple lien against their property and, in too many instances, ended up "buying" the property at a fraction of its actual value. He was openly charged with billing the bereaved for amounts far in excess of the services furnished, and he is credited with having purchased coffins shorter than normal at a price that had been trimmed accordingly and then fitting his too-tall clients into these in a manner that would not show when they were viewed in the usual waist-up fashion. His fees, however, were not cut to match.

Once he began to make money as an undertaker, Andrew Borden's investments extended to other parts of the city's economy. He owned one of Fall River's banks and had four fingers and at least one foot in three others. His properties began on South Main Street, just yards from the city's banking center; it was easier to point out those he did *not* own than those he did. He was a firm believer in public transportation, and, as a stockholder, his belief made a bundle for him. In what is now called a hostile takeover, two battling factions forced stockholders of the local horsecar line to choose a side and sell out. Andrew stood pat, defied everyone, and flatly refused all offers until his stock was absolutely essential to the takeover barons who were forced to make him the proverbial offer that he couldn't refuse.

Andrew collected his many rents personally, and it was not uncommon to see him on his rounds with a basket of eggs. These were a product of his farm holdings, and he offered them for sale at just one penny more a dozen than the leading local grocer. It is difficult to picture a more-than-six-foot-tall, slim, seventy-year-old, dour-faced man dressed in his trademark morning clothes maintaining his dignity with a rent book in one hand and a basket of eggs in the other.

About two years before his death, Andrew used some of his heaped-up savings to achieve his proudest personal goal. He erected a huge (for the time) office and commercial building in the heart of Fall River's business district. He named it, fittingly, the A. J. Borden Building. He owned it and all his other property outright. He loved telling anyone who would listen that he had never borrowed a cent from anyone at any time nor had he ever signed a note.

There are as many stories about Andrew Borden's money-grubbing ways as there are about Lizzie's misuse of hatchets. The difference is that the stories about Andrew are true.

Andrew refused to have his home connected to gas mains (the primary use of gas at that time was illumination—cooking and heating quickly followed). Kerosene was good enough for his household, and he sternly restricted its use.

Electricity was not yet commonly available, but telephones were. Andrew did not have one because he could see no use for it nor for the added expense.

There was no hot water in the house other than what a teakettle or pot could produce. The better wood- and coal-burning kitchen ranges had water-warming reservoirs built in; the range in the Borden kitchen did not. When Andrew bought the house, it had running water. He declared the running water on the second floor an unnecessary luxury and had the plumbing changed to cut it off and limit the running water to a sink room off the kitchen and one in the basement. The basement had a coal-burning furnace for central heating and—another wonder of the age—a water closet, the one and only one in the house. For whatever reason, it was not used extensively by the household.

On the day after his death, Andrew Borden was eulogistically characterized in the Fall River *Daily Globe* (August 5, 1892) as follows:

## MR. BORDEN'S CHARACTERISTICS

### Strictly Honest and Upright and Devoted to Money Getting

Andrew J. Borden was a peculiar man in many respects. While his tall, neatly clothed figure was familiar to all the older citizens, he had few intimates and was reticent to a marked degree. When he started in life his means were extremely limited and he made his money by saving it. The habits of economy and thrift which he formed then, clung to him to the last and although his income of last years was very large, he lived modestly and continued to count the pennies.

The firm of Borden & Almy, in which he was senior partner, long had a monopoly in the undertaking business, and it made them rich. They buried the wealthy and the indigent, the foreign-born and natives, and for years, with the single exception of Westgate's establishment, they had no competitors.

It was generally supposed that when Messrs. Borden & Almy retired, the former invested the greater portion of his

*The A. J. Borden Building on South Main, circa 1900*

accumulations in real estate but those who are informed regarding his affairs, state that this is not the case. He acquired property, centrally located, when land was considerably cheaper than it is today, but he also put much of his capital into mills and bank stock and was uniformly successful in his ventures.

It will be seen from the brief account published yesterday, that he was a director in several older corporations which have long paid large dividends and it is said that he was a heavy owner in many of the younger companies. He was regarded as one of the wealthiest men in town.

Mr. Borden had the manners of a gentleman of the old school. He was always dignified, but at the same time he was courteous and kindly, and as has been reported, was scrupulously upright in all his dealings and expected the same fairness in others. He was positive in his views, unbending in will, and at times appeared to lack sympathy. Deceased was domestic in his tastes and although he had considerable leisure time, was rarely to be found where men are accustomed to congregate.

*       *       *

The writer of these kinds words, published the day after the murders, used unmitigated restraint. Andrew Jackson Borden had no socially redeeming qualities. "He was rarely to be found where men are accustomed to congregate" because his contemporaries labeled him a despicable miser and considered him loathsome, repugnant, and worthy only of total social avoidance and ostracization. The day he was murdered, the area around his house was shoulder-to-shoulder with citizens, a few in tears, some rendered speechless by genuine and absolute shock. But for each mourner, ten others cheered and whooped and celebrated with unrestrained joy and delight. Andrew Borden was dead.

Writing the history of Fall River in the mid 1940s, Arthur S. Phillips reported that Andrew Borden was "a man of large wealth . . . mostly accumulated through his own parsimonious thrift and by means which fell within the letter of the law. . . . When the death of Mr. Borden was first announced on the street, general comment was that 'someone had done a good job'" (pages 3, 4, and 6).

By any standard Andrew Borden was wealthy. One of the first questions asked of Lizzie at the inquest was the value of her father's estate. She said she had no idea. Andrew Borden was worth much more than half a million dollars. In this age when millionaires are commonplace, this figure is not impressive. But these were 1892 dollars. At the time, bread was a nickel a loaf, a live-in maid was paid $3.50 a week, a millhand who worked all his eighty-hour week and met his quotas could earn as much as ten dollars. A well-built two-family house on a sizable piece of land might go as high as $2,000. Prime farm land close to town brought as much as $20 an acre. And the total outlay of the U.S. government was $364 million per year. Half a million dollars was a lot of money.

### Lizzie Andrew Borden

Miss Lizzie was born July 19, 1860, of Sarah A. and Andrew J. Borden. She was two years old when her mother died, and she was in her thirty-second year when her stepmother and her father were murdered. She professed no memory of her natural mother. Emma, who was almost ten years older,

*Lizzie Borden in her late teens or early twenties.*

became sister, companion, and surrogate mother. A second sister, Alice Esther, had been born five years before Lizzie's birth, but she died at the age of two.

Lizzie was everything a young lady of the age was expected to be. She belonged to Central Congregational Church, The Hill's "in" church, and was unquestionably one of its most active members. She conscientiously served in many capacities, on many committees, and in many organizations. If she did not serve as treasurer (in a group's vain hope for access to her father's resources), she was usually secretary.

Lizzie was not unattractive in face, figure, or personality. She had red hair and a temper to match, and she was stubborn and set in her ways. At the time of the murders, she had a number of escorts and suitors. She was, however, doomed to eternal spinsterhood by The Hill, as had been her sister before her. As far as marriage was concerned, her father, her stepmother, their residence, and their lifestyle coalesced into an alabaster albatross. Both Lizzie and Emma were tarred by the "not acceptable" rating from The Hill on the one side and by their father's rulings on the other. Any acceptable male of acceptable breeding *without* independent means or expectations would have been branded a fortune hunter by Andrew and chased away. Any available male *with* means or expectations would have had more acceptable prey to hunt. She was a poor little rich girl.

While some who proclaim Lizzie the murderer of Andrew and Abby Borden give hatred of Abby as the motive, others cite her lack of social acceptance and the denial of the pleasures that Andrew's money could have provided as her motive for the killings. It would not have been improbable.

*John Vinnicum Morse*

If a betting pool to determine the murderer had been established in the first forty-eight hours after the Bordens' murders, John Morse would have been the hands-down favorite and poor little orphan Lizzie would have been listed at about a thousand-to-one, if at all. In fact, if the good people of Fall River had not been restrained by their proper Yankee upbringing (and an inherent sense of fair play well reinforced by scores of police), they might have happily strung up John Morse within hours of the murders.

John Morse was a mysterious, tall, handsome stranger. He dressed like a hobo; he was a Westerner; he was highly suspect.

Although John Morse had been born and reared in Fall River, as a young man he took Horace Greeley's advice by going west. After first settling in Illinois, he moved on to Iowa where he spent about twenty-five years as a horse breeder. He was quickly absolved of any responsibility for the murders. The good people of Fall River were slightly red-faced over the error in their collective judgment, and when everything had been straightened out, they accepted John Morse as fully believable and trustworthy.

The Fall River *Daily Globe*
August 11, 1892

EVIDENCE HEARD AT THE OFFICIAL INVESTIGATION
OF YESTERDAY

After a full investigation by the authorities, John V. Morse is completely exonerated from suspicion of being connected with the Borden murders. It has been conclusively shown that he left the Borden house on Second Street not later than 8:45 o'clock on the morning of the tragedy. His story of his where-abouts until his return to the scene of the crime at 11:40 o'clock, had been corroborated in every particular, and the cloud that circumstances had placed him under during the past week is fully lifted.

Mr. Morse has felt his position keenly but has acted throughout with patience and discretion, talking with the utmost candor to both the police and the press regarding his movements on that fatal day. The hand of the law is not relaxing its grip, however, on the Borden house.

In a few short days, interest in John Morse faded into nothingness.

As the legal proceedings were getting under way, Andrew Jennings, Lizzie's lawyer, sent Pinkerton Detective Superintendent O. M. Hanscom to Iowa to investigate John Morse (for reasons we shall learn later). The paper in Hastings, Iowa, must have considered this visit by an honest-to-goodness Pinkerton man on a don't-that-beat-all murder case a reportable event and filed the following wire story:

### ECCENTRIC, BUT HONEST

John V. Morse as Known by His Far Western Neighbors

Hastings, Ia., Aug 14—This place was for about 25 years, and in a sense is yet, the home of John V. Morse. Miss Lizzie Borden has sent Detective Hanscom out here to investigate relative to Morse's past life.

Morse came here in 1860 from Illinois, where he had been a farmer with the exception of two or three years, during which, while a young man, he learned the butcher's trade. Morse has been a farmer ever since.

In Illinois he was a renter. During this period he saved up something less than $1,000, and then came here and bought land; he owns two farms, 220 acres in all, as well improved as any farm in the county.

Morse has never married. He was always regarded by his neighbors as a very eccentric and peculiar man. He never, apparently, formed any close friendships, always maintaining a close reserve and in all his dealings was close almost to the point of penuriousness.

But he was always strictly honest.

The years he spent there were years of the strictest frugality, of self-denial that amounted almost to miserliness. He would drive to town in an old rattle-trap lumber wagon using a pine board for a seat when he could have just as well afforded a buggy.

He would wear the same suit of clothes everywhere. It is pretty certain that the suit he is now wearing at Fall River is the same he wore when he left here two years ago.

Only once during his long residence here did he show any inclination to take any comfort in life as he went along. One winter he electrified everybody who knew him by purchasing a nice, new buggy and a new suit of clothes. He suddenly showed a disposition to go into society and all that winter he attended parties and some other social gatherings. It was rumored that he was looking for a wife.

When the winter was over, he re-sold his buggy, laid aside his store clothes and was still a bachelor.

Those who knew him best, however, agree that he was never anything more than eccentric. He was close, hard-fisted, almost avaricious, but scrupulously honest. On one occasion in making a settlement with a brother of Hon. L. G. Gerung, who lives here, Morse recalled and paid for items and services which Gerung had entirely forgotten.

It is somewhat singular that in the discussion as to the possibility of Morse's connection with the Borden murder, Morse's brother-in-law, whose farm adjoins that of Morse, and who has known Morse since 1857, manifests almost no feeling. Some years ago Morse lived with the Davidsons, and the result of this was a coolness amounting almost to an estrangement which was continued up to the present.

Mrs. Davidson, who is Morse's half sister, seems to hold an opinion of Morse which is hardly as favorable as that of her husband. She says Morse was a man who when crossed would never forgive, and in fact, she describes this as a characteristic of the family and one in which she herself shares. In speaking of the arrest of Lizzie Borden she became very indignant and exclaimed it is most preposterous to suppose that Lizzie could have murdered her parents.

Morse was never a horse trader, but he raised a good many horses on the farm, and when he had a surplus he sold them.

Two years ago when he went East, he took with him a carload of horses. None of the animals were blooded, and there are people who wondered at his taking so many ordinary stock.

But, however eccentric he may have been, he prospered and today he is considered quite well off for a farmer. Besides a farm he owns stock in the Botas Valley State Bank of Hastings. He has not been in need of money lately, for a short time ago he willingly gave one of his tenants who pays cash rent, an extension of time. And so, summing it all up, it appears that for almost 25 years, John V. Morse has been a very hard working farmer. He has prospered and now seems to be taking things easy.

It is altogether likely that his moroseness, cynicism and other eccentricities were largely the result of his lonely condition of life.

From the day Lizzie was arrested for her father's murder, we know almost nothing about Uncle John's movements, actions, fortunes, or lack thereof. We know he testified at the trial and some time after that he returned to Hastings where he died in the spring of 1912. That is all we know, for the only things written after the trial were reports of Lizzie's movements, as if everyone knew that someday she would run off to join the circus and they wanted to be reassured she had not done it yet.

John V. Morse must have entered the Borden world no later than his sister's marriage to Andrew in December, 1845, but we know little about his eastern-states existence until approximately five years prior to the murders.

During his first visit to the Borden house after he moved back East, an insignificant property transaction took place. The mother of Abby Borden, Andrew's second wife (*not* John's sister), wanted to sell the half of a duplex she owned. The other half belonged to Sarah Whitehead, Abby's half sister, who could not afford to buy out her mother and had good reasons for not selling the half she owned. Andrew bought his mother-in-law's half of the duplex and transferred the deed to Abby.

Lest there be any misunderstanding, this was not an act of charity on Andrew's part. His motive was the profitable acquisition of another piece of property, and he merely took advantage of two old ladies who happened to be in-laws. To him it was just another minute in a normal business day.

All previous accounts report this basically simple property transfer by Andrew as the onset of hate in Lizzie, the mistake of his life, the seed that grew death, the beginning of the end, and other such garbage. No such speculation has any truth.

During John Morse's second reported visit, the Borden house was burgled. This was no easy smash and grab robbery, for the house was uncharacteristically secure for the time. Doors were triple-locked; basement windows were heavily screened; all other windows were well above reach from the ground. The lot was fully secured, including a rear fence approximately six feet high with vicious barbed wire at both top and bottom. Neighboring houses pressed close on two sides. The house was seldom left unattended. Abby was almost always at home except for casual marketing and supper with her sister once every three or four months.

At the time the burglary took place, Abby had joined Andrew on a visit to a Borden farm property on the other side of the Taunton River—an extraordinarily rare event. However, the house was not unattended because Emma and Bridget were both at home, and Lizzie may have been there, although Uncle John's unclarified testimony gives reason to doubt this. In spite of all the normally effective defensive measures and at least two alert and somewhat paranoiac residents, the burglar made off with Abby's jewelry and gold watch, cash in greenbacks and gold, and a booklet of street railway tickets. These items were taken from the elder Bordens' upstairs rooms, and nothing was reported touched in any other part of the house. Most surprisingly, the two people known to have been in the house say they heard, saw, or knew nothing.

Uncle John testified that he was in Fall River that day, although he said little more. At the time he lived in a New Bedford suburb, less than fifteen miles from the Bordens. Although we do not know where Lizzie was, it has always been assumed that she was at home when the theft took place. By innuendo, every written account of this theft points a finger at her. Uncle John did say he was at the house and testified that he did not see Lizzie. His testimony was not questioned.

Andrew reported the crime to the police who dutifully investigated it. Lizzie volunteered that she had found the cellar door unbolted and wide open, and she gave the police a common nail she said she had found in the lock. Within a few weeks, Andrew asked the police to drop the whole thing, hinting that pursuit would be hopeless. If he was happy, so were they, and this crime, like the murders, was never solved.

From that day until the day of their deaths, Mr. and Mrs. Borden's upstairs rooms were always locked during daylight hours, but the key was left in open view on the mantle in the sitting room. Since Andrew never explained why he did this, any answer is pure supposition. The best guess is that he knew the theft was an inside job, and this was his way of saying he knew it.

For whatever reason, from that day on, not only was their bedroom door at the top of the rear stairs kept locked, the sole connecting door between their bedroom and Lizzie's was locked on each side and a chest of drawers placed in front of it on their side. This *locked* bedroom door is of major importance when we study the murders, but for now just remember how the locking came about.

Uncle John's next recorded visit to the Bordens occurred some time after Andrew announced there was no longer a reason for his household to keep a horse. The barn's sole occupants became Lizzie's pigeons. No one ever questioned Lizzie's love of animals, and as far as we know, these pigeons were her pets and the only pets she had, allowed by Andrew for the simple reason that, on occasion, they graced the dinner table. (Eating pets—and pigeons at that—is almost unknown today, but anyone who knew Andrew would understand it fully; his credo was "You do not feed animals who do not feed you.")

After the horse was gone, the barn was broken into on more than one occasion, and pigeons were stolen. In an action totally out of character for Andrew, he killed the remaining birds by chopping off their heads with a hatchet when Uncle John was visiting.

When she was questioned about bloody hatchets, Lizzie denied knowledge of any such thing, but she told of her father's using a hatchet a few months earlier to kill pigeons. Andrew's motive for this is incomprehensible to ordinary logic.

Uncle John, who was a houseguest when this strange event took place, claimed Lizzie was not at home at the time.

John Morse arrived for his last reported visit to the Borden house in the early afternoon of the day before the murders. He had no luggage, not even a toothbrush, even though he knew he was staying overnight. He arrived on foot, saying he had taken the train from New Bedford. In previous visits he had used his own horse and buggy and had stabled them in the Borden barn. Not so this trip.

Andrew Borden had no social life or friends outside of the circle forced into his company during business hours. The exception was his brother-in-law. Opposites may indeed attract, especially when they have important things in common. Andrew was respected for his position and his wealth; John was the forerunner of the stereotypical used car salesman and had money. Andrew had made some successful investments based on John's advice, and this may have been reason enough for Andrew's genuine affection for his brother-in-law.

Real or pretend, Lizzie professed a strong dislike for her Uncle John Morse.

# Chapter 3

Wednesday, August 3, 1892, the day before the murders, was not a routine day at 92 Second Street. It began on a most unusual note and continued in an abnormal vein to well after nightfall.

Abby Borden was not known as an alarmist, nor had she, as far as we know, ever expressed to anyone any fear for her personal safety or well-being. Early on August 3, however, she was in a panic for her life. Just after 7:00 A.M. she appeared in Dr. Seabury W. Bowen's office, which was almost directly across the street from her own house. She told him she feared for her life and was sure the entire family had been poisoned. She outlined in graphic detail the horrible night both she and Andrew had spent and underlined her own illness by vomiting ungraciously in his office. Dr. Bowen was most comforting, told her he guessed it was nothing serious, did agree that she "looked sick," and sent her home.

After he ate breakfast, Dr. Bowen went across the street to check on Andrew. Andrew Borden was not at all cordial, made it perfectly clear that the doctor was neither needed nor welcome, and, not too politely, told Dr. Bowen what he could do with any bill he might consider submitting.

Although Bridget said that she, too, had all the physical symptoms of Mrs. Borden's "poisoning" the next morning, no other evidence of it was found. Officially, autopsies performed by those trained in nineteenth-century techniques found no poison in the stomachs removed from the murder victims and submitted for examination.

Later that morning, Lizzie, it was testified, went shopping

for a poison called prussic acid. Of all the facets of the Borden murder case that have intrigued its followers over the years, Lizzie's visit to Smith's Drug Store is one of the most fascinating and worth looking at in detail.

Eli Bence was a well-respected young citizen of Fall River who was employed as a "drug clerk" at Smith's Drug Store on the corner of Columbia and South Main Street, a three-block knight's move from the Borden house. He testified that on Wednesday morning, August 3, Lizzie Borden entered the store and requested ten cents' worth of prussic acid to apply to a sealskin cape to protect it from moths. (Prussic acid, also called hydrocyanic acid, is a very weak solution [2 percent] of a most poisonous liquid used chiefly in fumigating against insects, rats, and mice; in 1892 drug stores were more like chemist shops where medicines were compounded from standard materials). Bence informed her that prussic acid was sold only on a doctor's prescription, that it was extremely dangerous, and that, in fact, they did not sell it. She stated she had purchased it before, turned, and left.

The first account of this incident appeared the day after the murders in the "sensational, hostile, and inconsiderate" newspaper, the Fall River *Daily Globe*.

### LIZZIE BORDEN VISITS A DRUG STORE TO INQUIRE ABOUT POISONS

At police headquarters Thursday night at 7 o'clock, Captain Desmond was posting himself on the murder by reading the papers and receiving reports.

Marshall Hilliard was busy with his men and inquiry for Assistant Fleet revealed the fact that he had gone to supper.

In a few minutes Mr. Fleet returned and then a conversation took place between him and the marshall. Officers Harrington and Doherty were given instructions and passed out.

Within thirty minutes after that the most important clue yet discovered was in their possession.

The two officers made their discovery on Main Street.

At D. R. Smith's drug store in the city they got the first important evidence.

They approached the clerk, Eli Bence, and from him learned that Miss Borden had been in the store within 36 hours past and had enquired for a certain poison.

The clerk was asked to accompany the officers and closely questioned as to the exact facts relative to the time, the girl's condition mentally, the amount and the quality of the poison she had bought or called for.

The officers then led the drug clerk to a residence on Second Street where Miss Lizzie Borden was stopping for the time being.

The young man was not previously well acquainted with the young woman but he had told them that he could identify her on sight.

He did identify her and in the presence of the police officers informed them that she was in his place of business and made inquiry for a bottle of poison.

Miss Borden's reply to this accusation as well as the exact language which was used at the time is known only to the two policemen and herself.

The statement above made is absolutely correct and was verified in every particular by a Globe reporter last night within minutes after it happened.

As to the source of information of the above facts it might be well to state that the policemen mentioned did not, nor any other policemen or detective give out one shadow of a suggestion for the reporter to work upon but he gained his knowledge from as reliable a source as they did.

Testimony was taken from Eli Bence at the preliminary hearing (August 9–11) and at the inquest (August 25– September 1), but not at the trial itself (June 1893). At the preliminary hearing, Bence was positive in his identification of Lizzie. District Attorney Hosea Knowlton asked, "Is this defendant the woman?"

"Yes, sir."

"Are you sure?"

"Positive."

In cross-examination, the defense showed that Mr. Bence could not remember the exact color of the dress, hat, purse, or gloves of the woman in his store, nor could he remember other sales he *had* made that morning to other women. At one point in the questioning by defense attorney Melvin Adams,

Bence was asked, "What did you refuse to sell them?" and he replied, "Who? I refused to sell Miss Borden prussic acid," undoing Adams' effort to undermine Bence's testimony. Finally Adams did elicit Bence's admission that he had never sold Lizzie anything in Smith's Drug Store, but "possibly in Riddell's Drug Store," where he worked "six years ago."

Adams then allowed Bence to reveal something that could have been damaging for the defense, asking, "Have not you talked to some people about it?"

"I talked to the authorities about it."

"Have you talked to any others?" Adams asked. "You need not name them."

"I talked to one other."

"Did you talk to anyone other than this person, whom you have in mind now; that makes three people?"

"Not to my knowledge," Bence answered. "Excuse me, I will say Mr. Phillips [the newest member of the law firm defending Lizzie and thus the one having to do the legwork in the case] came to see me and wanted to talk to me about it. I told him I did not care to say anything about it. He said Mr. Jennings [the defense attorney] would come up. I told him to send him, if he wished to."

Since this is all we know of the visits of Mr. Phillips and Mr. Jennings with Mr. Bence, we are free to speculate as to the intent. A major obligation of the defense in any trial is to neutralize harmful or adverse testimony. Bence's testimony of her attempt to buy poison was a most serious threat to Miss Lizzie and had to be neutralized. It is possible that money was offered to accomplish this. As occurs many times in the Borden trials, what was not asked speaks with thunderous volume. If District Attorney Knowlton had any interest in the truth, he would have jumped into this opening and hammered away. He did nothing.

With the exception of an account of the case written in 1893 by Edwin Porter which was upsetting to Lizzie, *all* written accounts of the case belittle and discount the entire prussic acid incident and offer as proof of its insignificance the "fact" that Bence did not know Miss Borden on sight because, say these accounts, he was taken to the murder house and placed *outside an open window* and asked to identify her by *hearing her speak.* At the preliminary hearing, however, after establishing that when he was taken to the murder house Bence could easily hear the conversation between Lizzie and Officer Harrington, he was asked, "When you were at the Borden house, you say you stood in the doorway?"

"Yes, sir."

"Did you stand in view of Miss Borden?"

"I did. I stood in view of her."

"Did she see you, were you in the open door, or behind the door?"

"I was in the doorway."

"You were not behind a door or obstruction? You stood right out, open?"

"I did. Yes, sir."

At the inquest Lizzie denied ever being in Smith's Drug Store and even denied knowledge of its location. Bence most certainly did not agree. He had never seen her in that drug store prior to the day before the murders, but he was unshakably adamant about the one time she was there and about her intended purchase. Bence's testimony was backed by two other witnesses.

Frank H. Kilroy, a medical student who was in the drug store talking to Bence when Miss Lizzie Borden entered and made her request, knew Lizzie by sight and positively identified her. He testified, "I was sitting in the front shop, under the fan, and conversing with Mr. Bence, and this lady came in, and Mr. Bence left me, and went behind the counter, and I heard her say, 'prussic acid.' Mr. Bence says, 'I cannot sell it without a prescription.' She said something that I could not understand, except 'sealskin cape'; and she left the store."

Mr. Kilroy was followed to the stand by Frederick B. Harte, who was also a drug clerk in Smith's Drug Store. He, too, testified at the inquest that Lizzie Borden came in, asked Bence for prussic acid, was refused by Bence, and left. There was no question in Mr. Harte's mind that the lady in the store was Miss Lizzie Borden. Like Bence and Kilroy, Harte could not say what she had been wearing that day, nor could he fix the time any better than "after ten and before half past eleven."

At the inquest, Lizzie first said she was out of the house

Wednesday morning. Later she changed that to not having left the house until the evening. One of those statements is wrong; one *must* be a lie.

The August 30 edition of the *Globe* reported:

> When the testimony of Messers. Kilroy, Harte, and Bence was going on, and they testified to seeing her in Smith's drug store asking for prussic acid, she whispered to her friend, Mrs. Brigham, "I was never in that store in my life."
>
> After the court adjourned, Mrs. Brigham was asked if she made this remark. She said, "Yes," and added, "Lizzie said that she was not out of the house in the morning, when three witnesses claim they saw her, but she says there is only Maggie [i.e. Bridget—all Irish maids were "Maggie"] now to prove that. The only other witness who could swear she stayed at home that day is dead. She means her stepmother."

Three days earlier, on August 27, Lizzie's "Maggie" had testified to Lizzie's whereabouts on the morning before the murders. It was important to Lizzie to demonstrate that she did not try to buy prussic acid. If she had paid off Bridget—as some have said—she didn't get her money's worth when it came to Bridget's providing an alibi for Lizzie's staying at home that morning. See for yourself.

Mr. Adams for the defense asked Bridget Sullivan, "And Lizzie complained of being sick?"

"Yes, sir."

"Lizzie stayed in her room all that forenoon, did she not?"

"I suppose so; I did not see her until she came to dinner."

"You knew she was upstairs? They were all sick and ailing that day?"

"Yes, sir."

"She did not go out at all that day, did she, so far as you know?"

"Miss Lizzie? I did not see her."

"So far as you know she did not go out?"

"I could not say whether she went out or not."

"They ate a little breakfast, and Lizzie went back upstairs to her room?"

"I suppose so. She went out of my sight. I do not know where she went."

We would not have this testimony if Jennings' copy of the preliminary hearing transcript had not been made available. Because no one has used that transcript until now, all pro-Lizzie fans through the years have avowed that Bridget did swear that Lizzie did not leave the house before early evening. This is how legends are made.

One other element about Smith's Drug Store must be mentioned. In 1892 the store was on the *wrong* end of town. Main Street was *the* shopping street, with city hall and its clustered banks the center. Smaller banks, acceptable shops and professional offices ran several blocks up *North* Main Street, and then the street ran into one of the better residential areas. In fact, The Hill began on this end of North Main.

*South* Main was different. The good shops and stores began at the foot of South Main and continued south for two short city blocks. Unlike North Main, the acceptable part of South Main ended abruptly at the same corner on which Smith's was situated. The street continued beyond that corner, but no one not Portuguese or not traveling south out of Fall River would have ventured down it. In fact, old timers from The Hill would tell you that there was nothing south beyond McWhirr's Department Store, and Smith's was a good city block beyond McWhirr's. Bridget Sullivan *might* have been persuaded to shop there, but Miss Lizzie Andrew Borden? *Never!*

However, this logic is a two-edged sword. Smith's was close to her home and in a direction Lizzie was not known to travel. The fact that it was in the wrong direction and on the wrong side of town would have made her feel secure in going there, knowing no one she knew would possibly see her or, should the worst happen and someone report her visit, no one would believe she would occasion herself to be in such a neighborhood.

Although many have belittled their testimony, no one has ever offered any evidence that could discredit what Bence, Kilroy, and Harte said. No one but Lizzie has denied their claims.

Many years later Arthur Phillips said that Bence's testimony was "immaterial . . . she had sought to purchase [the prussic acid] for an innocent purpose." Arthur Phillips was part of the defense team and for the rest of his life defended Lizzie's innocence. He must have known the truth, at least as to whether Lizzie was trying to buy the acid if not her real reason in doing so. If he were going to lie, he would say that Lizzie had *not* tried to buy the acid. But he said that she had.

The incident must have happened, and it must have happened just as the much maligned *Globe* reported it. More of this later.

Early in the afternoon before the murders, John Morse appeared at the Borden house for his final visit. Lizzie claimed several times (and Uncle John swore to it just as many) that she did not see her uncle at all on his last visit until after her stepmother and her father were dead. She said she knew her uncle was in the house, but she avoided him by staying in her upstairs bedroom when he was there.

In the midafternoon, Uncle John left the house to visit relatives on the other side of the Taunton River. He invited Andrew to join him, but Andrew was still feeling "poorly" (even though he would not see a doctor) and begged off. Because he had chosen to travel to Fall River by train, Mr. Morse was forced to hire a team for his trip to Swansea. For Mr. Morse to travel by train is a totally out-of-character action that was never questioned. It should have been questioned, for it is an act akin to a farmer with a herd of two hundred cows sending out to the corner grocery for a quart of unpasteurized milk.

Lizzie left in the early evening to visit Alice Russell, an especially dear friend of both Emma and herself. Miss Russell had known both sisters for many years, and neither sister professed to having a friend she considered closer than Alice Russell.

For whatever reason (and you can speculate to your heart's content), Lizzie poured out her heart to Miss Russell that evening. It may have been a cry for help; it may have been the unloading of a troubled soul; it may have been anticipation of the events programmed for the next day that caused the outburst. We don't know. It was as strange as Abby Borden's visit to Dr. Bowen earlier that day.

Lizzie told Miss Russell that *someone* was planning to do *something*, with neither "someone" nor "something" defined.

That it would be done *to* the Bordens was implied, but implied beyond any question or doubt. Because of the danger she sensed, Lizzie had written to friends near where her sister Emma was vacationing and said that she had decided to join them as she had previously said she would, but because of an upcoming church committee meeting scheduled for Sunday, she would not be able to get there until the following Monday (this was Wednesday evening). Miss Russell noted the tension in Lizzie and encouraged her to get out of Fall River. Lizzie volunteered she had something hanging over her she could not shake off and went on to describe how most of the household (Andrew and Abby) were sick to the point that Lizzie said she believed they had all been poisoned. She echoed exactly her stepmother's words to Dr. Bowen that morning.

As of the evening of August 3, neither Bridget nor Lizzie had been affected by the poison or sickness, although Bridget testified that she displayed the symptoms the next morning, the day of the murders. That only some of the members of the household were affected would tend to indicate that whatever was wrong was not food poisoning; all four people in the house ate the same things. It has been suggested, however, that this *is* proof of "selective" poisoning. No one could testify that Lizzie ever reached the same level of sickness as the others did, but later on Lizzie went out of her way to imply that she had.

Lizzie continued to reveal more to Miss Russell than anyone has ever bothered to consider seriously. She stated that her father had an enemy, someone who had caused him much trouble and was a real danger to him. The prosecution later used these words to suggest that she was pointing the finger at herself. Neither the prosecution nor the defense, however, wanted to reveal who the real murderer was and they were forced to *ignore* the implications of what Lizzie told Alice Russell. Listen to what Lizzie said—with an open mind and with the assumption that she was telling the simple truth.

Lizzie told Miss Russell of an unknown man on the property one night recently and of the barn break-ins when pigeons were stolen. She told of the daylight burglary and of the nail she found in the cellar door and gave to the police. She said the thief would be caught when he used the street railway tickets because they were numbered; in his love of counting things, Andrew Borden had recorded the numbers.

Lizzie's parting words to Miss Russell were later called prophetic. She vowed she would sleep with her eyes half open—one eye open all the time in fear *they* would burn the house down over them. As she left, she reiterated, "*I am afraid somebody will do something; I don't know but what someone will do something.*"

No one has ever accepted those words as meaning exactly what they say. No one has ever accepted the "somebody" or the "someone" as being anyone but Lizzie Borden herself, but she may have known exactly who that person was and it may not have been herself.

Miss Russell listened but took no action. It is doubtful she considered Lizzie's words anything more than the rantings and ramblings of a frustrated young old-maid. At the inquest and later at the trial, however, these ramblings counted heavily against Lizzie.

Lizzie arrived home about nine o'clock that evening (about fifteen minutes after Mr. Morse), locked all three locks on the front door, and immediately climbed the front staircase and went to her room. Uncle John (whom she had not greeted or even seen since his arrival) and the Bordens were talking together in the sitting room about ten feet from the door Lizzie entered. She ignored them and they ignored her.

At every chance, Uncle John stressed that on this particular visit he had not seen Lizzie at all before the murders. He volunteered that he had visited the Borden house three or four weeks earlier, but he had not seen Lizzie at that time either. Actually, he claimed, he had not seen her for three or four months before that. Lizzie agreed with all of this. For some reason, avowed and demonstrated separation between Lizzie and her uncle seemed important to both of them. Like her uncle's alibi, the story is stressed in such perfect two-part harmony that it forces suspicion.

Lizzie testified that a loud, argumentative conversation was taking place in the room below her room and that it was annoying, but she would not admit to hearing what was said.

No one else has ever indicated what the conversation was about. It may have been (as the district attorney insisted *after* the trial) of utmost importance to the case; it may have been the key to the whole situation; it may have been the cause of the deaths of both Abby and Andrew; or it may have been a retelling of the Iowa blizzard of 1883.

Many have stated with much conviction that a replay of the property swindle of five years earlier was in the making (another property transfer to Abby), and this, overheard by Lizzie overhead, triggered her murderous attacks the next morning. The conversation in the sitting room that evening may have been related to the next day's events, but those events did not begin that evening. The die had been cast long, long before.

Bridget, too, was out of the house that evening. She arrived home a few minutes after Lizzie, triple locked the rear door, and went directly up the rear stairway to her attic room. Abby soon retired up the same rear stairs, leaving Andrew and Uncle John to continue their conversation. A few minutes after ten o'clock Andrew went up the back stairs to his bedroom, and Uncle John went up the front stairs to his bedroom next to Lizzie's. Lizzie's door was closed, but Uncle John left his open. We have no more reports of any actions or activities inside the Borden house that evening, but let us not be too hasty in saying good night.

At Lizzie's trial, the first witness for the defense was Miss Martha Chagnon, daughter of Dr. Chagnon, the Bordens' neighbor diagonally northeast behind them. As she had stated at the preliminary hearing, Miss Chagnon testified that about eleven o'clock the night before the murders, she and her stepmother were disturbed by a noise of pounding on wood or on a fence. The noise came from the direction of the Borden fence and continued for four or five minutes. Her stepmother, Marienne Chagnon, was the second witness, and she repeated what Martha had said. In cross-examination, the prosecution muddied this testimony, forcing both Chagnons to admit that they did not investigate at the time and that the noise could have come from other sources.

As an example of testimony changing with time, the

"respectable" Fall River *Herald* had reported on August 8, 1892, that "Mrs. Chagnon and her daughter, Martha, say that Wednesday night about 12 o'clock they distinctly saw a man jump over the fence into the Borden yard and subsequently they heard a slight noise in the barn."

Suppose, for a moment, the noise was exactly what the Chagnons said, a pounding on the tall barbed wire reinforced fence at the rear of the Borden lot. The defense opened with this testimony but failed to pursue it, never referring to it again. Although the prosecution spent considerable time in neutralizing the testimony, they, too, never referred to it again.

We will.

# Chapter 4

The day of the murders began as all others normally did. Bridget came down the back stairs from her attic bedroom around 6:15 A.M. to begin her labors. Uncle John testified he was already up and about. Just before 7:00, Abby Borden came down from her upstairs bedroom as did Andrew Borden a few minutes later. These three joined in breakfast that was prepared and served by Bridget. Lizzie did *not* join them. She remained upstairs until just a few minutes after Uncle John left the house.

Uncle John left about 8:45 (Bridget is the only recorded witness to his departure), and he did not return for three hours. His alibi for part of those three hours was not just ironclad; it was double-wrapped in fifteen-inch-thick battleship armor. It was *so* good that it had to have been the product of a deliberate effort to establish an alibi.

Bridget testified to Uncle John's departure, but she did not see Andrew Borden leave the house that morning. Mrs. Churchill, Andrew's neighbor on the north side, however, stated she saw him leave his yard "around" nine o'clock. Andrew's usual leaving time was nine, and this morning Bridget was outside in the back yard, beyond a line of sight to the door he would have used. Since no one on Andrew's morning rounds reported his arrival as being at an unusual time, he must have left the house close to nine. This point is belabored because Lizzie first said it was about nine when her father left, then later changed that, not once but twice. Other than Abby, who could not be asked, Lizzie was the only household member who witnessed Andrew's departure from the house that murder morning, and she had him leaving at three different times.

Andrew Borden was well known and easily recognized in the financial district of Fall River, and his daily routine had been well established over the years. While no one came forward to pinpoint his minute-by-minute movements between 9:00 and 9:30, there was no major deviation this morning from his normal routine. The same people saw him in the same places as he was generally seen.

Andrew was president of the Union Savings Bank, and Abram G. Hart was the bank treasurer. Hart saw Andrew come into the bank the morning of the murder at "half past nine, as nigh as I can fix it." Mr. Hart said Mr. Borden stayed just five minutes or so, did nothing unusual, but did not look in the best of health. He also said he had been told that Andrew came back to the bank later that morning, but since Mr. Hart had been out at the time, he had not seen him. No time was asked or given for this second visit.

John T. Burrell, who was cashier at the National Union Bank, where Andrew was the majority stockholder, testified that Andrew had entered the bank between 9:15 and 9:45 and had stayed for five to ten minutes.

The Fall River *Daily Globe* reported that Andrew went into Pierre Leduc's barber shop for his daily shave, presumably after leaving the National Union Bank.

Everett Cook, cashier of the First National Bank—Andrew was director of a trust company connected with the bank—had looked at a clock and stated that Mr. Borden had arrived at the bank at 9:45 and had stayed about ten minutes, leaving at 9:55 by his best guess. He had failed to look at the clock when Andrew departed.

Each of these visits was a part of Andrew Borden's daily routine. He spoke to people, went to his office or his desk, conducted business, and took care of those details that made up his normal business day. What he did on this day was exactly what he did on most other days. All those who testified they saw him did not offer many details because it was all so routine. The record of the timing after Andrew left his banks is more precise.

Jonathan Clegg, a haberdasher who was about to become a

tenant of Andrew's, met him in the shadow of the city hall clock at the foot of South Main Street at 10:20 to discuss changes and renovations in the store he would soon be renting. Mr. Clegg said he could see the city hall clock easily from where they met and he checked the time at the beginning and at the end of their discussion. At 10:29, Clegg said, Andrew proceeded up South Main Street.

Andrew walked to the store Clegg was going to rent and discussed the remodeling with Joseph Shortsleeves and James Mather, two carpenters who were working there. Andrew left at 10:40 by the city hall clock, said Mather. He had checked it, he said, because he was getting hungry and he wanted to see how much longer he had to wait before lunch.

In *every* account of the Borden murders where the subject is discussed, it is said that on his rounds that morning, Andrew Borden picked up an old, broken, brass Yale lock, worthless even for scrap. He then went someplace never determined for a sheet of paper in which he wrapped this treasure and proudly carried it home. One unsubstantiated account states that he went to the post office and purchased a mailing wrapper for the salvaged lock. This is ludicrous. Andrew's life did not have the required minutes left in it for him to make that detour, nor, if there had been time, would he have purchased a throwaway luxury item like a mailing wrapper.

Without question, Andrew Borden picked up an old, worthless lock. Without question, he arrived home only a few minutes later holding in his hand a package wrapped in white paper. But also without question, the package did not contain the worthless lock. Dr. Kelly's wife, Caroline, had watched Andrew come home that morning. She had just left her house and was headed downstreet for an appointment. At the preliminary hearing District Attorney Knowlton asked her, "Did you see Mr. Borden that morning?"

"Yes, sir."

"Where was he when you first saw him?"

"He was coming around [the side of] his house," said Mrs. Kelly, "going toward the front door."

"Did you see him go up the steps?"

"Yes, sir."

"What did you see him doing, if anything, when he got up

*View down South Main Street (looking north), with the old City Hall and its all-important clock tower. Date before the turn of the century, probably between 1892 and 1900.*

the steps?"

"I thought he was trying to put the key in the door. I thought he was trying to open the door."

"Did he have anything in his hand at that time?"

"I think he had a small white package."

Mrs. Kelly's testimony about the "small white package" was of major consequence. However, at the final trial her important description given at the preliminary hearing was ignored. If the actual contents of that package had become public knowledge, the repercussions would have been severe. Defense Attorney Andrew Jennings also questioned Mrs. Kelly. He asked, "You said he had a white package in his hand?"

"I think he had a little square white package."

"Did it look as though it might be a letter, or something like that?"

"No," she said, "it was bigger, looked as though it might be a small box."

Jennings let it rest there, and Knowlton must have sensed something in this "small white package" because he, on re-direct, asked Mrs. Kelly, "Give me the size of the package or box as near as you can."

"It might have been five inches square, and perhaps an inch thick, as near as I can remember; it was wider than that book [indicates a note book]."

"Something that shape?"

"No, sir, it was square, about that square."

Bridget confirmed Mrs. Kelly's testimony at the preliminary hearing. Melvin Adams, for the defense, asked her, "When he came in, did he have anything in his hand?"

"A parcel."

"A white parcel?"

"Yes, sir."

"Any key or brass lock in his hand?"

"I did not notice it."

We will never know if, at that early stage in the case, Mr. Knowlton and Mr. Jennings knew the actual importance of the white square package. Jennings may have known because he worked to get an explanation for it when he questioned James Mather. He said, "You say he went to the window, and took something?"

"An old lock that was there, an old store lock," Mather replied.

"Was it an iron lock?"

"A Yale lock."

"Brass?"

"A brass bolt and brass springs inside."

"Did he wrap it up in anything?"

"No, sir," said Mather, "he took it in his hands."

"Did he have anything else in his hand that you noticed at the time?"

"I did not notice."

"Did he carry that away with him?"

"Yes, sir."

"Did he have it in his hand when you last saw him?"

"Yes, sir."

Jennings ended with Mather testifying that the route Andrew Borden took when he left the store was the most direct one to take if he was heading home.

Jennings' objective was to get *something* into Mr. Borden's hand for Mrs. Kelly to see. He did a credible job, one that has lasted through the decades. It is difficult to picture a brass lock as something white, an inch or more thick, and five or more inches square. But every account tells that Andrew Borden returned to his home that day with a worthless lock clutched in his hand and proudly exploits this as a fitting tribute to the last vestige of his miserly existence. The legend is wrong. What he was carrying was a fair-sized wrapped "box."

With all the police searches that took place the murder day and in the days that followed, no brass lock was ever mentioned. Of course, no white-paper-wrapped package was ever found either, but that is explainable. It was a package of great value.

That morning when Andrew visited his bank, he removed a small package wrapped in white paper from its repository to take to his home where he had an appointment with a man to whom it would be given. This man was well known to him and to all of the Borden clan. Andrew kept the appointment, and when the man left the Borden house, both Andrew and Abby were dead.

The determination of the time of the murders is important, but in the 1890s most people were not as aware of the exact time as they are today. This was before wrist watches, before electric wall clocks, and only the gentry had pocket watches. Factory whistles kept the masses informed of when they should begin work during the week, and on Sundays the important hours were marked with bells instead of whistles. Each hour of each day was chimed by the Fall River city hall clock. Those within its range listened for it and relied on it. Other accounts have tried to hang suspects for the murders based on a one- or two-minute discrepancy in their testimonies. Requiring such accuracy is impractical. Any reference to time in *this* account is reinforced by overlapping testimony.

Medical experts established that Abby did not die before

*The Borden house on Second Street, 1892. The barn is in the background.*

9:00 nor after 10:00. Their consensus was that she died about 9:30. At that time Andrew Borden was alive and well in the business district, Uncle John was out of the house en route to his relatives' home, Bridget was outside the house washing windows, and Lizzie was inside the house as, of course, was Abby.

Lizzie herself swore that Bridget was outside the house during the time Abby Borden was slaughtered. This testimony was supported by several reliable passers-by who saw her and said so under oath. It is another fact we can depend on: Bridget Sullivan was not inside the house when Abby Borden died.

Just one person steadfastly swore she was the only person in the house at the time Abby was killed, and that person was Lizzie herself. She denied she was out of the house, and she said that, other than Bridget, she saw no one on the property outside the house at that time and no one inside the house at that time. She said she heard nothing unusual. While telling us she was the only one who could have killed Abby Borden, Lizzie also vehemently denied that she had done so.

Lizzie's defense was strange but basically sound. She thought her stepmother was *out* of the house at the time of the murder. Therefore, if Lizzie was inside the house and Abby was outside, Lizzie could not have killed her.

Andrew Borden returned to his home about 10:40 carrying the small packet wrapped in white paper. Bridget had finished her outside work and was inside washing the inner surfaces of the windows. Because the front door was secured on the inside, she had to unlock it for Andrew. At this instant, Lizzie was upstairs in her bedroom or on the landing halfway upstairs or in the kitchen or in the dining room. At various times in her inquest testimony Lizzie claimed all four. Bridget said Lizzie was upstairs because the locking device hung up, and Bridget, fumbling with it, uttered an expletive ("Pshaw!"). She testified she heard Lizzie laugh at this, and the laugh came from up the front staircase. She identified the laughter as Lizzie's because as far as she knew the only person in the house was Lizzie. We do know that Abby's body, lifeless now for more than an hour, lay upstairs within a few feet from where Lizzie's laugh came, according to Bridget.

Bridget went to her attic room about 10:55 to lie down. Andrew Borden went to the couch in the sitting room to do the same. Lizzie went to the kitchen, or to the back yard, or to the back yard and to the barn, or to the back yard and to the barn and to the loft in the barn. She was out of the house for half an hour or maybe twenty minutes. She saw no one although she had the side door of the house in view at all times, or she did not have the side door of the house in view at all times. Lizzie made all these conflicting claims.

During this time, Andrew Borden met the same fate as had his wife. While Lizzie placed herself inside the house and Bridget placed herself outside when Abby was murdered, Lizzie said she was outside the house and Bridget said she was inside when Andrew was murdered.

At approximately 11:10, Lizzie went back into the house, discovered Andrew had been hacked to death, and shouted up the rear stairs for Bridget to come down quickly. Andrew Borden had been killed.

At 11:15 a telephone call was received at the central police station and answered by Fall River City Marshal (i.e., the chief law enforcement official) Rufus B. Hilliard. The caller

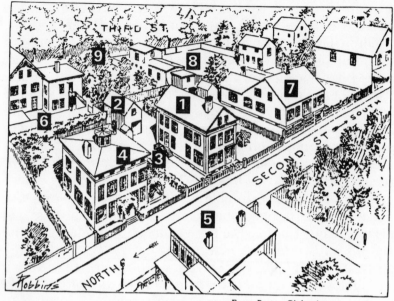

From *Boston Globe,* August 11, 1892

| | |
|---|---|
| 1 - Borden House | 5 - Dr. Bowen's House |
| 2 - Borden Barn | 6 - Dr. Chagnon's House |
| 3 - Side Entrance | 7 - Dr. Kelly's House |
| 4 - Mrs. Churchill's House | 8 - Dr. Kelly's Barn |
| 9 - Orchard - Third Street | |

*A bird's-eye view of the vicinity of the Borden murders.*

reported "trouble" at the Borden residence at 92 Second Street.

Somewhere, in the depths of all that was recorded of what took place that day is truth, truth that has, for whatever reason, never surfaced, truth that has never been uncovered. It is there; we shall find it.

# Chapter 5

There were several reports of unknown people around the Borden house the day of the murder. One of the better known ones was given by Dr. Benjamin Handy and reported in the August 10 *Daily Globe*.

## THAT STRANGE MAN

### Dr. Handy Tells of One He Met Near the Borden House.

In connection with the great mystery a report is circulated upon which more or less importance may be attached. Dr. Handy says that while driving by the Borden house at about 10:30 or 10:40 on the day of the murder he noticed a man walking slowly by the house.

In his profession the doctor meets and passes many people, but he says that his attention was never attracted to a person on the street before as it was to this man. So much so was he struck by his appearance that he turned about in his carriage to obtain a second look at him.

He described him as being a man about five feet four inches in height, of medium weight, and wearing a dark moustache. His face was deadly white but was round and full. The young man was apparently 24 years of age. This description tallies with that of a man whom Officer Hyde saw in the vicinity on the morning of the murder.

His description also answers to that of the man who is reported to have jumped on a wood team at Flint Village and asked to be conveyed to Westport. This man has had every opportunity to be miles away, but it is quite possible that if this same fellow was found something interesting would follow.

Note that this is the report that set off all the speculation about Dr. Handy's "wild-eyed" young man. Nowhere is there any mention of eyes. One can only speculate on how this description came into existence.

Another person seen around the Borden house on the morning of the murder was reported the next day, August 11, by the *Daily Herald:*

> Another woman dropped into the case Wednesday afternoon, but she did not stay long. A lad who drives for Wilkinson, ice cream man, said he saw a woman come out of the Borden yard about 10:30 o'clock Thursday. Officers Harrington and Doherty went to work to find this woman, and they succeeded in discovering that Ellan Eagan was passing that way Thursday morning when she was seized with a sudden illness. She went into the first yard she came to, but it was Dr. Kelly's yard, which is next to the Borden house, and the boy was mistaken.

Wilkinson's "lad" was a Russian immigrant named Hyman Lubinsky. His initial reports were rejected by both the defense and the police for two reasons: his report of the time of his sighting was not consistent with the crime, and Ellan Eagan's innocent presence on the scene was a possible explanation for the woman he did see. The defense worked diligently on his testimony. Later Lubinsky was promoted to the position of star witness to testify that he had seen Lizzie Borden outside her house at the time Andrew was murdered.

We will report what happened after the murders occurred by looking at the testimony of the witnesses at the legal proceedings. Dr. Handy was one such witness and told of the man he saw. However, Ellan Eagan, the witness who was, by far, the most important witness to the truth, was never called to the stand and is unknown to the legend. She is the woman the *Herald* says was seen by Hyman Lubinsky. She did contact the police, but since she was so uneasy at giving her story to authorities and since the officials got what they needed from Ellan to help build the case they had already developed, she was never given an opportunity to tell her whole story. Here's how it happened.

During the week following the murders, Ellan Eagan was troubled. The papers had been full of the awful things that had happened in the Borden house on Thursday and, as near as she could reckon, the murders must have happened about the time she passed the house. She knew the maid was outside, as she said she was, yet people were saying that the maid had murdered the Bordens because "you know how them Irish is." Maybe she *did* do it, but Ellan knew the maid was telling the truth when she said she was outside.

The man she had seen puzzled her. Ever since she had heard about the murders, she had wrestled with her memory. Somehow, no matter how she tried, her mind would not give her a good picture. She knew she had been real sick that day—summer grippe some called it—and she could easily remember some of what had happened, like the odor, but how do you tell somebody about a smell when you don't know what it was? How do you describe someone when you can't be sure of what he really looked like? She had told her family about the maid who was washing windows and about getting sick, but she had not said one word about that man. She wished she could get it clear in her own mind.

She wondered whether all her silliness about a devil had made her imagine some funny odor to go with one, something like brimstone. She remembered how she called the electrics on Main Street the devil's wagons and thought about the smell that people said was electricity. She had no idea what brimstone was supposed to smell like; she made a mental note to ask Father Patrick about it Sunday after mass. While she was at it, she would ask him if it was safe to ride the new electrics. He would know.

Ellan even wondered whether the odor had been her own because she knew she had been sick to her stomach when she was in Dr. Kelly's yard. Her family had laughed about that. "Imagine going to a young doctor just starting out," they said, "with that fancy Dr. Bowen right across the street. You should have got sick in *his* yard even if his visits do cost ten cents more than Dr. Kelly's."

*View up Second Street (to the south), with the Borden house just left of center. Portions of the Churchill house and Dr. Kelly's house are also visible, as is (on the side of the street from which the picture taken) Dr. Bowen's house.*

Maybe that was funny, but the way people were picking on the Bordens' maid was no joke. Ellan had watched the papers carefully, and no one admitted to seeing her outside as she had said she had been. They did say she was washing windows on the *third* floor, but that was silly. According to the papers, others had seen a person she assumed was the man she had seen. People were talking about a man seen by Dr. Benjamin Handy as "wild eyed." That sure was right! If anyone ever had "wild eyes," that man did.

Ellan did not want to get mixed up in the murder case. No Eagan she could remember had ever been in a police station, and the very thought made her legs feel weak. The papers said an arrest was going to happen any minute, and so the police must know who that awful man was. But she felt guilty because of the bad things she had thought about the maid who was, after all, just doing what someone told her to do. Ellan could at least tell the police that the maid had been outside.

She wrestled with her indecision and finally made up her mind. She would go to the police and tell them that the maid had been outside. Then, she figured, she could sort of tell them about the man she had seen, and when they caught him like the papers said they would any minute, she would ask if she could look at him and see if it was the right one. That would do it. Ellan Eagan was proud of her plan.

Ellan's thinking had been misled by the newspaper reports. The arrest warrant for the murders had already been issued—but for Lizzie, not "the wild-eyed man"—and Dr. Handy had never said that the man he had seen had "wild eyes." That was the *Globe*'s embellishment. Dr. Handy had described a man much younger and totally different from the man Mrs. Eagan had seen. In reality, two men were near the Borden house that morning. One was simply waiting for the other.

Within hours of the crime, almost everyone had accused the Fall River police of being less than professional in their initial investigation into the murders. By the Wednesday following the murders, the marshal was furiously trying to make up for it in show, if not in fact. All personnel were on full-time duty and under orders to *stay* on duty until they could no longer stand and then to rest for no more than an hour. Every clue, hint, or rumor, every letter, every report, every outrageous story, and every person connected with the Bordens, no matter how remotely, had been checked and sometimes re-checked, and then re-rechecked. Every hour brought another drunken or irresponsible confession, another maniac report, another bloody hatchet report, another wild goose chase, another irate citizen or another official screaming another change of orders.

City Marshal Rufus Hilliard turned to paperwork for help and demanded full, complete, and properly prepared written reports on everything, regardless of what the officer's personal opinion might be. The marshal was not a man to cross right now. He was always hard on anyone who took shortcuts, but now the entire force cringed whenever he appeared. Men with almost no formal training in criminal investigation and totally unaccustomed to exerting themselves were being pushed beyond their intellectual and physical limits. All were tired; some were close to rebellion.

Officer Mullaly was tired, hungry, hot, dirty, angry, and irritable to the snapping point. He was five minutes away from getting off an almost three-day-long shift when Ellan Eagan walked into the police station on August 10, the Wednesday after the murders took place. She wanted to report something about the Borden case. That meant he had to listen to her, and that meant time, and time meant his long longed-for relief was still out of reach.

"All right, young lady, what's the trouble?" he asked, knowing his voice was gruff and more fitting for a Saturday night saloon fighter than a lass like this one. But he didn't care.

"She was too outside, and that's no lie!" Ellan quaked. She was shaking all over, but she pressed on, in spite of her fast-forming better judgment. "When I went downstreet Thursday morning, I saw her outside washin' winders like she said she was."

"Who, in God's name, is *she?*" Mullaly knew he was acting like a horse's arse, but it felt good. For a few minutes, at least, he had someone *he* could kick.

"*She* was the maid at the Borden house!" Ellan felt she was shouting, but the constriction in her throat reduced her voice to a raspy whisper. Her lower lip was quivering, and she felt herself reddening shamefully. *Why is this policeman mad at me?* she thought.

"Thank you, *ma cushla*. We know she was. We know all about it, but I will personally tell Marshal Hilliard you was in to confirm it for us. Anything else?"

"Well, yes . . . there was this man. . . ."

"All covered with blood, carrying a bloody hatchet, and all wild and crazylike?" he teased threateningly.

"Well, no, ah . . . yes . . . well, sort of, but . . ." Ellan tried but quickly surrendered to silence and wished she could simply sink through a crack in the floor.

"Where was you?"

"Well, I went by the Borden house and saw him and got scared and ran into Dr. Kelly's yard next door and . . . and I got sick." Ellan's knees were beating. *This was an awful mistake*, she told herself, *but it's too late now. Sweet blessed*

*Jesus, get me out of here,* she pleaded silently.

"What time was this?" Mullaly asked with a sudden, genuine interest. There was a report an ice cream peddler had made about a woman in a yard around the Borden house that morning. Police officer Harrington insisted that it meant Miss Borden was outside the house when her father was murdered, just as she said she was. Everyone else on the force knew for sure that that nose-in-the-air-too-good-for-ordinary-people Borden female was as guilty as whaleshit! If only they could prove it.

"Well, the city hall clock had rung 11:00 when I wasn't sick no more and . . . and headed home." Her struggle for words was easier. She sensed that all of a sudden there had been a change in the policeman's manner. The change ended abruptly.

"Whoa, the maid was washing windows at 11:00?" he snapped.

"No, that was when I went *downstreet*, earlier, before 10:00 rung," she corrected. "I saw her clear as anything outside the house and standin' with a long pole so she could reach the winders she was washin'. It was when I was *goin' home* I got sick and saw the man. . . ."

"At 11 o'clock you were in Dr. Kelly's yard, is that right?"

"Yes sir, it was maybe a bit after that, maybe five minutes. . . ."

". . . and that's when you were chased by a wild man with a bloody axe? Thank you Mrs. Eagan. Now listen to me. You look like a nice proper lass and I'm sure you don't want to get in no trouble telling me a tale about some wild man with an axe. We know who done it, and we are tired and sick to death of all these crazy stories about wild men with bloody hatchets! You should be home taking care of your babies, and if you don't have none to take care of, get your man to take care of you! Now run along like a good girl before I lock you up!"

Ellan Eagan was in tears when she bolted from the police station. She was only trying to help. "Jesus, Mary, and Joseph, hear my vow," she pleaded with tears streaming down her cheeks. "Never, never, never will I say anything about that . . . devil . . . never, never, never again, I swear, I swear, I swear!"

She didn't know why, but that made her feel better. She dried the tears as she slowed her flight. *Maybe the policeman was right*, she thought. *It certainly would have been hard to tell and even harder for anyone to understand.*

She headed up Second Street as she had done nearly a week earlier. A small crowd was still in the street milling around in front of the murder house, as had been the case since the news got out. She slowed and followed the exact steps she had taken that morning. She stared unashamedly into the Bordens' side yard, and no matter how hard she tried, she had to admit she had no clear picture of what she had actually seen that morning.

She was very sure of one thing: she didn't want any trouble. The Borden girls could take care of themselves. She had her own business to mind. She had done her duty and would say nothing ever again.

Later on the afternoon of Wednesday, August 10, Ellan Eagen heard a knock on her door and opened it to find officers Harrington and Doherty ominously filling the tiny entryway. She panicked at the sight of uniformed policemen, and her panic turned quickly into a terror that released a flood of uncontrollable tears and tortured wails. The police officers were thrown off balance by this outburst, and several *cushla ma chrees*, some genuine sympathy, and lots of soft coos were required to calm her. She was finally convinced she was not in trouble because of her visit to the station house that morning and their only reason for being there was their need for her help. Even so, talking was not an easy task for her.

The officers spent most of an hour asking her question after question about the maid and the window washing and the sickness that had forced a visit to Dr. Kelly's yard. They tried to pinpoint time and, thanks to the city hall clock, she could offer a degree of accuracy that was helpful. She liked these two policemen. They were polite and seemed genuinely interested in what she said.

Her delicate confidence nearly turned to rice pudding when, as they were about to leave, Officer Harrington asked if there was anything else she could tell them. Because they had been so understanding, she decided to tell them about her man in the coat.

She would have, too, but in that split instant she remembered the vow made just hours earlier, a vow never to talk about *him* again. She also remembered a time when her school class had visited a convent and Mother Superior Mère Sainte Therese had talked to them about vows and had given each student a holy medal. The mother superior told how a girl would lose her soul and be sent to hell if she ever broke a sacred vow. When Ellan had left the police station that morning, she had made a vow not to talk about it *ever*. She remembered Mère Sainte Therese's words and froze in renewed panic. She could not force herself to form words, and so she stood mute.

The officers were happy with what she *had* told them, and they had no reason to connect any possible importance to her hesitation. They did not press her. They saw the beginnings of a chin quiver; they remembered the tears and the wails that greeted their arrival; and they were in a hurry. They thanked Ellan and took their immediate leave.

When the importance of the interview finally hit her, Ellan Eagan felt so happy she danced a little jig and sang a bit of a silly song. For the first time since the burden had been placed on her that frightful morning, she was free again. It was all over. She had done the right thing. The poor maid was safe from being called a liar, and her vow to the Holy Family had not been violated. She promised that she would make a special offering to the Virgin Mother for sending her that vision of the mother superior right at the second when she was so close to losing her soul. She knew she had been given a special blessing.

Officers Harrington and Doherty went directly from the interview to the court house where the inquest was in progress. They reported their findings to Marshal Hilliard, who was trying to show that Lizzie was in the house while her father was murdered.

"If this Mrs. Eagan was the woman Wilkinson's man saw, then Miss Borden has no one to back up her story about being outside the house when Mr. Borden was murdered, right? And if no one saw her outside and no one but that senile Dr. Handy saw anyone else outside, then it's all over. She hasn't got a leg to stand on! Good work, men. I'll remember it."

Within fifteen minutes, this summary had been shared with Mayor Coughlin and District Attorney Knowlton. The following day, Lizzie was placed under arrest. For the first time in almost eight long days, the Fall River police could relax.

# Chapter 6

lthough there were actually four opportunities for witnesses to give testimonies, most accounts of the Borden murders make primary use of the superior court trial testimony. In addition, we can glean information from events and opinions as reported in the newspapers and from early accounts of the case. While the testimonies frequently agree (and sometimes do not agree) from court appearance to court appearance, it is important to remember that the purpose of Lizzie's trial (the last of the court appearances) was to make sure the identity of the murderer was *not* revealed.

An agreement had been worked out (more of that in the next chapter) that called for the arrest of Miss Lizzie Andrew Borden on the charge of murder. This was to be done to ensure that the true murderer would not be considered and that his name would not even be brought up in the legal proceedings or in the newspapers. If the true murderer was identified, it would force the existence of Andrew Borden's will out into the open. It is not certain to whom Andrew wished his fortune to go, but since Abby was dead, it is certain that without a will it would go only to Emma and Lizzie.

This seemingly drastic and potentially dangerous step of arresting Lizzie was considered acceptable because the Mellen House gang (a group of powerful men in law enforcement who shall be discussed later)—at the direction of Lizzie—had a plan of what would happen. The preliminary hearing would bring a number of controlled facts into the open to satisfy the public's desire for information. The preliminary hearing would also direct the case to the grand jury where, under the cloak of secrecy, the charges would be dismissed for lack of evidence. Because of the testimony of Lizzie's closest friend, Alice Russell, however, events did not go as planned.

At the final trial, the defense had the advantage of what they had learned at the first three court appearances. They suppressed what they did not want in the record—those things that could hint at the identity of the real murderer. Thus, accounts of the earlier appearances are actually more helpful in uncovering the truth.

The official legal documents now on file are authentic and unquestionably bona fide. We have more information today than was available fifty years ago. The difference is not the *content* of the transcripts, but the *availability* of the transcripts. Material is now available that was "lost" in the early years after the trial.

Amazingly, the more one studies of past accounts of the case, the more convinced one becomes that no one who has ever written about the Borden murders knew what actually happened. Using identical "facts," authors have proved that Lizzie did it, that Bridget did it, that Emma (poor, sweet, mousy Emma) did it, that Uncle John did it, that Dr. Bowen did it, that Lizzie's mythical boyfriend did it, and on and on *ad nauseum*. In addition, there are accounts that name no "who-done-it," just that Lizzie didn't. What is available now—with one major exception—was available to each person who wrote about the case. The sources of information are the inquest, the preliminary hearing, the grand jury, the superior court trial, newspaper accounts, and other early accounts of the case.

*The Inquest.*

An inquest was called on Tuesday, August 9 (five days after the murder), and lasted three days. This short time span between the crime and the testimony should produce the best record and be closest to being pure and untainted. Unfortunately, except for what Lizzie herself said, most of the inquest testimony is lost because the inquest was private. Lizzie's inquest testimony was published *in toto* in June 1893 by several newspapers, with the New Bedford *Evening Standard* credited as being the first and the most complete.

This action did not breach any laws because the relevant 1877 Massachusetts statute did not require inquest testimony to be secret. It only permitted it to be secret: "The Court or trial justice shall thereupon hold an inquest which may be private." Neither was publishing Lizzie's inquest testimony ethically unacceptable because when it was published, the trial jury had already been selected and seated. Thus the jury was shielded from direct exposure to the published material. Lizzie's inquest testimony is reproduced in its entirety in the Appendix. Portions of that testimony seem innocuous and innocent because the truth of what happened has been unknown. The portion *most* necessary to understanding who actually murdered the Bordens has always been deleted in abridged presentations of the testimony because it seemed unimportant.

*The Preliminary Hearing.*

Within three weeks of the crime, a preliminary hearing was convened to determine "probable cause." Again, things said within so short a time after the crime have a fair chance of being borderline fresh. Yet testimony from this hearing is almost unanimously passed over by all but the earliest accounts. Each who omitted its study excused the action by claiming it was all repeated in the superior court trial. This is not true.

While not secret, the transcript of the preliminary hearing was sequestered immediately after Lizzie's trial and subsequently "lost." Verbatim accounts should have been obtainable, but they were not freely or easily accessed. Newspaper accounts were far from complete and generally far from accurate.

The personal copy of the hearing transcript owned by Andrew J. Jennings, Lizzie's defense attorney, complete with his hand-written marginal notes, underlinings, comments, and cryptic markings, is on display at the Fall River Historical Society Museum. The curator of the museum, Mrs. Florence Brigham, allowed me to peruse a copy of this transcript, a relatively new acquisition by the museum.

Mr. Jennings was well respected in Fall River and was an outstanding attorney. He entered into the defense of Lizzie with full faith in her innocence; he came out a sadder but wiser winner of a victory in which he took no pride. He was, in fact, ashamed of some of the actions he had been forced to embrace to achieve victory. Almost immediately after the trial, he severed all professional and social contact with Lizzie Borden and hung on tenaciously to a tin tub in which he had placed all materials and exhibits generated by and germane to the trial. He covered this collection with a droppings-speckled piece of old canvas, put the whole thing out of curiosity's reach, and gave orders that transcended his death that it should remain forever out of sight and untouched. He would not so much as discuss the tub or the case with *anyone*. His silence approached mania.

When Andrew J. Jennings died in 1923, his daughter, Mrs. Dwight Waring, inherited the tin tub and her father's attitude toward it. The contents continued covered, untouched, and unexplored. After Lizzie and her sister Emma both died in 1927, Andrew J. Jennings' tub and its contents *continued* covered, untouched, and unexplored.

In 1941 almost every adult who had any connection with the case had died except Arthur S. Phillips, Jennings' legal assistant. For whatever reason, Mr. Phillips in 1941 elected to comment on Mr. Jennings' collected hoard of evidence and the continued sequestration of "the mass of documents" by saying, "Mr. Jennings considered their secrecy important to her defense should there be any new phases of police investigation."

Because he made this statement *forty-eight years* after Lizzie's trial and *fourteen years* after her death, Arthur Phillips' statement seems to be idiotic. When he made it, he was openly ridiculed. However, when considered in light of what really happened at the trial, his words take on a most profound meaning. Andrew Jennings was scared to death of "any new phases of police investigation," not because of any damage they could do to Lizzie, but because he knew that a successful investigation would uncover *his* crimes relative to the case. Phillips knew well what Jennings' crimes were because he himself had been an accessory to them.

In early 1970 the material that had been privately sequestered for seventy-seven years was finally uncovered and donated to the Fall River Historical Society by Mr. Jennings' daughter. Its contents revealed nothing earthshaking to the eagerly curious who examined it in light of traditional interpretations of the crime and its investigation.

There were firm rumors (and firmer denials by those who took part) that one pocket notebook was taken back by the family because its pages were too revealing and the memory of poor Lizzie (or of someone else) was still too hallowed for its revelations to be made public.

One item *did* contain new information: Mr. Jennings' well-scribbled-in and marked-up copy of the preliminary hearing transcript. At this hearing—as at the inquest, but not at the trial—questions were exploratory and thus very revealing. As you may have guessed, we are concentrating on the preliminary hearing testimony others have always been forced to overlook. We will also examine the differences between testimonies given at the hearing and at the trial. These differences are important because they indicate which truths were deemed necessary to avoid at the trial to make sure that the finger was not pointed at the true murderer.

The preliminary hearing offers many examples of reporting errors that have became foundation for the legend. The testimony of John Morse is a case in point. Under cross examination by Andrew Jennings, he was asked, "Did you notice at all the cellar door, whether it was open or shut."

Morse's answer counters what has long been accepted as fact. "I think it was open; I won't say for sure, but I think it was."

"When you first went to the back of the house?" Jennings asked.

"Yes, sir."

"Wide open, or only partly open?"

"Well, I could not say," was Morse's final answer.

Under re-direct questioning by the District Attorney, Morse was equally indecisive. After being asked if the cellar door was open, he answered, "I think it was; I am not sure."

However, on August 27, 1892, the Fall River *Daily Globe* reported the exchange between Jennings and Morse as fol-

lows: "How soon was it that you saw the cellar door open?"
"Soon after I came."
"Are you sure the cellar door was open?"
"I am sure."
The Legend has been built on many such misrepresentations of trial testimony. Ironically, at the final trial the only door Uncle John was asked about was the door to the barn!

*The Grand Jury.*

The grand jury's deliberations in November 1892 resulted in Lizzie's indictment and her subsequent trial. There is no transcript of the grand jury hearing. By law, then and now, this hearing *was* secret, and any disclosure was a punishable offense. The records were sequestered, and they have never surfaced. The press covered this secret hearing as well as it could. In spite of the locked doors, the hearing made news.

For a full week, the jury heard testimony from witnesses and adjourned without handing down its verdict. This was a clear, strong signal that reasonable doubt existed and that Lizzie would not be indicted. Euphoria reigned in her camp, growing with each additional day that went by without anything being done. Then, after an uncommon ten-day hiatus, the jury was reconvened to hear just one witness: Lizzie's closest friend, Alice Russell. Alice had appeared already and had testified in full, but she had begged for a reappearance to amend her original testimony. Only minutes were required to hear what she now had to say, and when she had said it, the jury acted immediately and not only handed down indictments against Lizzie for the murder of her father, but also for the murder of her stepmother and, a most unusual *third* charge, the murders of *both* her father and her step-mother.

The twenty-one members of the jury voted twenty-to-one to indict Lizzie. The revelation of this vote was a crime, but no one took credit for leaking this information and no one was ever accused of having done so. It is the correct opinion of all who have commented on the case that without the few minutes of revised testimony of Alice Russell, the jury would have handed down a clean bill and Lizzie would have walked away relatively safe from any further investigation or trial. This damning testimony was not given by an enemy, but by the person that Lizzie considered her closest and dearest friend.

*The Superior Court Trial.*
The trial of Lizzie Andrew Borden occurred in June 1893, ten months after the murders. After thirteen days of testimony and thirty minutes of deliberation, twelve honorable men voted that Lizzie was not guilty of murdering either her stepmother or her father.

The 1,930-page transcript of the superior court trial is on file at the Boston Public Library. It shows that the trial was well orchestrated, well rehearsed, and predictable. It clearly shows the open cooperation between the court and the defense and their combined manipulation of the truth. When Lizzie was found "not guilty" by this court, she was safe from further prosecution under the state's constitutional safeguard against double jeopardy. A copy of the superior court trial transcript was made available to me through the kind offices of The Honorable Robert L. Steadman, then chief justice designate of the superior court of the commonwealth.

The complete transcript now available was not available to early writers. All they had were segments reported in newspapers or recorded by the reporters themselves. The official original transcript is lost. What is now on file is a late-surfacing carbon copy. Comparison with earlier reports of the trial indicates that it is a complete and correct carbon copy of the trial transcript.

*Newspaper Accounts.*
Every telling of the case of the Borden murders grasps at each newspaper report that furthers the author's premise. This is possible because newspaper articles were not always as accurate as we might hope; even today the media present "facts" to suit their conclusions. In 1892 the only medium for news other than magazines and word of mouth was the newspaper. The newspapers said it all and, most generally, said it any way they felt would increase their circulation figures.

The entire country (and some of the rest of the world) was caught up in following the investigation of the Borden murders, and many out-of-town reporters journeyed to Fall River, including ones from The New York *Times.*

One of the most outrageous and embarrassing newspaper accounts appeared in the Boston *Globe*. The *Globe* was then (and still is) a well established and well respected Massachusetts institution. But at least once in its history it fell flat on its bold-face type. On October 10, 1892, it devoted an entire edition to charges it accepted as fact. Even today, efforts to contact the public relations department of the *Globe* for comments or additional information about the event are fended off with a firmness that reflects the paper's everlasting embarrassment.

In 1892 the *Globe* had been in business for twenty years, and it had the largest circulation of any newspaper in New England. The Fall River police had hired a detective, Edwin G. McHenry, to assist in the investigation of the Borden murders. McHenry then sold the "evidence" the police had supposedly uncovered to a young, aggressive Boston *Globe* reporter named (believe it or not) Henry Trickey. We do not know who—if anyone—was behind McHenry's deliberate act of misdirection. But Trickey and the *Globe* were at fault because they did not trust McHenry's assurance of exclusivity and so rushed the story into print without any attempt at verification. The morning edition of the *Globe* contained the entire story. The overwhelming majority of what was published was pure fabrication on McHenry's part, combined with shameless sensationalism.

### LIZZIE BORDEN'S SECRET

Mr. Borden Discovered it and Hot
Words Followed.

Startling Testimony from Twenty-Five
New Witnesses.

Emma was Kicked During That Quarrel—
Family Discord and Murder.

Lizzie's secret, said the *Globe*, was that she was pregnant through the loving efforts of her Uncle John. Each of the twenty-five "new" witnesses reported some graphic aspect of the crime: bloody raincoats, screams, thuds, and semi-identifiable faces semi-concealed behind semi-closed shutters. All these witnesses were named, and their places of residence were given. *All* these named witnesses were fictitious; none of the addresses existed.

The afternoon edition of the *Globe* repeated the story from the morning edition, including every fanciful fact as stated by every fictitious character McHenry had invented. The afternoon headline added to what was printed in the morning edition:

### SEEN IN MOTHER'S ROOM WITH A HOOD ON HER HEAD.

Accused Sister of Treachery and Kicked
Her in Anger.

Theft of a Watch—Money Offered to Bridget
—Story of a Will.

In addition, the front page of the afternoon edition carried a huge, self-serving article that bragged of the paper's cleverness in scooping the world with the story of the century.

*LATEST!*

*ASTOUNDED.*

All New England
Read Story.

Globes were bought
by Thousands.

Lizzie Borden Appears
in New Light.

Belief in Her Innocence
Sadly Shaken.

Excitement Runs High
In Fall River.

Police Think the Scoop
is a Corker.

Lawyer Jennings Says Lies
Have Been Told.

Doesn't Believe There is
Any Secret.

Opinions on That Spying by
Detective McHenry.

The articles published on October 10, 1892, were out-rageous. Today we have become conditioned to such sensationalism by supermarket tabloids and soap operas. In 1892, however, nothing could be more horrible or more harmful or destructive of a woman's character than to say that she would have a child out of wedlock *and* that the child was a product of incest.

Lizzie was immediately visited in her cell by several official observers who announced there was no visible evidence to confirm the paper's claim of her pregnancy. Even after the paper's retraction, she was observed closely for several more months, but no evidence of pregnancy ever showed itself.

The next day's morning edition contained a brave attempt on the part of the *Globe* to admit its error and to deny that New England's flagship of the fourth estate was taking on water and in danger of going under. It headlined that the story had been furnished to it by Detective McHenry and that "It has been proven wrong in some particulars." The head-lines also said, "Globe Secures Best Detective Talent Available to Find Murderer." The afternoon edition fell all over itself to admit error:

## THE LIZZIE BORDEN CASE

The Globe is, first of all, an honest newspaper. To err is human, and, as newspapers have to be run by men and not by angels, mistakes are inevitable.

The Globe feels it is a plain duty, as an honest newspaper, to state that it has been grievously misled in the Lizzie Borden case. It published on Monday a communication that it believed to be true evidence. Among all the impositions which newspapers have suffered, this was unparalleled in its astonishing completeness and irresistible plausability [sic]. Judging from what we have heard, it impressed our readers as strongly as it did the Globe. Some of its remarkably ingenious and cunningly contrived story is undoubtedly based on facts, as later developments will show. The Globe believes, however, that much of it is false, and never should have been published.

The Globe, being thus misled, has innocently added to the terrible burdens of Miss Lizzie Borden. So far as lies in our power to repair the wrong, we are anxious to do so, and thereby tender her our heartfelt apology for the inhuman reflection upon her honor as a woman, and for any injustice the publication of Monday inflicted upon her. And the same sincere apology is hereby tended to Mr. John V. Morse, and any other persons to whom the publication did an injustice.

The Globe comes out in this manner because it believes that honesty is the best policy, and because it believes in doing what is right. We prefer to build up rather than to tear down, to help rather than to injure, to carry sunshine and not sorrow into the homes of New England.

When we make a mistake, whether through our fault or not, we believe that justice to our readers demands that we should fairly and honestly and boldly proclaim the fact in the same conspicuous place in the Globe where the error was committed.

Even in 1892, before society developed its current litigious nature, Lizzie Borden and John Morse could have successfully sued the *Globe* for practically whatever they wanted. The accusations made were outrageously damaging to their characters and provably false.

In 1971 Louis Lyons, who had been a reporter for the *Globe* from 1919 to 1946, published *Newspaper Story: One Hundred Years of The Boston Globe*. In addition to covering the glorious moments of the paper's history, he told of the Borden fiasco, concluding, "The Globe was lucky to escape ruination. Exposed as false as soon as [the story] was printed, it must have been the harried condition of the Borden lawyers, desperately seeking to contrive any plausible defense for Lizzie, that led them to settle for a complete retraction and apology" (page 86). Lyons then outlined most of the false statements in the articles. Without knowing it, he included the actual reason there was no suit.

The twenty-five "new" witnesses were false, but *some* of the other names published were of real people. What they were quoted as saying was never mentioned at the trial. For example, the paper said, "Bridget swears that on the afternoon of the murder, about 6 o'clock, Lizzie said to her in a whisper, 'Keep your tongue still and don't talk to these officers, and you can have all the money you want.'" The paper also quoted Bridget as saying, "I did not state these things on the witness stand because I was not asked and the district attorney told me not to be afraid and to answer only such questions as was asked me." The legend says that Bridget was paid off. And yet this issue was never raised at the trial. District Attorney Knowlton never asked her anything about it.

Sarah Whitehead, Abby's half sister and her only friend and confidante, was quoted by the *Globe* as having full knowledge of Andrew's will. She was never called as a witness. The paper also credited Bridget, Dr. Dolan, Dr. Bowen, and Mr. Jennings with knowledge of Andrew's will. Yet none of these was asked about it.

Mixed in with the twenty-five imagined witnesses is another interesting account:

> Bearing still stronger on the probable motive is the statement of Mr. Frank Burroughs, a well known New York city lawyer, who formerly lived in Fall River.
> He will testify that about eight months previous to the murder Miss Lizzie Borden talked to him in Fall River about property rights. Again about five weeks before the murder he saw her again. He was obliged to spend some time in New Haven, Conn., preparing a case at law for the New York, New Haven & Hartford railroad. While there he received a visit from Miss Lizzie and she again inquired closely into the subject of wills and property inheritance, with especial reference to the legal disposition of property in the event of a stepmother's death before that of the husband.
> He told her that he would look the matter up at his convenience, as he was a little rusty on Massachusetts law.

Lizzie again called on him in New Haven just one week before the murder, and he then gave her the required information and she went off.

The day after Mr. Burroughs' return to New York he read the facts of the murder, and his suspicions were aroused.

Burroughs is not mentioned anywhere else in accounts of the murder, and yet we can accept his testimony as a legitimate contribution by the *Globe* article. In his book, Lyons wrote, "A lawyer (a real lawyer) was quoted as saying Lizzie had consulted him about property rights under a will; this bit was probably true. Another testified the father had told him he was cutting Lizzie off in his will" (page 89). The parenthetical insert—"a real lawyer"—is Lyons'. Frank Burroughs was real. He existed, but he was never called to testify.

Lizzie, Uncle John, and Andrew Jennings never brought suit against the *Globe* for its accusations because mixed in with a great many libelously false statements were some true ones that revealed information never brought out anywhere else. When the entire story—including the true statements—was recalled as false, it was a more than a fair trade.

Henry G. Trickey, at age twenty-four, paid dearly for his part in this coup. He was dead within weeks of the incident, reportedly killed by a train in a Canadian railroad yard.

In its retraction headline, the *Globe* said it would secure the "best detective talent available to find murderer." The detective referred to was none other than Edwin G. McHenry. The only further mention of McHenry, however, was during the questioning of one of the Fall River police officers during the final trial. He said that when last heard from, McHenry was engaged in an investigation that had taken him to New York City.

*Early Accounts.*
One other important source forms a story in itself. After the trial, Edwin H. Porter wrote and published a book, *The Fall River Tragedy—A History of the Borden Murders*. Mr. Porter was the police reporter for the Fall River *Daily Globe* and had covered the murders from minutes after they happened through Lizzie's acquittal. He had been labeled "hostile and

inconsiderate" by Lizzie's defense attorneys, but no one on the outside of the crime had a more complete knowledge of it than Edwin Porter.

It is not known how many copies of *The Fall River Tragedy* were printed, but it had to be several hundred if not several thousand. Fifty years ago only two copies were known to exist, and one other copy was rumored. Mrs. Brigham at the Fall River Historical Society has reported that four copies are now held by the society, and she knows of one other held privately. Even the copy that should be held by the Library of Congress is missing. The overwhelming majority of the press run simply disappeared the day it was published. Miss Lizzie, the legend says, acting on the advice of Andrew Jennings, bought up and destroyed every copy she could. If Lizzie did not do that, *someone* did.

Porter himself, like almost everyone else connected with the case, dropped from sight. We assume that he was paid to disappear, just as the legend says Bridget Sullivan was. Like Bridget, he played the game honorably. He could have gone elsewhere and republished his book, but he did not. Porter was an outstanding reporter, and yet after 1893 there are no reported by-lines of his from anywhere in the country. He simply was never heard from again.

In 1985 Robert Flynn of Flynn Books, 466 Ocean Avenue, Portland, Maine, reprinted Edwin Porter's book. It is now available for anyone to study.

The last sentence in Porter's book is, "Thus ended, on the thirteenth day, the famous trial of Lizzie Andrew Borden, and she returned guiltless to her friends and home in Fall River." Porter was eminently qualified to pronounce judgment. He knew almost everything the police knew; he was privy to information that was never made known to the public; he was on the scene every minute; he knew most of those involved personally and talked with them on and off the record; and he could see reactions, sense attitudes, feel anger and hostility. And he said Lizzie was guiltless.

But he did not say she was innocent.

# *Chapter 7*

Before we examine the testimony given at the various legal proceedings following the Borden murders, there are several factors bearing on the case to consider.

## *The Silent Government*

Fall River, like most towns in 1892 and today, had ways of operating that were unwritten but were more important and influential than the official channels of command.

The police force, for instance, was run by the patronage system. In a city where unskilled labor was in perpetual oversupply, a man could gain immediate respect, opportunities for advancement, and excellent pay by becoming a policeman. The job required no special skills or training. If the requirement for able-bodiedness was met, the only thing absolutely necessary for the job was a sponsoring patron. Generally, patrons formed the Silent Government of the town.

When a new recruit entered the force, a simple favor had been done by the patron for the police recruit who was in a position to appreciate it and who would, someday, in some way, return it. Everyone ever nominated to the force knew and agreed to the rules of the game.

This arrangement guaranteed civic peace and tranquility while maintaining a professional and well-ordered network for the handling of graft, kickbacks, and the multitude of big and little payoff requirements. It also produced a strong fraternal order with unquestioned loyalty to command. The chief of police (in 1892 he was called "marshal" in Fall River) took his orders directly from the mayor. The mayor took his orders from the head of the Silent Government. Sometimes the head was an honestly elected public official; sometimes it was that official's patron.

The power of government was in the county courts. This power was most often used in civil actions where, unknown to most of the voting public, the court could generate magnificent fortunes for whom it wanted (or whom the Silent Government decided) through its decisions in cases involving such mundane matters as eminent domain, right of way, zoning, licensing, or contractual settlements, or in its appointments of supervision over public funds.

County criminal court action involving people with a lot of money (as in the Borden case) was totally different. Here the media aimed their arc lights at the center ring. In such cases, if the Silent Government was to maintain control, actions required finesse and contrivance far beyond the skills of the average politician. If in such a criminal case the verdict had been agreed to before the trial (as in the Borden case), it was necessary to produce a plausible sleight-of-hand act that satisfied the most discerning critic while guaranteeing the pretrial, well-paid-for-in-advance result.

There is no possible way the names of all those who were part of the 1892 Silent Government of Bristol County, Massachusetts (of which Fall River was part), could be known. It did include the following (listed in alphabetical order):

Judge Josiah C. Blaisdell (justice, Second District Court for Bristol County)

Dr. John W. Coughlin (mayor of Fall River in public life and a physician and surgeon in private life)

Dr. William A. Dolan (chief medical examiner for Bristol County)

Marshal Rufus B. Hilliard (Fall River chief of police)

District Attorney Hosea M. Knowlton (district attorney for Bristol County)

Attorney General Arthur E. Pillsbury (attorney general for the commonwealth)

George F. Seaver, who was connected in some way with the "Massachusetts District Police" and reported to the governor.

When the Borden murders occurred, the Silent Government established a covert (at first) command post in the back parlor of the Mellen, the most posh hotel in Fall River, and all its actions were directed from there. Except for Mr. Seaver, each of these public officials had an office in a public building, but the meeting place in the Mellen was determined more suitable. Access to the room could be restricted to those the group wished to speak with or those who required an audience without fear of excessive exposure to the public or an alert reporter. By the time this "smoke-filled" command post had been hunted down and exposed to the public, the room had been sanitized of its curtain of smoke and identified as "Parlor B."

The members of the Silent Government directed most of the initial police investigation of the Borden murders and conducted the subsequent orchestration of the trial procedures. The first meeting of this group was reported by the Fall River *Globe* as being "within the first twenty-four hours of the crime," which would mean the evening of August 4 or Friday morning, August 5. Rumor indicated that Andrew Jennings, Lizzie's lawyer, met with the group at its first meeting.

Step One of the agreement called for Lizzie's arrest on the charge of murder. While potentially dangerous, this step was tempered with firm agreements on the groundwork that must be laid to guarantee that she would go free. However, unplanned events created unexpected problems.

The same evening the agreement was made—Friday—John Morse left the murder house to post a letter at the post office. Because he was the public's *prima facie* suspect for the crime, the police had warned him not to leave the house.

His mission successful, Uncle John began his return to the house, but mob action made his journey a near fatal one. Some three thousand people who had been milling around the Borden house followed him, and when the crowd became unruly, the police had to rescue him from them.

Early Saturday evening, Mayor John W. Coughlin and Marshal Rufus B. Hilliard—both unimpeachable witnesses—took the first short step to insure Miss Lizzie's future. They arrived together at the Borden house after battling their way through the mob gathered outside.

Finally inside, the mayor met with Miss Emma, Miss Lizzie, and Uncle John Morse. "I have a request to make of the family," he began, "and that is that you remain in the house for a few days, as I believe it would be far better for all concerned if they [*sic*] did so."

Miss Lizzie asked immediately, "Why? Is there anybody in this house suspected?"

The mayor's response contained all the tact and finesse of his office. "Well, perhaps Mr. Morse can answer that question better than I, as his experience last night, perhaps, would justify him in the inference that someone in this house was suspected."

Lizzie was not mollified. "I want to know the truth."

When this failed to extract an immediate answer from the mayor, she demanded, "*I want to know the truth!*"

"Well, Miss Borden," he replied, "I regret to answer, but I must answer—yes, *you* are suspected."

Lizzie's retort was immediate ("earnestly and promptly, without hesitation," were the words the mayor later used to describe it). "I am ready to go now."

Emma jumped in here with a comment that defies a normal, logical explanation. "Well, we have tried to keep it from her as long as we could." Some have suggested that Emma was referring to Lizzie's living in a news blackout since the murders and not knowing that the newspapers had been screaming her name in their headlines; others considered it something typically "Emma."

It is important to understand what Emma's words did mean. Neither side attempted to explain them at the final trial. Her words are most revealing, but only if one understands the deal that had been struck at the Mellen House.

Prior to this meeting, Mr. Jennings had signed on as the Bordens' official legal advisor. He had been present while the authorities made extensive searches earlier that day, and he had met with the family in several previous sessions. The fact is, Lizzie had established the parameters of the investigation and its final outcome; Jennings' only responsibility was to ensure that no one stepped beyond the limits of Lizzie's restrictions.

In this context, Miss Emma's statement meant, quite simply, "Lizzie, if you insist on this course, there is no option. You must shoulder the full responsibility." It was Emma's voice of resignation. She was giving in to the arguments she and the rest of the Bordens had had with Lizzie in attempting to make her soften her stand. Lizzie would not yield, and so Emma told her, in so many words, "I told you so."

Uncle John Morse had provoked the need for this visit by his near disaster of the previous evening. Even so, his only question during this meeting was, "How shall we get our mail from the post office?"

The mayor offered to have a policeman get the Bordens' mail for them, which they refused. Letters to and from the Borden clan were most important at this juncture. Control was essential, and they were not absolutely sure they had it. Time proved that they did, or at least they did in short order.

At the final trial, all of Lizzie's statements beyond this point, including that of the inquest, were thrown out of court. The action was justified by saying that the city's "mouthpiece," the mayor, had called her a "suspect," and the Massachusetts constitution afforded her the right not to testify against herself from that point forward.

The first step of the plan had been successfully taken.

One thing is certain. In the private room at the Mellen House, Lizzie Borden's defense and the court's ultimate verdict were agreed upon, signed, and sealed; and full payments were pledged—all within twenty-four hours of the murders. What followed is epilogue.

*The Will*
Andrew Borden's will was never found and never probated. Both Lizzie's testimony and testimony given in the preliminary hearing indicated that a will existed. Much speculation has been made concerning it.

On August 17 and 18, 1892, articles in the *Globe* offered a possible reason why Lizzie might have considered committing, murder. These were published several days before any testimony had been given in open court, but after the "private" inquest.

On the first day of the inquest, Lizzie had been asked, "Did you ever know of your father making a will?" Lizzie knew that the very day she was testifying, a locksmith had been contracted by the authorities to open her father's safe. Mr. Jennings had promised her he would take charge of the safe's contents, but she did not know if he would be able to keep a will secret if one was found. And so Lizzie answered, "No, sir, except I heard somebody (whom she identifies as Uncle John Morse) say once that there was one several years ago." We can be sure Lizzie and John Morse (who, remember, was the brother of Lizzie's dead mother, not of Abby Borden) had spoken about the will. At the inquest, this revelation is followed up with a host of questions about the will, all of which Lizzie honestly answered with enough negatives to leave the impression that she knew nothing about a will.

However, knowledge of Lizzie's inquest testimony was not available to the readers of the *Globe* articles.

August 17, 1892

VERY IMPORTANT MOTIVE IN THE
UNMADE WILL.

Developments of a most startling nature are promised for the preliminary trial.

The State will, THE GLOBE is informed on very good authority, prove that Andrew J. Borden did and was making preparations for the drawing of his will. It may be shown that he talked to several persons interested and also to some of his personal friends about the will which he intended to make.

The making of that will could not possibly affect anyone except Lizzie and Emma Borden *and other persons connected to them by blood relationship* [italics mine]. When all the evidence is in it will be seen that to some of those with whom he talked about the making of this will Mr. Borden said that his second wife Abbie had been a faithful and devoted wife and a loving and careful mother to Lizzie and Emma.

A better mother than they had had before and a woman who was as such entitled to more recognition in the will than that of a widow's dower. That Mr. Borden was devoted to his second wife there are none who will deny.

When the trial is called and Miss Emma Borden takes the

stand she may be asked some pointed questions as to what she knows about the family talk previous to the arrangements for making the will. She will be required to tell about her prolonged visit to friends in Dartmouth and Fairhaven and her conversation with John V. Morse relative to the matter of the will.

From reliable authority it is stated that the State will prove that Mr. Borden expressed his desire to make a will favorable [to] his second wife and that the daughters did not approve of this method of disposing of the property. The evidence will show what has been taking place in this connection for a long period of time previous to the murders.

This first article in the *Globe* clearly suggests Andrew's will is a most viable motive in the murders and uses language that is incredibly frank:

The "will could not possibly affect anyone except Lizzie and Emma Borden and other persons connected to them by blood relationship."

"Abbie had been . . . a better mother than they had had before and . . . entitled to more . . . in the will than . . . a widow's dower." [This is the only indication we have that Emma and Lizzie's mother Sarah was anything other than beyond reproach.]

"Miss Emma . . . may be asked some pointed questions . . . the will . . . visits to Dartmouth and Fairhaven . . . conversations with John Morse relative . . . to the will."

The last paragraph of the article states with frightening authority that Andrew Borden planned to leave most of his vast holdings to his dear wife Abby. Such a will might readily be accepted as a possible motive for murder by Lizzie.

This article must have caused Andrew Jennings considerable consternation. He knew that at the inquest reference was made to a will that would be harmful to Lizzie and that some of that testimony must come out in open court. He also knew that a will existed, and he could not deny it if anyone had a way of forcing him to talk about it. He himself had drawn up the will, and the original copy was in his possession.

He countered the first article by leaking information for a second article that appeared the next day.

August 18, 1892

THE WILL THEORY

Did Emma and Lizzie Know of Their
Father's Going to Make One?

Public interest in the Borden murders now centers in the will which Andrew J. Borden proposed to make just before he was killed. That this subject occupied his mind is known; what he said to members of his family regarding it can only be conjectured. Soon after the tragedy, Marshal Hilliard learned that Mr. Borden had said to Charles C. Cook, who had more or less to do with Mr. Borden's real estate transactions, "I must make a will. I am getting to be an old man and I have put it off too long already."

The government had to have a motive for the crime which had been committed, and here was the most reasonable motive. It was money. If dollars and cents were cast aside, hatred must figure in the killing. If it were neither dollars and cents, nor passion, then the deed was the work of a maniac. Proceeding on the theory that the property had inspired some member of the family to butcher Mr. Borden and his wife, Inspectors John Parker and Frank Hathaway of New Bedford, were engaged to collect information bearing on this point.

They have been working on the case for nearly two weeks and are still busy. Parker and Hathaway have been able to give the government considerable valuable information. An out of town official had this to say regarding their movements yesterday:

"There had been considerable travel between the cottage of William Davis (where John Morse lived) on the South Mill road and the Borden house on Second street, just before Mr. and Mrs. Borden were butchered. I have not talked with Parker and Hathaway for three or four days, but I know what their line of work has been and the suspicions of the government. They have proceeded far enough to make it possible for me to talk a little without embarrassing them.

It was natural of course for the government to attempt to find out what took Miss Emma to Dartmouth and what business John Morse had in Fall River. The latter was not in the habit of running over to Fall River every few days and anything out of the usual course that anybody connected with the murder does, is important. I hear that Miss Lizzie also visited Dartmouth, but I am not positive whether that is true or not.

The government has cause to believe that Mr. Borden's family knew that he was going to make a will and that his intentions did not make the relations between the daughters and their stepmother any more friendly. Mr. Borden meant to give his wife considerably more than the law would have given her had there been no will. He was not blind to the situation in his household. He was very fond of his wife and appreciated all that she had done for him and his daughters.

He knew she had worked hard and been economical and, like a good many other men, felt that his fortune was as much hers as his, though he meant to hold on to it as long as he lived. It is believed that the girls resented their father's views in this matter. They were loyal to their own mother and knew that when they were in comparatively humble circumstances, she had worked hard to save money and assist her husband.

They felt that her interest in the estate should be preserved for them and not go to their stepmother and the latter's relatives. I can only give the general outline because I do not know just what discoveries Parker and Hathaway have made. I do not pretend to be giving facts, but simply a reasonable assumption on which the police have been working. Mr. Borden may have said that he was going to make a will and dismissed the subject from his mind.

It may be that he never mentioned it again. But if he did, and his daughters heard that their stepmother was to have a larger share than they thought she was entitled to it would be natural for them to act as I have stated. In the absence of other evidence, it might explain their visits to Dartmouth, where their uncle was stopping, and their uncle's trips to Fall River.

That is all there is to it. Mr. Morse was interested in his nieces, and if there was a dispute, he might be expected to take sides with them. At all events his prejudices would be with them and against the second wife as he was their own mother's brother and would be apt to feel as they did regarding their rights in the property.

As I first heard it, Mr. Morse learned that the girls were to receive $25,000 apiece and informed them of their father's intentions. Mr. Borden would not be likely to tell them or to talk much about his money affairs. He was a man who kept his business to himself for one thing, and he would have known that the subject of a will would have increased the bitterness between his wife and daughters. Now this theory may be founded on nothing more substantial than the imagination, but there is the Dartmouth cottage and Miss Emma's visit to it and Mr. Morse's trips to this city, and the only safe course to pursue was to investigate thoroughly."

Jerome G. Borden, Abrams G. Hart and others who were reported to have talked with Mr. Borden about a will, were seen this morning, but they had never heard the subject mentioned by Mr. Borden and did not believe he had ever talked about it with anyone.

Charles C. Cook was seen at noon today and asked if he had said that Mr. Borden had spoken to him about the making of a will. Mr. Cook said that he had never been interviewed on the subject but once and that he had a certificate copy of that interview locked up in his safe. He didn't propose to be misquoted and to prevent that thing he would have nothing to say about the will. "If I was in the habit of swearing," said Mr. Cook, "I would say that the statement in the morning papers is a blank lie."

"Then you never told any man that Andrew J. Borden spoke to you about the will."

"No, sir, I never did. Mr. Borden never mentioned a will to me."

This article, published one week *before* the preliminary hearing, is a masterfully conceived "leak." It both counters the potential damage done by the previous day's article and preempts some of the testimony that would be given the following week. Most of it is credited to what is today called a "reliable source," which, in this case, is "an out of town official." The crafting of this leak required that new facts were given in trade for what was received. The foremost trade item received was a repetitive stressing that Andrew was planning in the future to make a will. If Andrew *was going* to make a will, there was no point in looking for one. John Morse will say that there *was* a will, but we already are told that "Mr. Morse was interested in his nieces and, if there was a dispute, he might be expected to take sides with them."

In return for stressing that a will did not exist, the article reveals that "the girls were to receive twenty-five thousand dollars apiece." Releasing this bit of information was a gamble on the part of Jennings, Knowlton, and those in the Mellen House group. It is probable that Jennings thought it might come out anyway. In 1892, $25,000 was a fortune, and Andrew may have bragged to someone unknown or outside the control of the Mellen House group that after his death his daughters were guaranteed comfort for the rest of their lives. It is also possible that, not wanting to give his daughters their inheritance without supervision or some form of restriction, Andrew could have established a trust account for each of them in his own trust company. Jennings would have known of such trusts if they had been set up and would have realized that they could, in any number of ways, float to the surface and require explanation. The best defense against this was to announce it as fact.

Also revealed in the second article are the names of inspectors John Parker and Frank Hathaway who, it is said, were engaged for the purpose of digging into the details of Morse's frequent visits to Fall River and of Emma's most unusual trip to Dartmouth (a town near the Davis cottage where Morse lived) and Lizzie's rumored trip to the same area. There was no danger in releasing information about these travels, for it would become public knowledge the next week anyway. What is strange is that Parker and Hathaway, who were said to have worked on the case for more than two weeks and had "been able to give the government considerable valuable information," were never called to testify. Their names are never mentioned again. In fact, there is no proof they ever existed.

As curious as Emma's travels are, she was not called to testify at the preliminary hearing. At the final trial, she was asked nothing about Mr. Morse, her travels, or her father's will.

*Hiram C. Harrington*
The Borden murder case seems full of characters who appear with a fanfare, whip up a maelstrom, and then sail off serenely leaving us with an overwhelming desire to know

more and a frustrating impossibility of asking our questions. One such character is Hiram Harrington.

Harrington had married Andrew's only sister, Lauanna (or Laurana, according to the *Daily Herald*). He had been despised by Andrew, was detested by Lizzie, and was tolerated by Emma because she genuinely adored her Aunt Lauanna. He stated his occupation as "blacksmith," certainly an ironic expression in view of his owning and operating an 1890s version of a Cadillac dealership on Fourth Street, two *very* short blocks from the murder house. In spite of his Irish name, Hiram Harrington was accepted by The Hill.

The evening of the murders he visited his nieces and claimed to have a "long interview." Because of his status, he reported that interview in full in the next day's *Daily Herald*. The *Globe* published an abridged version of the interview, but the shorter version cut many of the cleverly concealed hints and threats present in the longer version the *Herald* published.

The Fall River *Daily Herald*
August 5, 1892

CLOSE IN MONEY MATTERS

Hiram Harrington, 40 Fourth Street, is married to Laurana, Mr. Borden's only sister. A reporter who interviewed him gathered the following story: "My wife, being an only sister, was very fond of Mr. Borden and always subservient to his will, and by her intimacy with his affairs I have become acquainted with a good deal of the family history during years past. Mr. Borden was an exceedingly hard man concerning money matters, determined and stubborn, and when once he got an idea nothing could change him. He was too hard for me.

"When his father died some years ago he offered my wife the old homestead on Ferry Street or a certain sum of money. My wife preferred to take the money, and after the agreements were all signed, to show how close he was, he wanted my wife to pay an additional $3 for water tax upon the homestead."

"What do you think was the motive for the crime?" asked the reporter.

"Money, unquestionably money," replied Mr. Harrington. "If Mr. Borden died, he would have left something over $500,000, and all I will say is that, in my opinion, that furnishes the only motive, and a sufficient one, for the double murder. I have heard so much now that I would not be surprised at the arrest any time of the person to whom in my opinion suspicion strongly points, although right down in my heart I could not say I believed the party guilty.

"Last evening I had a long interview with Lizzie Borden, who has refused to see anyone else. I questioned her very carefully as to her story of the crime. She was very composed, showed no signs of any emotion or were there any traces of grief upon her countenance. That did not surprise me, as she is not naturally emotional. I asked her what she knew of her father's death, and, after telling of the unimportant events of the early morning, she said her father came home about 10:30. She was in the kitchen at the time, she said, but went into the sitting room when her father arrived. She was very solicitous concerning him, and assisted him to remove his coat and put on his dressing-gown; asked concernedly how he felt, as he had been weak from a cholera morbus attack the day before. She told me she helped him to get a comfortable reclining position on the lounge, and asked him if he did not wish the blinds closed to keep out the sun, so he could have a nice nap. She pressed him to allow her to place an afghan over him, but he said he did not need it. Then she asked him tenderly several times if he was perfectly comfortable, if there was anything she could do for him, and upon receiving assurance to the negative she withdrew. All these things showed a solicitude and a thoughtfulness that I never had heard was a part of her nature or custom before. She described these little acts of courtesy minutely.

"I then questioned her very carefully as to the time she left the house, and she told me positively that it was about 10:45. She said she saw her father on the lounge as she passed out. On leaving the house she says she went directly to the barn to obtain some lead. She informed me that it was her intention to go to Marion on a vacation, and she wanted the lead in the barn loft to make some sinkers. She was a very enthusiastic angler. I went over the ground several times, and she repeated the same story. She told me it was hard to place the exact time she was in the barn, as she was cutting the lead into sizable sinkers, but thought she was absent some 20 minutes. Then

119

she thought again, and said it might have been 30 minutes. Then she entered the house and went to the sitting room, as she says she was anxious concerning her father's health. 'I discovered him dead,' she said, 'and cried for Bridget, who was upstairs in her room.'

"'Did you go and look for your stepmother?' I asked. 'Who found her?' But she did not reply. I pressed her for some idea of the motive and the author of the act, and, after she had thought a moment, she said, calmly: 'A year ago last spring our house was broken into while father and mother were at Swansea, and a large amount of money stolen, together with diamonds. You never heard of it because father did not want it mentioned, so as to give the detectives a chance to recover the property. That may have some connection with the murder. Then I have seen strange men around the house. A few months ago I was coming through the back yard, and, as I approached the side door, I saw a man there examining the door and premises. I did not mention it to anyone, The other day I saw the same man hanging about the house, evidently watching us. I became frightened and told my parents about it. I also wrote to my sister at Fairhaven about it.' Miss Borden then gave it as her opinion that the strange man had a direct connection with the murder, but she could not see why the house was not robbed, and did not know of anyone who would desire revenge upon her father."

Mr. Harrington was asked if he knew whether or not there were dissensions in the Borden family. "Yes, there were, although it has been always kept very quiet. For nearly ten years there have been constant disputes between the daughters and their father and stepmother. Mr. Borden gave her some bank stock and the girls thought they ought to be treated as evenly as the mother. I guess Mr. Borden did try to do it, for he deeded to the daughters, Emma L. and Lizzie A., the homestead on Ferry Street, an estate of 120 rods of land with a house and barn, all valued at $3000. This was in 1887.

"The trouble about money matters did not diminish, nor the acerbity of the family ruptures lessen, and Mr. Borden gave each girl ten shares in the Crystal Spring Bleachery company, which he paid $100 a share for. They sold them soon after for less than $40 per share. He also gave them some bank stocks at various times, allowing them, of course, the entire income from them. In addition to this he gave them a weekly stipend, amounting to $200 a year.

"In spite of all this the dispute about their not being allowed enough went on with equal bitterness. Lizzie did most of the demonstrative contention, as Emma is very quiet and unassuming, and would feel very deeply any disparaging or angry word from her father. Lizzie, on the contrary, was haughty and domineering with the stubborn will of her father and bound to contest for her rights. There were many animated interviews between father and daughter on this point. Lizzie is of a repellent disposition, and after an unsuccessful passage with her father would become sulky and refuse to speak to him for days at a time. She moved in the best society in Fall River, was a member of the Congregational church, and is a brilliant conversationalist. She thought she ought to entertain as others did, and felt that with her father's wealth she was expected to hold her end up with others of her set. Her father's constant refusal to allow her to entertain lavishly angered her. I have heard many bitter things she has said of her father, and know she was deeply resentful of her father's maintained stand in this matter.

"This house on Ferry Street was an old one, and was in constant need of repairs. There were two tenants paying $16.50 and $14 a month, but with taxes and repairs there was very little income from the property. It was a great deal of trouble for the girls to keep the house in repair, and a month or two ago they got disgusted and deeded the house back to their father."

The *Daily Globe* handled the story in its usual more restrained manner:

August 6, 1892

HIRAM HARRINGTON TALKS

Hiram Harrington, a blacksmith and brother-in-law of the murdered man says:

"If Mr. Borden died, he would have left something over $500,000, and all I will say is that, in my opinion, that furnishes the only motive, and a sufficient one, for the double murder. I have heard so much now that I would not be surprised at the arrest any time of the person to whom in my opinion suspicion strongly points, although right down in my heart I could not say I believe the party guilty.

"Last evening I had a long interview with Lizzie Borden who has refused to see any one else. I questioned her very carefully as to her story of the crime.

"She told me she helped her father to get a comfortable reclining position on the lounge, and asked him if he did not wish the blinds closed to keep out the sun, so he could have a nice nap. She pressed him to allow her to place an afghan over him, but he said he did not need it. Then she asked him tenderly several times if he was perfectly comfortable, if there was anything she could do for him, and upon receiving assurance to the negative she withdrew.

"All these things showed a solicitude and a thoughtfulness that I never had heard was a part of her nature before. She described these little acts of courtesy minutely.

"Lizzie is haughty and domineering with the stubborn will of her father and bound to contest for her rights. There were many animated interviews between father and daughter. Lizzie is of a repellent disposition and after an unsuccessful passage with her father would become sulky and refuse to speak to him for days at a time."

Mr. Harrington testified at the inquest, but there are no clues as to what he said. He was *not* called to testify at either the preliminary hearing or at the superior court trial, which indicates he either said nothing that was of any interest or he said too much and the Mellen House group didn't allow him to take the stand again. The only other possible explanation would be that his "interview" with his nieces was imagined and would therefore not be admissible testimony.

No one who has ever written on the Borden murders has considered Hiram Harrington particularly important. Henry Hawthorne, however, says that he was essential to the killer's successful escape. After killing Abby and Andrew, he went to Harrington's place of business as he had planned to do.

In her inquest testimony, Lizzie named Hiram Harrington as a possible suspect in the murder of her father. In spite of this accusation, he was of no overt interest to the police or to the attorneys. Her remarks were considered to be merely vindictive.

Although he reported a lengthy "interview," Hiram Harrington seems unimportant. Remember him. Remember that his place of business was on Fourth Street, two short blocks from the Borden house, and that he lived on Turner Street.

# Part Two

# Chapter 8

T he first legal proceeding, the inquest, was called on Tuesday, August 9, five days after the murders. It lasted three days. The court consisted of a judge—Josiah C. Blaisdell—and an examiner—District Attorney Hosea Knowlton. Both were empowered with the right to ask questions. Other than a court stenographer and high ranking police officials, *no one* was permitted in the hearing room while the witnesses were questioned. There were no spectators, no press, and no counsel for the witnesses.

As Lizzie Borden's attorney, Andrew Jennings argued in vain for the right to be present when she was interrogated. He based his request on the grounds that his client had been accused of the murders by the mayor himself, the city's highest ranking law enforcement official. Jennings' protest was important when the inquest testimony was disallowed at the superior court trial. At that point, Jennings wanted to *prevent* Lizzie's testimony from being entered into the record as evidence; the judicial error of not allowing her representation by counsel helped him to do that.

It was Judge Josiah Blaisdell's legal duty to warn witnesses of their rights before they responded to any questions. When Lizzie was called, he did not mention her rights or warn her in any way. Later, he said he *assumed* Mr. Jennings had warned her and there was no need for him to repeat it.

What was amazing was not that these kinds of errors were made. Rather, it was amazing that the public accepted these errors almost as if they were an integral part of the judicial system. It is not surprising that shortly after the inquest began the Providence *Journal* quipped that the final outcome of the case was no longer in doubt because those who represented the Borden family had "made their influence felt."

Bridget was the first witness called at the inquest. She was quizzed for hours, on both the first and third days. Lizzie was questioned all three days, but only half as long as Bridget. If Lizzie could not be found guilty, *someone* should be, and Bridget was a logical choice. In addition to Bridget and Lizzie, Eli Bence, Fred Hart, Frank Kilroy (all three were druggists), Emma Borden, Dr. Seabury Bowen (the Borden family doctor), Adelaide Churchill (a Borden neighbor), Hiram Harrington, Marshal Rufus Hilliard (chief of the Fall River police force), John Morse, George Seaver (of the Massachusetts state police), and possibly others testified.

Lizzie's testimony is the only part of the inquest of which we have a record. It is not clear where the New Bedford *Evening Standard* obtained its copy, but it was published on June 12, 1893. Those who knew said that what was published was accurate.

Before we examine Lizzie's testimony, a few words of explanation must be given. First, at that time the generic name for all Irish maids was "Maggie," just as all Irish males were called "Patty." It was as if the names "Rover" and "Kitty" were used to differentiate one group of animals from another. Appellations of this type were given in all social strata. For example, Bridget, who was a "Maggie," labeled anyone in a social position lower than hers as a "Portuguese." At one point she called a laborer on the Borden farm, who was actually Swedish, a Portuguese.

Second, within the Borden household the responsibilities, duties, and restrictions were carefully laid out. Bridget's domain was the first floor, the basement, and her third-floor garret. She had no duties on the second floor. Abby had nothing to do with Emma's or Lizzie's bedrooms, and Emma and Lizzie had nothing to do with the senior Bordens' half of the second floor. The guest bedroom was neutral territory—everybody used it. This division meant, for instance, that Bridget did the family washing and ironing and left it folded in neat piles in the dining room. She never would have considered delivering it to the respective rooms where it belonged.

Third, in spite of the fact that a great many people talked about a note that was brought to Abby, they all learned what they knew from Lizzie. She was the sole source of information about this note, which was to have been the reason for Abby to leave the house. No note was ever found, no one ever acknowledged authorship, and no one claimed a $500 reward as the messenger who delivered it.

Overall, Lizzie's testimony is basically the truth. It is not the whole truth, and it is nowhere near nothing but the truth, but it is a masterful job of answering questions in a credible fashion.

Immediately after the murder, the young ladies with whom Lizzie had planned to stay in the seashore town of Marion the following week were interviewed relentlessly by the press. Each woman proclaimed her faith in Lizzie and the improbability of her being guilty. More emphatically, they insisted that had Lizzie actually killed anyone, it would be absolutely impossible for her to lie about it. They intended this as a testimony to Lizzie's character. We should assume, where possible, that Lizzie's answers are true.

Lizzie said that she had no idea of her father's worth (Q-2, 3, Appendix), but she did name some of his holdings with no hesitation at all. She readily outined (Q-3) the dastardly (from her viewpoint) deed of five years earlier in which Andrew had given her and Emma some property. Others have proclaimed this to be the conception of the double murder, but Lizzie told of a $5,000 buy-back that should have cleared that account from the books. Most other accounts tend to discount or overlook this fact. Accepting it weakens Lizzie's motive for murder, especially since the property had a value of less than $3,000.

The confrontational nature of Lizzie's testimony at the inquest appeared right away when Knowlton asked Lizzie about her father's children (Q-4). It is an important series of questions, deleted from all other reports of the inquest because it seemed unimportant and was without meaning to them.

"How many children has your father?" Mr. Knowlton asked her.

"Only two," Lizzie responded.

"Only you two?"

"Yes, sir."

"Any others ever?"

"One that died."

The significance of this exchange is that Lizzie lied. Andrew Borden had not fathered "only two" children. In addition to a daughter who was dead, he had, by a woman named Phebe Hathaway, fathered an illegitimate son whose existence was whispered on The Hill and was more than common knowledge within the Borden clan. Without that knowledge, this exchange seems to have no significance whatsoever. William Borden, the bastard son, was never publicly acknowledged or recognized by Andrew. But Knowlton, a native of the area, was well aware of this gossip. In addition, he knew that Lizzie had an older sister Emma and was well aware that Andrew's second daughter, Alice, had died in childhood. Read his question again: "How many children *has* your father?"

Andrew was dead. The tense was present and was not intended to include Alice. However, if Lizzie's father had chosen not to recognize his son publicly, neither would she. This was the stand she had taken with the others in the family and with Mr. Jennings. She was adamant. "Only two."

Knowlton followed this answer with, "Only *you* two?"

This question makes no sense at all *unless* Knowlton was telling Lizzie he knew a lot more than she thought he did. He was telling Lizzie that he knew of her half brother William Borden and that it would cost her dearly if she did not want him to be made known. Knowlton had tendered his bill. It was later paid in full.

At this juncture Lizzie could have cleared the air once and for all, but she had a forthright love for her father. She would keep her trust with him even in death. There is no question about it—she was a devoted, loyal, and most loving daughter. But while she may have kept quiet out of loyalty or Victorian restraint, she had another more compelling reason for her unrevealing answers, one much stronger than those two: a selfish lust for money. So she answered, "Yes, sir."

"Any others ever?"

Again, Lizzie was offered a chance to tell the court about

her half brother. She declined.

"One that died."

She stuck by her guns. She would not broadcast the product of her father's dalliance.

Having dropped one bombshell on Lizzie, Knowlton did not wait. He dropped a second by bringing up the subject of Andrew Borden's will. It was five minutes into the proceeding, and things were not going Lizzie's way. The district attorney's message had been delivered clearly and unmistakably. He first brought up her half brother and then her father's will and the revelations *it* could produce if Andrew had decided that, in death, he would be honorable and remember his son or his son's mother.

Lizzie was caught so far off base she blurted out John Morse's name (Q-5) as the person that told her of her father's will. There is no honest reason why this should have caught Knowlton sound asleep, but he missed a fabulous chance to force Lizzie to admit that she and her Uncle John *had* spoken to each other. In spite of all her protestations later, Lizzie did not lie here.

When asked if there was anyone with whom Andrew "was on bad terms," Lizzie again told the truth, to a point. "There was a man that came there that he had trouble with, I don't know who the man was." The man had an interest in a Borden property. "'I would like to have that place,' he said. I heard father order him out."

On the evening before the murder day, Lizzie had told Miss Russell, "Father has an enemy, someone who had caused him so much trouble, someone who was a real danger to him." At the inquest she said it again. Someone had an interest in a Borden property, was "from out of town," and had a partner. Her only withholding of truth was in her statement, "I don't know who the man was." She *did* know who he was, and she knew he was the murderer. But Lizzie would not name him.

Because of the agreed-to ground rules, Knowlton (Q-6) jumped in quickly and steered Lizzie away from saying too much.

"Beside that do you know of anybody that your father had bad feelings toward, or who had bad feelings toward your father?"

Miss Lizzie had been the one who said the murderer could not be named. Knowlton was extremely talented in directing witnesses away from thin ice, and he did a masterful job at it later with John Morse at the preliminary hearing.

She answered Knowlton's question with the name of Hiram Harrington (Q-7) but gave no further details.

Knowlton then went into a long series of questions (Q-8 through 12) to prove Lizzie and her stepmother were not on the best of terms. Lizzie freely admitted they were not close, but Knowlton was not able to get her to admit to any instances of extreme animosity between them.

Lizzie paused just once (Q-12), and Knowlton called attention to it. The question "Were your father and mother happily united?" stopped her. Perhaps she had never considered them as a couple whose union had anything at all to do with happiness, or perhaps it was a difficult question to answer because of her loyalty to her real mother. When Knowlton pushed her for the reason for her pause, she said, "Some of your questions I have difficulty in answering because I don't know just how you mean them"—an honest response.

Knowlton next asked three questions (Q 13) about the clothing Lizzie was wearing the morning of the murders: "What dress did you wear the day they were killed? Did you change your clothing before the afternoon?" ("No") and "You dressed in the morning, as you have described, and kept that clothing on until afternoon?" ("Yes"). The answers are of almost no consequence if you know who really committed the murders, but much was made of them during the following ten months in Fall River.

Knowlton next turned to Uncle John Morse, his visits to the house, and the events of the evening before and the morning of the murder day (Q-13 through Q-22). Lizzie had recovered from her initial uneasiness by this time and defended herself by being vague and elusive. Not much is revealed, although Knowlton did miss a chance to follow up Lizzie's statement that she spent three or four days at 20 Madison Street in New Bedford (a rooming house, just a long stone's throw from the house where John Morse lived) (Q-15). Why she would have stayed in a rooming house there is beyond comprehension unless, like the Boston *Globe*, you

*Hosea M. Knowlton*

want to accuse Lizzie and Uncle John of having an affair.

Lizzie said, a little too definitely, that the first time she saw John Morse on his latest visit to Fall River was "Thursday noon," after the murders (Q-16). Her answer seemed too prompt and too exact to be anything but memorized from a prepared script.

Question 15 contained a damning slip on Lizzie's part. She had been identified as the woman who attempted to buy prussic acid on the morning before the murders. Later in her testimony, when that came up (Q-79), she was adamant about being home all day. However, when asked when John Morse arrived at the Borden house, Lizzie said, "I don't know. I was not at home when he came; I was out."

After questioning Lizzie concerning the events of the evening before the murders (Q-16 through Q-19) and the whereabouts of the family members and whether she had seen anyone else around the house (Q-19 through Q-24), Knowlton turned to the matter of Bridget's washing the windows, a focal point in the case. Because of the record high

131

temperatures that day, it was inhumane to have Bridget, who was not feeling well anyway, outside washing the windows. However, it was important because her being out of the house afforded an opportunity for murder. The crimes could not have been committed if she had been in the house performing her normal household duties.

It was planned for both Bridget and Emma to be out of the house the morning of the murders. Emma was no problem; she had agreed to a two-week vacation. The importance of Bridget's absence from the house makes it worthwhile to determine who ordered her to wash the windows.

According to Lizzie (Q-24 through Q-25), Abby gave the command. She said that when she came downstairs that morning just before nine o'clock, Andrew was reading, Abby was dusting, and Bridget was "going to wash windows around the house. She said Mrs. Borden wanted her to. . . . Maggie went out of doors to wash the windows and father came into the kitchen."

Knowlton asked Lizzie (Q-26), "Did you say anything about washing windows?"

"No, sir."

"You do not remember of talking about washing windows?"

"I don't remember whether I did or not; I don't remember it. Yes, I remember; yes, I asked her to shut the parlor blinds when she got through, because the sun was so hot."

Lizzie said it was Abby's idea for Bridget to wash the windows. But we might assume from a newspaper article in the *Daily Globe* (August 11, 1892) that Bridget testified otherwise.

It is definitely fixed that Andrew J. Borden left the house about 9:45 o'clock the day he died: he was 30 minutes behind Mr. Morse. About 10 minutes after Mr. Morse's departure, and 20 minutes before Mr. Borden went out, Bridget Sullivan last saw Mrs. Borden alive. She was at that time downstairs in the sitting room.

Not over 15 minutes after Mr. Borden's exit, Miss Lizzie Borden instructed Bridget to go out of doors and wash all of the windows outside in the first floor. Bridget did as she was told. She left Lizzie in the kitchen. For fully an hour Bridget was thus engaged and at no time was in the house except to get hot water. She completed her labor and returned in doors just in time to admit Mr. Borden when he returned from down town. It was then fully 10:40. Lizzie was in a room off the dining room ironing. During the hour or more that Bridget had been out of doors Lizzie Borden and her stepmother were the only persons inside. During that time Bridget heard no noise, and saw no one enter or leave the premises.

Although we could assume Bridget testified that Lizzie told her to wash the windows, we might also question the accuracy of the article. Later testimony established 1) Mr. Borden left the house much closer to 9:00 than 9:45; 2) Bridget saw Mrs. Borden alive and well *after* both Andrew and John Morse had left the house; 3) Bridget entered the house for a dipper with which to rinse the windows, not for hot water; 4) Lizzie ironed in the dining room, not a room off the dining room; and 5) Lizzie and Abby were not the *only* persons inside the house while Bridget was outside. Other than these few minor errors, the article is quite accurate. It illustrates why those who have based their investigation solely on contemporary newspaper reports tend to come to conclusions that conflict with the truth.

The remainder of Lizzie's first-day testimony (Q-25 through Q-36) was spent discussing the events of the morning before the discovery of the murders. There are two major points of confusion. The first is the time Andrew left the house. At first Lizzie said, "I don't know; it must have been after nine o'clock" (Q-26). The second day, she said, "My father did not go away, I think until somewhere about ten" (Q-40, also Q-70). She may simply not have remembered accurately, or her contradiction may have been the result of Jennings' after-hours coaching in an attempt to have Andrew in the house at the time Abby was murdered. Fortunately, we are not dependent on Lizzie's memory to establish the time of Andrew's activities that morning.

The second point of confusion was the establishment of where Lizzie was physically when Andrew returned. She played a game to create confusion. One almost feels sorry for Mr. Knowlton. Lizzie wanted him to know she had received his message and that she did not like him. It came through in rich, brilliant, vivid colors, his being radiant reds and lustrous purples on several occasions. First she said she was in the kitchen (Q-27), then in the dining room (Q-27), in her room (Q-29), on the stairs (Q-29), then in the kitchen again (Q-30), and the next day she implied she was in the cellar (Q-37).

Lizzie's disclaimer (Q-32) of any knowledge of her step-mother's whereabouts sounds reasonable. She accounted for her inability to see Mrs. Borden's body lying on the floor when she went up and down the stairs by saying that the guest chamber door was shut (Q-33). Since others testified later that it was easy to see Abby's body with just a casual glance into the room while climbing or descending the stairs, it follows that if the door had been open, Lizzie should have seen the body. Much was made of this, and it is often cited as a telling blow against Lizzie. Her answer was simply that the door was closed.

Lizzie admitted making one or two trips to the cellar (Q-33 and Q-35) and concluded the day's testimony by telling about the note Abby was said to have received.

Knowlton asked, "Had you any knowledge of her [Abby's] going out of the house?"

"She told me she had had a note," Lizzie began. "Somebody was sick, and she said 'I am going to get the dinner on the way,' and asked me what I wanted for dinner."

"Did you tell her?"

"Yes, I told her I did not want anything."

"Then why did you not suppose she had gone?"

"I supposed she had gone."

"Did you hear her come back?"

"I did not hear her go or come back, but I supposed she went."

"When you found your father dead, you supposed your mother had gone?"

"I did not know. I said to the people who came in 'I don't know whether Mrs. Borden is out or in; I wish you would see if she is in her room.'"

"You supposed she was out at the time?"

"I understood so; I did not suppose anything about it."

"Did she tell you where she was going?"

"No, sir."

"Did she tell you who the note was from?"
"No, sir."
"Did you ever see the note?"
"No, sir."
"Do you know where it is now?"
"No, sir."
"She said she was going out that morning?"
"Yes, sir."

The second day of Lizzie's testimony had the appearance of a club fight between Mr. Knowlton and Miss Borden. The district attorney's outbursts revealed his frustration at Lizzie's masterful refusal to bow to his almost brutal attack. He did not treat Lizzie with excessive respect, either from frustration or as an act of good faith with the voters who elected him. But she proved that she could take care of herself.

Knowlton began the second day with more questioning about the morning of the murder. Lizzie said Abby had said she intended to leave the house (Q-37) and she would shop for something for dinner while she was out.

"Dinner" in 1892 denoted the meal served at noon every day of the week. The evening meal was always "supper." Because of the rapid spoilage due to lack of refrigeration, the perishable food for each day was normally purchased on that day or the day before. An icebox would keep food only slightly below room temperature. Much has been made over Lizzie's statement that Mrs. Borden had planned to shop for dinner while Bridget later testified that dinner for the day of the murder would be leftovers from the day before.

Lizzie admitted going down into the cellar, a potentially damning admission if the cellar door had been open; it would have had to be unbolted from the inside. It was safe for Lizzie to admit her trips to the cellar. Mr. Knowlton was forced to assume her trips to the cellar were made in connection with the water closet, and he would not ask her anything that could produce so shocking a revelation. Lizzie used this to her advantage by saying that Mrs. Borden *could* have left the house during the interval of the cellar visit (Q-37). If Lizzie thought her stepmother was out of the house, there is no way she could have killed her. This strange defense almost makes sense.

135

After the magnificent shambles Lizzie had made of Mr. Knowlton's composure the previous day when he asked about her physical location when Andrew arrived home, Lizzie placed herself in the kitchen where she thought she had been in the first place (Q-38). One can sense Knowlton's blood pressure begin to climb. Very patiently (Q-40), as if to remind her of possible consequences if she refused to cooperate, Knowlton asked her if she was alone in the house during the critical time period. He made three attempts before she gave a qualified answer, "So far as I know, I was," which again raises the question of who Bridget heard laugh upstairs when she let Andrew Borden in the house.

Lizzie said (Q-41) that when her father came home, she was in the kitchen reading a magazine, eating a pear, and waiting for her "flats" to heat up on the wood stove so that she could iron eight or ten of her best handkerchiefs.

Lizzie did make one statement that is probably false. She stated (Q-43) that she went out of the house when her father had "laid down on the sitting room lounge, taken off his shoes, and put on his slippers." Later she said, "I saw him taking off his shoes." However, photographs of his dead body show Andrew wearing his street shoes. Either Lizzie was mistaken on this point, or she had left her father before he laid down and, knowing his habits, thought she remembered seeing him taking off his shoes.

Hosea Knowlton then set out on a crusade to nail down Lizzie's location when her father was killed. It was not an easy task. When he questioned Lizzie about Bridget's movements, she answered with a series of "I don't know's" that finally caused him to exclaim (Q-46), "Miss Borden, I am trying in good faith to get all the doings that morning of yourself and Miss Sullivan, and I have not succeeded in doing it. Do you desire to give me information or not?"

Here Knowlton made his point very clear by saying, in essence, "It is either you or the papist—take your pick. If we are to clear you, it must be because someone else seems more guilty than you, and your Maggie is the logical choice. You can, of course, clear the air and tell us what *really* happened." Lizzie dug in her heels—by blood, she was a Borden!—and replied, "I don't know it—I don't know what your name is."

Lizzie said that after leaving her father she went out of the house, picked up some pears that had fallen off the pear tree, and then went to the second story of the "very hot" barn where she spent fifteen to twenty minutes first leisurely eating three pears while looking out of the window and then looking for some lead to use as sinkers. Lizzie was planning to go to Marion the next week and wanted to do some fishing there. Her claimed search for sinker lead is not too far removed from the realm of the possible, but the details are almost laughable as she sets out to frustrate her inquisitor. She was paying Mr. Knowlton and had decided she would get her coerced money's worth and intended to enjoy herself doing it (Q-43 through Q-58).

The truth is that although Lizzie left the house before her father was murdered, she did not go to the barn. She went out of the house through the cellar door, which she unbolted and opened, and sat in the shade of the pear tree, calmly eating some pears. In her only testimony at the inquest, Lizzie said she was in the barn. And yet in the closing arguments at the superior court trial, the defense stated as fact that Lizzie was under the pear tree when her father was murdered. As a follow-up to this, in his charge to the jury, Justice Dewey also said that Lizzie was outside the house sitting in the shade of a pear tree calmly eating pears when Andrew Borden was being hacked to death. Lizzie had not testified in this way. Her attorney did it for her, and to ensure fairness to all, the judge suggested that anyone who placed her anywhere other than under the pear tree was mistaken.

When Lizzie came inside from eating the pears—in the barn, according to her, or under the tree, according to Robinson and Dewey—she checked her flats, found the fire in the stove had gone out, and "thought I would wait till Maggie got dinner and heat the flats again" (Q-59). Her answer has the solid ring of truth. Lizzie was spoiled rotten and lazier than any modern-day couch potato. She would delight in putting off *any* chore she could foist on someone else. The fact that she checked her flats *before* discovering her father's body indicates that she did not expect to find him dead. Although she knew Andrew had met with the person who killed him, she did not know the meeting had ended in murder. Her panic, her fright, and her horror were all genuine.

When Lizzie found her father, she said, she did not look for Abby because she thought she was out of the house. Lizzie called for Bridget and sent her to get Dr. Bowen. Knowlton questioned Lizzie about the details of her father's body more than was necessary, and she understandably lost control (Q-62). He then asked her about Abby and any conversations they might have had the morning of the murder. Just as Lizzie's account of the fire in the kitchen had a ring of truth in it, her reported conversation with Abby (Q-63) had the thud of falsehood. Lizzie said she asked Abby if she were going to change her dress before going out, and Abby answered, "No, this is good enough." In 1892 no woman of Abby Borden's position would appear outside her house in clothing she wore inside when she did housework. It just was not done. Both Dr. Bowen's wife and Miss Russell said they changed their dresses before responding to Lizzie's panicky plea for help. Either Abby did not have on an old dress (as Lizzie classified it), or she did not make the statement Lizzie quoted her as making. A very old dress was on Abby's body.

Most of the rest of Lizzie's testimony the second day was merely a rehash of the same subjects for the third or fourth time. She did disclose, however, that it was Emma who suggested calling Mr. Jennings (Q-72). She also used an interesting phrase in her retelling the story of the house sale of five years earlier (Q-73). She testified, "I said what he [Andrew] did for her [Abby's] people, he ought to do *for his own children.*" This choice of words is not one that would be used by Lizzie to refer to Emma and herself. It would, however, be appropriate if she was referring also to her half brother.

One interesting bit of background information is necessary to understand Lizzie's comment (Q-76) that she had fleas when asked to explain small bloodstains on her undergarments. In Victorian America ladies did not "have the curse" or "receive monthly visits from Mother Nature" and certainly didn't menstruate. The subject of menstruation was seldom discussed, but when it could not be avoided, ladies alluded to having fleas. At the trial, Lizzie's physical condition was mentioned, but not discussed.

The second day's questioning ended with an interesting insight into how thorough the investigation was. Six days after the murders, Mr. Knowlton asked Lizzie to turn over to the police the shoes and stockings she wore on the day of the murder. She was not sure whether the stockings had been washed or not.

The last day of Lizzie Borden's testimony was short. Mr. Knowlton tied up a few loose ends and brought up some of the same subjects discussed earlier.

No unexplained blood was ever found on any of the clothes Lizzie gave to the authorities as the clothes she was wearing the morning of the murder. When this fact became general knowledge, surprise was expressed as to how, guilty or innocent, she could have been on the murder scene without getting blood on some portion of her clothing. Lizzie's explanation (Q-80) was that she did not enter either death room. The other possible explanation is that the clothing she turned over to the police was *not* the clothing she had actually worn that morning.

Halfway through the day's questioning (Q-82), Mr. Knowlton asked Lizzie, "I now ask you if you can furnish any other fact, or give any other, even suspicion, that will assist the officers in any way in this matter?

"About two weeks ago—" she began.

It is here that Knowlton begins to earn his keep. "Was you going to tell the occurrence about the man that called at the house?"

He stopped Lizzie dead in her tracks. He was afraid she was going to tell more about the man who was "a real danger" to her father, the "someone" who had caused him so much trouble. Knowlton knew the rules that had been negotiated with the Silent Government, and part of his obligation was to halt any testimony that might point to the murderer. He was an honorable man, and he was now dedicated to protecting his new clients.

In Q-84 is an exchange that has never been challenged. Mr. Knowlton had tried to stop Lizzie from telling too much, but she persisted and referred to the man who had come to the house and argued with her father.

"You have not been able to find this man?" Knowlton asked.

"I have not; I don't know whether anybody else has."

"Have you caused a search to be made for him?"

"Yes, sir."

Lizzie Borden had described a suspect, one that should be a *prime* suspect. How does District Attorney Hosea Knowlton, this defender of law and order for the County of Bristol, respond to this lead? He says, "Have *you* been able to find this man? . . . Have *you* caused a search to be made for him?" Was it not the responsibility of the local police force to search and find the murderer?

Actually, it was not their responsibility. The pact agreed to at the Mellen House made it clear that the murderer would not be apprehended unless Miss Lizzie Borden changed her mind and so dictated. In the meantime, she accepted all responsibility, posted a blank check, and agreed that *she* would be charged with the crime. All she asked in return was freedom for the murderer (unless she intervened) and a directed verdict of not guilty for herself.

History tells us all these terms were met.

If you find this rape of justice hard to accept, be assured that it is not unusual even today, given the right circumstances and the right number of dollars.

On August 17 an unknown reporter for the *Daily Globe* wrote, under the headline "Too Many Lawyers,"

If the people of this city have officers occupying positions of honor and trust, in whom they have no confidence or on whose integrity there rests the slightest suspicion, it is the people's fault and they have themselves to blame. No official connected with this murder case is a new man. Every one of them has been tested, and if any one of them has been found wanting, the people made no attempt to remove him.

True words then. True words today.

# Chapter 9

T estimony was given at all four legal proceedings. Except for Lizzie's testimony, we have no record of that given at the inquest. Nor is there any record of testimony given before the grand jury. Most accounts of the murders have relied on testimony from the superior court trial. Since the Jennings transcript came to light in 1970, we have the opportunity of looking at both the final trial testimony and the testimony given at the preliminary hearing.

The following account of the testimonies given is arranged by witness with the most important part of each person's preliminary hearing testimony and final trial testimony given together. Where important, the source of the testimony is clearly identified. Admittedly, this has the effect of telling the same story a number of times from different perspectives, but it is the best way of presenting the mass of evidence surrounding the murders.

*Miss Bridget Sullivan*

The murder day began with Bridget "not feeling well," for she possessed all the physical symptoms of Mrs. Borden's "poisoning." She told the court she came down to the kitchen at 6:15 and proceeded with the usual morning chores. She brought in the milkman's delivery, started her fire in the kitchen stove, and began preparing breakfast. When she went out for the milk, the back door was triple-locked, just as she had locked it the previous night. She left the back door open and hook-locked the screen door. It stayed that way until she opened it for the ice man.

She stated with conviction that nothing out of the ordinary took place that morning. She said no one went to the cellar in the early morning to use the water closet.

She herself went to the cellar three times during the morning: first for wood to start the kitchen stove fire, the second time for coal to maintain it, and later on for a pail to use for washing the windows. She paid no attention to the cellar door to the outside on any of these trips. As far as she could tell, it was last opened two days earlier when she had hung out the family wash. She was sure she had bolted it then when she finished.

She did not see anyone in the house when she came down, and she was alone until Mrs. Borden joined her at 6:30 or 6:40. Mr. Borden came down about ten minutes later. Lizzie remained upstairs, and the senior Bordens were not joined by Mr. Morse until the three of them sat down for breakfast at what, Bridget stated, "I should judge was quarter past seven."

Much has been made of the conflict between Bridget's story and Mr. Morse's. He testified he came downstairs at 6:20 and saw no one until Mr. Borden came down approximately fifteen minutes later. John Morse had not seen Bridget. He referred to her as "the servant," and it is doubtful he even knew her name. In his mind she was part of the house, not a person. Thus he simply did not "see" her.

There is, however, a serious disagreement between them regarding when Bridget was assigned to the significant window-washing detail. Bridget testified it was after Mr. Morse left. He testified he heard the instructions given.

Because he returned to the Bordens' house just before noon, all past accounts state as fact that John Morse was expected there to join the family in the noon meal. Bridget heard and reported Andrew's invitation, but neither she nor anyone else heard Uncle John's acceptance or regrets.

"Did Mr. Borden go out when Mr. Morse did?" she was asked.

"No, sir," she replied.

"He went to the door?"

"Yes, sir, with him."

"Did you hear him say anything to Mr. Morse?"

"I heard him ask him to come to dinner."

"What did Mr. Morse say?"

"I do not know."

Just as all others have readily *assumed* John Morse accepted Andrew's invitation to lunch and returned to the house for that reason, we will assume he refused it and was on his way back to his home in the New Bedford area. The murders changed his plans.

Bridget reported Mr. Borden's movements prior to his leaving the house, such as his going up to his bedroom for his collar and tie, coming back down and brushing his teeth in the kitchen sink, and going into the living room for his Prince Albert pseudo-uniform coat. She did not, however, see him leave. Her breakfast had not settled well on her "poisoned" stomach, and she spent ten or fifteen minutes in the back yard retching. Mr. Borden left the house at that time.

"When you came back, did you see Mrs. Borden?"

"No, sir."

"Did you see her after you came back?"

"Not until nine o'clock."

"When you went out in the back yard, was it before Mr. Morse went off?"

"No, sir, it was after he went off."

"How soon after he went off?"

"Maybe ten or five minutes; I cannot tell."

"When you came back again, where did you go?"

"Into the kitchen."

"Where did you see Mrs. Borden after that?"

"In the dining room, dusting," Bridget replied. "She wanted to know if I had anything particular to do that day. I told her no. Did she want anything? Yes, she said she wanted the windows washed. I asked her how. She said on both sides, inside and outside; they were very dirty."

"Did you see Mrs. Borden after that?"

"No, sir."

"Where did she go to then?"

"I cannot tell you. I came out, and shut the dining room, and was in the kitchen."

"You shut the dining room door and went to the kitchen?"

"Yes, sir."

"When did you next see her after that?"

"Not until I saw her dead."

"Was that before Lizzie came down?"

"No. Lizzie was after getting through her breakfast."

"When Mrs. Borden spoke to you."

"Yes, sir."

"You had seen Lizzie before then?"

"Yes, sir, before that, when she came downstairs."

"Did Lizzie come downstairs before you went out in the yard?"

"Yes, sir."

"When Mrs. Borden said that to you about washing windows, do you know where Lizzie was then?"

"No, sir."

Bridget's testimony to this point has never been seriously challenged for either accuracy or duplicity. The *Globe* claimed that Bridget said Lizzie told her to wash the windows, but this is not supported by her testimony. It is another piece of the legend that is incorrect. The window washing was ordered by Abby Borden.

Bridget's testimony continued with surprisingly little substance. Basically she gathered together her window washing equipment, went outside, and washed the windows. She did not see Mrs. Borden alive again, and she did not see Lizzie again until she had washed and rinsed the windows on the outside and had come inside to finish them. During her time outside, she made only one trip into the house and that was to the sink room to get a tin dipper, which she used to throw water on the windows for their final rinse. The trip for the dipper reinforced the fact that the side door was not hook-locked the entire morning.

Bridget was outside the house and starting on her window-washing project some time between 9:00 and 9:30. During this period, ten minutes or so were devoted to an over-the-fence gossipy chat with Dr. Kelly's maid next door. Neither could pinpoint the time, but Bridget said it was before she started on the first window.

Before going outside and after talking to Mrs. Borden, she ". . . cleaned up my kitchen, and straightened up things."

"Then what did you do?" she was asked.

"Washed the windows."

144

"What preparations did you make about washing the windows?"

"I went down cellar and got a pail, and came up, got a brush out of the closet, and went out to the barn and got a stick."

"When you started to go out to the barn, do you remember how you found the door then?"

"Miss Lizzie came through the kitchen then, as I started to go out in the barn with a pail. She was at the back door."

"You had the pail?"

"Yes. I was outside. She was at the back door. She wanted to know if I was to wash windows. I said yes. I told her she need not hook the door, for I would be around there; but I told her she could hook it if she wanted to, and I would get the water in the barn."

"Did you get the water in the barn?"

"Yes, sir."

"Have you any idea how long that was after Mrs. Borden told you to wash the windows."

"Half an hour, I should judge. . . ."

"Were the windows shut?"

"I shut them before I went out."

"When you were around shutting up the windows, did you see anything of Mrs. Borden or Lizzie?"

"No, sir."

Bridget then estimated that her outside portion of the chore was finished by 10:20, and she came into the house to wash the inner surfaces. When she came in, she did not see or hear Lizzie or anyone else until Andrew Borden came home.

"How did you know he had come?"

"I heard him at the door. I cannot tell did he ring the bell or not, but I heard a person at the door trying to get in; and I let him in."

"It was Mr. Borden, was it?"

"Yes, sir."

"Have you any idea what time it was?"

"It might be later than half past ten; I could not tell."

"Up until the time you had let Mr. Borden in, had you seen Miss Lizzie?"

"She was upstairs at the time I let him in."

"Where upstairs?"

"She might be in the hall, for I heard her laugh."

"At the time you let Mr. Borden in?"

"Yes, sir."

"Was that the first time you had heard or seen her since you spoke to her at the back door?"

"Yes, sir."

"You had not seen her or Mrs. Borden during the intermediate time?"

"No, sir."

"What was the occasion of her laugh?"

"I got puzzled at the door, I said something, and she laughed at it; I supposed that must make her laugh—I don't know."

"Did she laugh out loud?"

"Yes, sir."

"Say anything?"

"No, sir."

"Did you see her then?"

"No, sir."

"How soon did you see her?"

"It might be five or ten minutes after, she came downstairs; she came through the front hall, I don't know whether she came from upstairs. She came through the sitting room, I was in the sitting room.

The legend insists that Bridget not only heard Lizzie laugh at her expletive, but she *saw her* on the stairs as well. Bridget did not say that, and if you read her exact words, she actually had no idea where Lizzie was at the time.

When Mr. Borden came into the house, he went into the dining room and sat down to read. Bridget was finishing the windows in the sitting room when Lizzie went into the dining room to speak with her father. She asked if she had any mail and told her father that Mrs. Borden had received a note and had gone out. The note, Lizzie added, was from some sick person. Bridget qualified this by saying, "Of course the conversation was very low. I did not pay any attention to it, but I heard her telling her father that."

When Bridget moved her window washing into the dining

room, Mr. Borden had taken his bedroom key from the shelf in the living room and gone upstairs. Bridget had no idea where Lizzie was. Mr. Borden returned from upstairs, placed the key on the shelf again, and sat in an easy chair in the sitting room "with a book or a paper in his hand." As Bridget was finishing up in the dining room, Lizzie entered with a small ironing board used for small personal items and with several handkerchiefs that had been dampened ready for ironing. Bridget could not say where Lizzie had been since she heard her speaking with her father.

"What did you do when you finished washing the windows?" she was asked.

"I went out in the kitchen, and Miss Lizzie was talking to me a little while, not very long."

"What was she saying?"

"She asked was I going out that afternoon. I told her I did not know, I might, and I might not. I was not feeling very well. She said Mrs. Borden was going out, or gone out—I could not catch the two words she said; that somebody was sick. I asked her who was sick. She said she did not know, but she had a note that morning. 'If you go out, be sure and lock the door, because I may be out.'"

"What did you do then?"

"Hung up my cloth I had to wash with and threw away the water and went upstairs to my room."

"Where was Miss Lizzie?"

"She came out in the kitchen, as I was starting to go upstairs."

"What for, if you saw?"

"She came out, and she told me there was a sale in Sargeant's that afternoon for dress goods for eight cents a yard. I told her I would have one."

"Did she say anything else to you?"

"No, sir. That was all."

"When you went upstairs, what time was it?"

"It might be four or five minutes to eleven."

"How do you know?"

"By the length of time I was upstairs when it struck eleven o'clock."

"Where were you at the time?"

"I was laying on the bed."

"You did not take your clothes off?"

"No, sir."

"How long did you say it was after you got upstairs before the clock struck?"

"I should say it was three minutes."

"Did you go to sleep, so far as you know?"

"No, sir."

"Was it your habit to go upstairs that way?"

"Yes, sir."

"When?"

"When I got through with my work downstairs, if I had not anything else to do, I always went upstairs before I started to get dinner, if I had time."

"How did you leave the fire when you went upstairs?"

"I did not see the fire at all."

"When was the last time you had anything to do with the fire?"

"After getting the breakfast and washing my dishes, I did not see the fire again. I had no business with it."

"You were coming downstairs at half past eleven to get the dinner?"

"Yes, sir, probably sooner."

"Did you hear anything downstairs?"

"No, sir."

"Did you go in or out of the screen door after you came in from washing the windows?"

"No, sir."

"Did anybody else, so far as you saw?"

"No, sir."

"When you came in, you fastened it?"

"Yes, sir."

"After you let Mr. Borden in, did you shut the front door up again?"

"He shut it up."

"When did you next see anything or hear anything?"

"Not until Miss Lizzie called me."

"What time was that, as near as you can fix it?"

"I might be upstairs ten or fifteen minutes, as near as I can think, after I went upstairs."

"Have you any way of fixing that, or is it just your estimation?"

"That is what I think, I did not look at the clock when I came down. That is the length of time I thought I was there."

"You were still lying on the bed . . ."

"Yes, sir."

". . . when she called to you. What did she say?"

"She holloed to me. Of course I knew something was the matter, she holloed so loud. I asked her what was the matter. She said, 'Come down quick,' that her father was dead."

"She called your name, Maggie?"

"Yes, sir. I came down and asked what was the matter and was going into the sitting room. She told me to go quick for Dr. Bowen."

"Where was she when you went down?"

"Standing in the back door, leaning against it, right by the screen door."

"Did she say anything when you got downstairs?"

"She said, 'Go for Dr. Bowen.' I ran ahead. I did not know what was the matter. She told me to 'go quick and get Dr. Bowen.'"

Bridget went right over to Dr. Bowen's. Only Mrs. Bowen was at home, and so Bridget returned to the Bordens' house.

"Who was there when you came back?" Mr. Knowlton asked.

"Nobody but Miss Lizzie. I told her he was not in. I told her what Mrs. Bowen told me. She told me to go after Miss Russell."

"How far away is that?"

"I do not know—it is a good ways away. I could not tell you exactly how long it is."

"Had anyone else come in when you came back there, telling that Dr. Bowen was not there?"

"No, sir, I did not see anyone."

"At the time when you went out after Dr. Bowen, did you find the screen door locked?"

"No, sir."

"Did you come back with Miss Russell?"

"Ahead of her."

"When you came back, who did you find there then?"

149

"Dr. Bowen was ahead of me; he stepped out of his carriage as I came up Second Street. Dr. Bowen went in ahead of me."

"When you got in, who did you find there?"

"I think Mrs. Churchill was in when I got in there."

"Who else was there besides Mrs. Churchill?"

"That is all I remember, Mrs. Churchill and Dr. Bowen." At this point Mr. Knowlton questioned Bridget's actions after the bodies had both been discovered. After the official police investigation began, total chaos took over and trampled the truth into oblivion. In all candor, what happened *after* the police arrived on the scene is of almost no interest.

Mr. Knowlton asked Bridget several questions in regard to another trip to the cellar when she acted as tour guide to the police in their final search of the house.

"Did you see whether the outside cellar door was open then?"

"No, sir, I did not."

"Did you notice it was, or was not?"

"I did not notice anything about it."

Again, Mr. Jennings' handwritten comment at this point in the preliminary hearing transcript is more revealing than the words. Bridget's "No, sir, I did not" is underlined, and his notation is "Matter of news for Mr. Morse." Without question, Mr. Morse *and* Mr. Jennings were convinced either that Mr. Morse had seen an open door or, at the very least, that he wanted the cellar door to appear open to create a reasonable doubt. Here Bridget had another chance to earn her rumored payoff. She could have made it so easy for them. She did not.

"Did you hear Miss Lizzie say at any time where she was when her father was killed?"

"I asked her where she was. She said she was out in the back yard."

"Did she say what she was doing in the back yard?"

"No, sir."

Bridget was the first of many to ask Lizzie her whereabouts when her father was being murdered. Lizzie had not had time to review the danger inherent in her simple statement of truth, but she soon did and her answer to Bridget was the first *and only* time she placed herself outside without being in the barn and/or its loft.

Miss Lizzie had not lied to Bridget.

\*     \*     \*

We now arrive at the one area where Bridget's answers have been universally accused of being other than the truth. She was asked, "Do you remember the dress she had on that morning?"

"No, sir."

"You have no idea at all?"

"No, sir."

"You could not tell whether she had a dress on and waist of the same kind, or different?"

"No, sir, nothing about it."

"Could you tell whether she had an apron on?"

"I could not tell whether she did or not."

Those who accuse Bridget of lying in this series of questions are actually accusing Lizzie of having bloodstained her first outfit of the day and changing into something different before the police began collecting evidence. If you review all of Bridget's testimony, you will find that she and Lizzie are in full agreement. They had little physical contact that morning. Bridget was sick and in no mood for fashions.

Under cross-examination, Mr. Adams stressed the locks on the front door and the fact that all were secure and required Bridget's undoing. In Mr. Jennings' copy of the transcript is the notation, ". . . every lock fastened. (If L. did it—after she killed Mrs. B. she would have unlocked & left ajar—so would think person came in & had gone out)."

This notation offers a rarely available chance for us to share in Mr. Jennings' thoughts. By his reasoning here, *if* Lizzie had killed Mrs. Borden, the front door should have been unlocked. It was not. This proved to him that Lizzie had not killed Abby. Mr. Jennings seems to forget there were *two* murders. If the door was still locked, it would also prove *the killer had not left the house*, at least not via the locked front door. Lizzie was the only known person who had not left the house, so unless Mr. Jennings knew of a second person, his reasoning condemned Lizzie rather than helped her. It would make perfect sense if the killer was someone other than Lizzie (or Bridget), someone who simply stayed concealed between the two events.

Mr. Borden had attempted to enter the house by his usual route, the side door. It was hook-locked, and so he came around the front and found another locked door through which he was finally admitted, but one that he relocked immediately. The basement and its door grew in importance in the mind of Mr. Jennings (see his interrogation of John Morse).

Bridget had testified she was the only member of the household to go to the cellar that morning. In her inquest testimony, Lizzie hinted that in a break with family tradition, she used the water closet about the time Bridget went outside to wash windows. (Bridget had not lied. She was outside at the time and thus had no knowledge of Lizzie's visit.) In the cellar was running water should one care to wash stains away, plenty of concealment, and its own almost private door, one that had been reported to the police as the possible entry point in an earlier burglary. Jennings should have had a deep interest in the cellar and its door. If the police and the authorities had not been so cocksure of Lizzie's guilt and no one else's, so might they.

Mr. Adams tried desperately to make Bridget change her recollection of when Mrs. Borden gave her the window-washing instructions. He could do nothing to change her testimony.

Bridget then described some of the other chores she performed that morning, one of which was folding the laundry she had ironed the previous day and piling it for those to whom it belonged. The stacks for Emma and Lizzie had been removed from where she had stacked them, implying that Lizzie had gathered her laundry and her sister's and had taken it upstairs at some time near the time when Mrs. Borden was murdered. In her inquest testimony, Lizzie stated she did, indeed, go to her room for this very purpose.

Mr. Adams ended his questioning with a review of Bridget's inability to remember what dress Lizzie was wearing that morning and the fact that Lizzie was totally without bloodstains on her skin, hair, and whatever it was she was wearing. His last questions:

"What dress did *you* have on?"

"A calico dress."

"Where is that dress now?"

"Down here where I am."

This was a cheap shot but one the legend loves. Pro-Lizzieites will tell you that Bridget's clothing was never checked by the police for any signs of blood and that her belongings, which she was allowed to remove from the house, in part on the murder day and in total the day after, included any number of incriminating items that no one bothered to check. However, common sense must prevail here.

The first suspect in the crime was an unknown "Portuguese," a member of the lowest rung of the social ladder. When none could be found, the second suspect was Bridget, "that papist girl." There can be no doubt that Bridget and anything she possessed was checked far more closely than anything associated with a Borden daughter.

Emma and Lizzie had posted a $5,000 reward almost immediately. In 1892 that was a staggering amount, but especially to anyone who traveled in Bridget's circles. She had no family to turn to; and on her first night out of the Borden house she shared the servant quarters with Minnie Green, servant to Dr. Bowen's neighbor who lived across the street. Minnie and Bridget were nodding acquaintances, not strong friends. Five thousand dollars represented more than a lifetime's earnings to Minnie, and one can be sure that a bloodstained dress in Bridget's wardrobe of two non-Sunday dresses or a dripping hatchet in her handbag would have been noticed and reported with glee.

So, here the legend is, at best, wishful thinking. All common sense dictates that Bridget and her every belonging were minutely inspected long before she left the scene. Anything even slightly suspicious that might have been smuggled out of the house would have been reported by the first person who gave her shelter.

In her testimony, Bridget gave a concise, definitive report of the murder morning. Wherever their testimony overlaps, there is no disagreement between her remembrances and those of Miss Lizzie, Dr. Bowen, Mrs. Churchill, or Miss Russell. Nothing she said placed her above suspicion; she pointed no fingers at anyone, and she said nothing that is overwhelmingly for or against Lizzie.

*Miss Alice M. Russell*

One of the most frustrating witnesses was Alice Russell, the close friend of Lizzie and Emma. At the preliminary hearing, she admitted to being a maiden lady (but she never did tell her age); she did not know how far away she lived from the Borden house (but she admitted she had been told it was three hundred yards); she was acquainted with the Bordens (she had known Miss Lizzie eleven or twelve years); and her first word of the event had been delivered to her by "Maggie."

Mr. Knowlton asked her, "Do you know what time of day it was?"

Miss Russell replied, "I am not positive."

"As near as you can fix it, when was it?"

"I thought that day it was quarter past eleven; I do not know why I thought so, now."

"Have you come to any different opinion now?"

"No, sir. I have forgotten how I placed the time."

"Bridget called you; what happened then—what did you do?"

"I went over. I changed my dress, though, before I went."

"Did you hurry to get over?"

"I thought I hurried; I do not know whether I did or not."

"When you got there, who did you find there?"

"I am not positive who I found. I saw Lizzie."

"Where did you see Lizzie?"

"As near as I can remember, she was leaning up against the frame of the door between the back entry and the kitchen."

"Was Mrs. Churchill there when you got there?"

"I cannot remember whether she was or not."

"Did you say anything to Lizzie, or she to you then?"

"I do not remember."

"What did you do when you got there?"

"I think I got Lizzie to sit down in the rocker."

"Was anyone with you when you got Lizzie to sit down?"

"I do not remember. I do not think there was."

"When you got there, do you remember whether Dr. Bowen was there or not?"

"I do not think he was."

"Did you see the policeman, Mr. Allen, come?"
"I do not remember seeing him at all."
"You did not see him?"
"I do not remember of seeing him."
"Do you remember how Lizzie was dressed?"
"No, sir."
"Do you remember anything that took place at all?"
"I remember nothing very connectedly."

Miss Russell proceeded to prove she remembered very little, "connectedly" or otherwise. She did not know if she talked to Lizzie, and she certainly did not remember asking Lizzie any questions. She did hear some *answers*, however. Lizzie said she had come in from the barn and saw her father "lying on the sofa with his face all. . . ." Miss Russell did remember she asked Lizzie why she went to the barn, and Lizzie told her it was to get a piece of tin or iron to fix her screen or window.

Miss Russell remembered she went upstairs with Lizzie at some time or other, but she had no idea who was in the house after that. "I do not know how many were in the house. It seemed to me there had been a great many coming and going; it was confusion all downstairs." She revealed that she stayed in the Borden house "four nights and about three days and a half" after the murders. She slept two nights in Emma's room and two nights in Mrs. Borden's room.

Miss Russell stressed she was friendly with the sisters but not with Mrs. Borden. The friends visited upstairs in the guest room, and she repeated that her going there was never planned. It was "just as it happened."

Under cross-examination by Mr. Jennings, her memory did tend to improve, but she continued to exhibit her nonloquacious, circumspect, aggravating, and exasperating foot dragging. She wasn't sure, but she thought that maybe it was as soon as she entered the house that she was able to get Lizzie to sit in a rocking chair in the kitchen.

"Was it while she was there that Mrs. Churchill was there fanning her? Do you recollect that?"

"I remember we fanned her with a paper. I do not remember who fanned her. I remember we were both there fanning her—or doing something."

"Where were you standing?"
"I think I was sitting."
"Where were you sitting?"
"Right beside her."
"Did you notice whether there was any blood on her or not?"
"I did not see anything."
"On her hands?"
"No, sir."
"Did you see her hands?"
"Yes, sir, I rubbed them."
"Were there any signs of blood on them?"
"No, sir."

Miss Russell was sure there was no blood on Lizzie's face or her hair. In fact, she bathed Lizzie's face, and there was no sign of blood. Her hair was in place as usual; there was no blood on Lizzie's clothes, dress, or shoes, but Miss Russell could not remember what kind of shoes Lizzie was wearing. She did remember there was nothing unusual that attracted her attention, and, no, Lizzie was not panting from exertion.

At the combined urging of Miss Russell and Mrs. Churchill, Lizzie moved from the kitchen chair to the lounge in the dining room where she remained until well after the police arrived.

"Do you remember the time when the officers first went upstairs?" Jennings asked her.

"No, I do not remember."

"Do you remember whether they went up the back or front stairs?"

"I do not remember anything about that."

"Do you remember anything they did upstairs?"

"I remember being up in Mr. and Mrs. Borden's rooms with some officer," she replied. "I remember their asking me about the rooms that went out of it. The door into Miss Lizzie's room was hooked. They pulled the screw out, I judged. I remember I asked them to let me look in first; I did not know what the condition of the room was. I pulled the portière aside, looked in, and said it was all right, and they went in. I do not recollect whether I went in or not."

Miss Russell immediately reverted to her standard form.

She did not know whether they searched Lizzie's room or not. She did know Officer Doherty and didn't have the faintest idea if he was one of the maybe three, more or less, policemen in the house at the time who may or may not have been searching the house at the time. She had no idea.

She could affirm positively, however, that some policemen had been in Lizzie's room at some time and for some length of time before Lizzie went upstairs. She stressed, and it is of primary importance, the police were looking for "someone," not "something," and she did remember one of the officers, Mr. Fleet.

Miss Russell said that officers were "coming all day" on the day of the murders and searched Lizzie's closets. On Saturday afternoon a thorough search was made from the top to the bottom of the house with Andrew Jennings present. She did not know whether the officers went into all the rooms or the spare rooms or Miss Emma's room or the clothes closet. She did know they went into Miss Lizzie's room before Miss Lizzie went upstairs and, yes, they went into Mr. Borden's room. She did not know if another search was made on Monday. She left the house Monday morning.

It is difficult to believe from the above account that Miss Russell's testimony at the grand jury hearing held approximately three months after the preliminary hearing could have been the only reason Lizzie Borden was bound over and tried on the charge of murdering Andrew and Abby. But it was.

### Adelaide B. Churchill

Mrs. Adelaide B. Churchill lived in the Buffington House on the north side of the Borden house. This house had been part of an estate, and when the land became too valuable for single ownership, portions had been sold off. In approximately 1850 (about twenty years before Andrew Borden purchased it), the Borden house had been built on a south side-lot of the estate.

Mrs. Churchill was the daughter of the city's most respected and beloved late Mayor Buffington. Her mother (the mayor's widow) lived with her in the former manor house. They employed a male servant named Tom Bowles as handyman and carriage driver. The space separating the two houses was typical for a subdivided city lot, and calling to a neighbor across the fence was accepted practice when the space was less than shouting distance. In this case, it was much less.

On the murder morning, Mrs. Churchill was returning from her morning downstreet shopping when, walking up Second Street toward her home, she saw a "frightened" Bridget Sullivan come out of Dr. Bowen's house and enter the Borden yard. Mrs. Churchill entered her house, went into the kitchen (the room closest to the Bordens' side door), looked out a window, and saw a "distressed or frightened" Lizzie Borden standing inside the screen door.

Mrs. Churchill opened a window and asked, "Lizzie, what is the matter?"

Lizzie replied, "Oh, Mrs. Churchill, do come over; someone has killed Father."

Mrs. Churchill closed the window, went out her front door to the Second Street sidewalk, through the Bordens' north gate into the yard to the side door, and joined Lizzie in the rear entry.

She asked Lizzie where her father was, and Lizzie told her he was in the sitting room. She asked Lizzie where she had been when this happened, and Lizzie told her she had gone to the barn to get a piece of iron, came back and heard a distressed noise, found the screen door open, went into the house, and found her father.

Mrs. Churchill was the first outsider on the murder scene. She asked Lizzie where Mrs. Borden was, and Lizzie told her about a note her mother had received asking her to come to someone who was sick. Lizzie added that her mother might be killed, too, for she thought she had heard her come in and she wished someone would try to find her.

Lizzie then repeated some of the things she had told Alice Russell the evening before: her father had an enemy, they had all been sick, and they thought the milk had been poisoned. She finally got around to adding the more germane fact that Bridget had not found Dr. Bowen at home, and she had to have a doctor. At this point, Mrs. Churchill asked, "Will I go and try to find someone to get a doctor?" Lizzie said yes to this, and Mrs. Churchill hurried out of the house to seek medical help, leaving Lizzie alone once more. (Bridget had returned and had been sent to fetch Miss Russell before Mrs. Churchill arrived.)

The Bordens' next door neighbor to the south, Dr. Kelly, was a qualified physician. Unfortunately, he was also Irish and, as such, simply did not exist in the Borden-Churchill mind. Mrs. Churchill went to Hall's stable down the hill from Dr. Bowen's house where she found her hired man in a group of several men. She told him there was "trouble" at the Borden house and sent him to find a doctor, "any doctor," which meant religion and national origin were suddenly secondary to knowledge and ability.

John Cunningham was near the group Mrs. Churchill had approached, and he overheard what she said to Tom Bowles. Mr. Cunningham would later testify, "It called my attention; her actions were rather peculiar for a lady." He went into Hall's and made four reported telephone calls: the first to the police where he talked directly to the marshal, the second to the Fall River *Globe*, the third to the *Herald*, and the last to the *News*. Mr. Cunningham listed his occupation as "news dealer," and he dealt out his scoop to all the town's players. The *Globe* later reported he had called it *before* he called the police. That may be true. A call to the police was solely Cunningham's idea. Neither Lizzie, Bridget, nor Mrs. Churchill had suggested any need for the police; their request was for a doctor.

Nothing critical was lost if several minutes were misspent. Andrew and Abby Borden were both sadly beyond help, and their murderer was well on the way to safety from police detection.

The second person to appear on the murder scene was Dr. Seabury W. Bowen. Mrs. Churchill could not state with certainty if, when she returned after talking with her hired man, Bridget had returned from her second mission. If not, Bridget arrived a very few seconds after Mrs. Churchill's return, as did Dr. Bowen.

Dr. Bowen was directed to Mr. Borden's body in the sitting room. The women did not accompany him. When the doctor rejoined them, he asked for a sheet to cover the body. Bridget got the key to the Borden bedroom, and she and Mrs. Churchill went up the rear stairs to Mrs. Borden's dressing room to find one. Mrs. Churchill stated that immediately after he covered the body with the sheet and before the police or any other medical assistance arrived, Dr. Bowen left the house.

Because Bridget was not sure where Miss Russell lived, the trip to her house took much more time than the one to Dr. Bowen's had. Lizzie would have been alone for all of that time if Dr. Bowen had not appeared or if Mrs. Churchill had not been at home or had been less nosy or not quite so neighborly. Bridget did find Miss Russell who, after taking time to change her dress, arrived shortly after Dr. Bowen left.

Miss Russell, Mrs. Churchill, and Bridget were consoling Lizzie when she again insisted that someone hunt for her stepmother. Mrs. Churchill and Bridget went up the front staircase and found Abby's body in the guest room.

This produced a most controversial point that resulted in total disagreement between the prosecution and the defense that generated page after page of useless testimony and argument. Mrs. Churchill testified, "Soon after Miss Russell came in, I think Miss Lizzie said she wished we would try and find Mrs. Borden. She thought she heard her come in. Bridget did not want to go alone. I went with her halfway up the front stairs. I could see across the floor of the spare bedroom. I saw something at the far side of the bed, the north side, that looked like a prostrate form. I did not go any farther. I turned and went right back again."

Bridget continued on into the guest room and went to the foot of the bed where she could see Abby's bloodied, mutilated form. Mrs. Churchill returned to the kitchen, and Bridget soon followed. Miss Russell asked, "Is there another?" and Mrs. Churchill answered, "Yes, she is upstairs."

Under direct examination, Mr. Knowlton asked, "Was the bed between you and the prostrate form when you saw it?"

"Yes, sir," Mrs. Churchill answered.

"Did you see it over the bed or under the bed?"

"Under the bed."

"Where were you standing when you saw what you think was the prostrate form?"

"About halfway up the stairs, I think."

"So your head was above the level of the floor?"

"My eyes were on a level when I looked."

There is no reason to doubt Mrs. Churchill, but experts did. Tests were conducted that disputed her: the bed was too low to see under; the light was too dim to see with; and on and on it went. The point was critical to Lizzie because Bridget placed Lizzie upstairs or on the stairs when her father came home, and Lizzie herself admitted to making at least one quick trip up and down those very stairs. The prosecution insisted that Mrs. Churchill's testimony proved that Mrs. Borden's body was in plain view and Lizzie could have seen it with the same ease as had Mrs. Churchill.

The defense conceded nothing, saying that *if* one knew what to look for, *if* one knew in what direction to look while at the exact height above the landing *and* while standing stock-still on the stairs *and* with the light much brighter than it had been that morning, *then* one would still not see a thing. Neither side won the point.

Under cross-examination, Mr. Jennings asked Mrs. Churchill, "Did you go up ahead, or Bridget?"

"I do not remember. I think Bridget was ahead, but I do not remember."

"You think she went up ahead of you; cannot you recollect whether she opened the door or not?"

"The door was open."

"Are you sure about that?"

"Yes, sir."

At the inquest, Miss Lizzie had said that door was shut.

Here we have what seem like two concise, straightforward statements of fact that are in absolute, direct conflict. Like so much of the Borden mystery, the answer is so simple when you know who did kill the Bordens. Both Miss Lizzie and Mrs. Churchill are correct. When Lizzie last came down that staircase, the door was shut; when Bridget and Mrs. Churchill first went *up* those stairs, the door was open. Lizzie, you see, was not the last one to come down from upstairs. The murderer was.

\*     \*     \*

\*     \*     \*

Mrs. Churchill had witnessed Mr. Borden leave the house that morning about 9 o'clock. She had also seen Bridget outside, "rinsing or washing off the parlor windows, rinsing it, throwing water on it with a dipper," although she did not know what time that was. She had gone to Lizzie's aid something after 11 o'clock. In spite of the best efforts of both the defense and the prosecution, she could not fix the time more accurately. She offered no guess, no "might have been." She was an excellent witness.

She described Lizzie's dress that morning as "calico cotton, blue and white with a figure on it, the shape of a diamond in a darker blue, in fact, the figure was navy blue." This description does not fit the dress Lizzie turned over to the police as the dress she said she was wearing on the murder morning. It does, however, sound like the one Lizzie destroyed a few days after the tragedy.

Mrs. Churchill saw no blood on Lizzie's skin, hair, clothing, or shoes. Lizzie did not appear wet from recent washing. Her hair was neat, in place, and worn up as it usually was worn.

In Mrs. Churchill's testimony we have an outstanding record of all that took place from the time Lizzie "holloed" up the rear stairs for Bridget to come down to the arrival of the first policeman, Officer George W. Allen, about ten minutes later. The record suggests that Lizzie Borden did not act like a loving daughter confounded and shaken up by the gruesome butchery that had befallen her father. There were no tears or cries of anguish. There was nothing in Lizzie's demeanor or actions that even showed emotion, let alone the degree of emotion the situation should have suggested. She may well have been in shock.

When Bridget left her the first time to get Dr. Bowen, Lizzie remained alone inside the house where, unless she knew better, a brutally vicious killer could still be lurking. Lizzie could have found more safety outside the back door, but she elected to stay inside. The fortuitous appearance of Mrs. Churchill was not the result of any direct action taken by Lizzie. In sending Bridget on her second trip away from the house to fetch Miss Russell, Lizzie again lost the protection of a strong and capable young woman and, once more, remained alone inside the house. If she knew the killer had left the house, she would have no reason to be afraid.

Dr. Bowen's arrival is an incredible example of perfect timing. No doubt one quick look at the bloody mess that once had been his neighbor was enough for an experienced physician to realize that nothing could be done for Mr. Borden, but how could he know from those few moments he had been in the house that it was more important for him to leave the premises than it was for him to stay? How could he possibly know that a loving daughter who had discovered her world smashed to bits did not need some comforting words and, at the very least, the strength gained from a hug or a held hand? How did he know that his masculine presence was not necessary as some measure of protection for the three women during the scant minutes remaining before the authorities arrived? In other words, why was it so all-fired imperative for him to leave the house and leave with all due haste?

It is time to take a close, hard look at the good doctor.

### Dr. Seabury W. Bowen

According to the available-to-all *final trial* testimony, Dr. Seabury Bowen arrived at the murder house, determined immediately that Mr. Borden was beyond medical help, and requested a sheet with which to cover the grotesquely mutilated body. Then, at the request of Miss Lizzie and in the role of friend and neighbor rather than that of doctor, he left the house to send a telegram to Lizzie's sister Emma to apprise her of the tragedy. Rather than leave the helpless women alone, he waited for the first policeman to arrive and then headed for the telegraph office.

Nothing in these attested actions can be faulted, and this is the picture usually painted of the doctor. His testimony in the final trial shows him to be a mite stupid and bumbling, but forgivably funny.

However, Mr. Jennings' long-buried copy of the *preliminary hearing* transcript gives a different picture. Before hearing what has not been available or presented until now, what has been accepted as fact all these years should be reviewed in detail.

At the final trial, Dr. Bowen told of having completed his initial examination of Mr. Borden's body and of asking for a sheet with which to cover it.

"What was done in consequence of your request?" he was asked.

"Bridget Sullivan brought me a sheet."

"In the meantime, had you had any conversation with the prisoner?"

"No, sir."

"What occurred after the sheet was brought back and used upon the body?"

"Miss Lizzie Borden asked me if I would telegraph to her sister Emma."

"And in consequence of that, did you go to the telegraph office?"

"Yes, sir."

"Now have you told us all that occurred up to the time of your return from telegraphing?"

"I wished to notify the officers and as I was going out Officer Allen—supposed to be, I didn't know him at that time."

"You know him now?"

"Yes, sir, I have seen him since to know him. He is a short, thickset man. I know that. I didn't know him at the time. He came in, and I satisfied myself that the officers knew of the affair."

This *final trial* testimony shows Dr. Bowen to be a man dedicated to his patient, Andrew Borden. When Dr. Bowen determined that the patient was beyond help, he turned his attention to his patient's grieving daughter to offer her aid and comfort. He could best serve Andrew in death by making things as easy as possible for Andrew's daughter whose only concern at the moment was how her sister Emma should be informed of the awful tragedy. That is exactly Bowen's projected image in reports of the case. At the *final trial*, Dr. Bowen claims: 1) Miss Russell was in the house and she and 2) Mrs. Churchill were with Lizzie while 3) Bridget brought him the required sheet; 4) he had had *no* conversation with Miss Lizzie, and 5) he consulted with Officer Allen before leaving to send the telegram Miss Lizzie asked him to send.

No one can fault those actions, but before passing final

*Dr. S. W. Bowen*

judgment on the good doctor, let us take a look at Mr. Jennings' transcript of the *preliminary hearing* and learn what Dr. Bowen had said when questioned ten months earlier, within days of the event.

Under direct examination by Mr. Adams for the defense, Dr. Bowen established the facts that he had been a practicing physician and surgeon in the city of Fall River for twenty-five years and had lived in the house diagonally across the street from the Bordens for about the same number of years as the Bordens had lived in their house. He characterized himself as the Bordens' neighbor, family physician, and friend.

On the day of the murders, he had just driven up to his house from Tiverton, Rhode Island, when his wife and Tom Bowles (Mrs. Churchill's manservant) met him simultaneously and explained in no uncertain terms that there was an immediate need for his presence in the Borden house. His best guess as to the time that he had arrived was ten to twenty minutes after eleven. This estimate is well within the limits of truth, but at the final trial it would be revised to between "11:00 o'clock and 11:30 o'clock" to fit his new testimony.

Mr. Adams asked, "What took place?"

"I was excited myself because I received the message in such a manner that I knew something was wrong," Bowen replied. "My wife was very much excited indeed, and Mr. Bowles at the same time told me to go across; and I was prepared for something unusual. I said, 'Lizzie, what is the matter?' She said, 'Father has been killed' or 'been stabbed'—I would not say which."

"What did you do?"

"I asked her where her father was [pause] or perhaps I asked her [pause]. She said he had been killed or stabbed. I says, 'Did you see anyone?' She said she did not see anybody. I asked her if she heard anybody. She said she did not. Then I asked her where her father was. She said he was in the sitting room. I went directly through the dining room to the door of the sitting room, the door from the dining room to the sitting room.

". . . and saw Mr. Borden?"

"Yes, sir."

"After seeing Mr. Borden, what did you do?"

"I examined him and satisfied myself that he was dead. I went directly out the door going from the sitting room to the kitchen, and told whoever was there that Mr. Borden had been killed, that he had been murdered."

"What was done? Was anything done about a sheet then?"

"I asked very soon for a sheet—I won't say how long afterwards."

"After this sheet was brought, you went away?"

"Yes, sir."

"Where did you go?"

"As I was going out, Miss Lizzie asked me if I would not telephone or telegraph her sister. I said I would do anything for her that I could."

"You did telegraph—or cause a telegram to be sent?"

"Yes, sir."

"Where did you go to send it?"

"The Western Union Telegraph Office on Pleasant Street, between Second and Main."

"How many minutes walk was it?"

"It was a ride—I rode."

"You drove?"

"No, I went to my home before that."

"You went to the house?"

"To my home across the street."

"Then you did what?"

"I told my wife what had happened and consulted the Old Colony timetables to see if she [sister Emma] could come on the first train, to see if she was able to."

"After consulting the timetables, what did you do? Did you drive to the telegraph office?"

"Yes, sir, my boy drove me down to the telegraph office."

"Then right back again?"

"I went from the telegraph office into Mr. Baker's drug store on Main Street. I had a few moments conversation with Mr. Samuel Flint. Then I drove directly to the Borden house."

You have now twice heard Dr. Bowen's explanation for leaving the murder house when he did. The accounts are similar but also very different. Some testimony, like fine cheese, changes its texture (and its aroma) with age. He has told you he left to send a telegram to Lizzie's sister Emma. Each and every account ever written, by either Lizzie-friend or Lizzie-foe, states this as his justification for leaving the scene. Lizzie requested him to telephone or send a telegram to her sister to notify her of her father's death. We might think how thoughtful of Lizzie to finally show some concern for someone other than herself. But that is pure hogwash!

Mrs. Churchill had heard this conversation between Lizzie and Dr. Bowen. Under prodding from Mr. Knowlton, she testified. "Anything about telegraphing?" Knowlton asked.

"Oh, yes," Mrs. Churchill replied. She asked Dr. Bowen if he could send a telegram to her sister Emma."

"Did she say anything more than that?"

"She told him not to say the worst, because the lady was old where her sister was visiting, and it would shock her. Something to that effect."

Either Mrs. Churchill misunderstood what had been said, or it contains some hidden caveat from Lizzie to Dr. Bowen. Emma Borden was at a seaside cottage with the Brownells. Since Mrs. Brownell was a contemporary of Emma's, it was not nice of Lizzie to have called her an "old lady."

By the separate testimonies of Mrs. Churchill, Bridget, and

Miss Russell (and each confirms the other *exactly*), we know that, after sending Bridget out of the house for help, Lizzie had spent a brief period alone. Mrs. Churchill arrived first and then left to give the alarm (leaving Lizzie alone again), and she returned before Dr. Bowen arrived. Similarly, Bridget returned from her second sojourn (to summon Miss Russell) at the same instant as the doctor arrived. Miss Russell will tell us she arrived some minutes later *as the doctor was leaving*. Miss Russell had not arrived when Mrs. Churchill and Bridget went upstairs *together* to get the requested sheet. *The doctor and Lizzie had that time alone.*

Admittedly, this time span was probably no more than a minute, but many words and many things can pass between two people in sixty seconds. Whatever passed between them in those precious seconds was important enough to chase Dr. Bowen from the premises immediately and then later force him to reconstruct his testimony for the final trial to ensure that this time element, as small as it was, and the opportunities it offered disappeared.

Did Dr. Bowen leave the house for the primary purpose of sending a telegram to Miss Emma as all reports state? He testified here, "As I was going out, Miss Lizzie asked me if I would not telephone or telegraph to her sister. I said I would do anything for her that I could."

Dr. Bowen's testimony at the preliminary hearing makes a mockery of his trial testimony that had been expertly revised to eliminate any hint of his primary reason for leaving the house. Lizzie made her most noble request *as he was leaving*; it was strictly an afterthought on her part, but it soon became the primary reason for his departure from a major crime scene *before the arrival of the authorities*!

With regard to Dr. Bowen's *final trial* reference to short, thickset Officer Allen (adjectives that scream of coaching), at the preliminary hearing, he was asked: "Did Officer Allen get there before you?"

"I do not know the man. I should not know him if he was here. As I was going out the first time, I think I said I wished someone would notify the police."

"Do you know whether Officer Allen came there before you did the second time?"

"I do not."

What a far cry it is from "wishing someone would notify the police" to his final trial claim of having a long conversation with short, thickset Officer Allen *before* he left the house to send Lizzie's telegram. No one challenged his conflicting testimony.

From Dr. Bowen's hearing testimony we learn some seemingly innocuous facts. Because of the later effort expended to bury these facts, they must not be as innocuous as they might seem.

Here he admits he went to his home, to the telegraph office, and then to a drug store. Certainly there is nothing incriminating in any of these moves. Unlike the Borden house, Dr. Bowen's house had a telephone. If nothing else, its use could have served as an alibi or an excuse had he been pressed for why he went there first. He was never pressed, and so the alibi was never used. Remember, in those days all telephone calls went through switchboards and were placed by operators with memories and billing pads in which each and every call was recorded for charges. However, calls to Western Union were made direct and were gratis. Public telephones, being prepaid, had less switchboard memory, but were far more scarce in those days than they are today. Baker's drug store had a public telephone. (The newspapers will tell you about a telephone call later. It was not to Miss Emma. All those in a position to check seem to agree that Miss Emma received the telegram he promised Miss Lizzie he would send. Emma arrived home about seven hours after the telegram was sent. This delay was never questioned.)

Dr. Bowen was never asked or questioned about the Samuel Flint whom he met and talked to at the drugstore.

All his errands, telephoning, telegraphing, and whatever else completed, Dr. Bowen returned to the murder house to find a crowd. Mrs. Churchill met him and told him Mrs. Borden had been found murdered in the same manner as her husband. The doctor went upstairs to the front guest room, examined Mrs. Borden, and confirmed that she was, indeed, dead. Beyond that, Dr. Bowen had little to contribute other than a strong suggestion to Lizzie that she retire to her bedroom and stay there.

Dr. Bowen admitted he was seldom a visitor to the Borden house except for "business, financial, or professional" reasons. He had last seen Mrs. Borden alive the morning before the murders when she came to his office, and he had last seen Mr. Borden alive later that same morning after breakfast when he went across the street to the Borden house to check on him.

Dr. Bowen went on to admit confusion as to the events and personnel during that first half hour, and he was quick to admit that listening to others testify had "revived" his memory. He went on to say that Mr. Borden was a "horrible" sight to see, ghastly enough to effect tears. One wound went through the left side of his nose, through both lips, and down into the chin. Another began at the angle of the left eye and went down to about an inch above the lower jaw. Another began about where the forehead met the right side of his head. Yet another began by the eye, cut the eyeball in half, cut the cheekbone in half, and stopped just above the mouth. Another blow crushed portions of Andrew's skull into the brain. All in all, ten vicious, horrifying blows were rained upon his head.

Dr. Bowen returned to the Borden house after his errands and stayed there most of the remainder of the day, but contributed very little. He did examine Mrs. Borden several more times and acted as tour guide to fellow medical associates as they appeared on the scene. Belatedly, he decided Lizzie needed some aid and comfort. Mr. Knowlton's last questions of Dr. Bowen were, "Did you ask Lizzie at any time where she was when her father was killed?"

"Yes, sir. That was the first visit—I omitted that."

"What did she say?"

"She said she was out in the barn."

"What did she say she was doing out in the barn?"

"She said she was looking for irons, or something to that effect."

On redirect by Mr. Adams, the doctor said he had not been concerned about Abby's poison complaint because "at the time the weather was warm, and it was not unusual for people to be unwell that way." He did add that Abby did look sick. Not poisoned, mind you, just "sick."

At the *final trial*, Dr. Bowen provided some of that trial's most damaging testimony against Miss Lizzie. It had almost no bearing on the determination of who murdered the Bordens. But since that was not the purpose of this judicial charade anyway, it fit in beautifully.

The district attorney did a masterful job here against overwhelming opposition. Dr. Bowen, most reluctantly, all but proved for the prosecution that the dress Lizzie had turned over to the authorities as the dress she was wearing the murder morning was anything but that. He had seen her within minutes of her father's death. Here again, his inquest testimony, which has never surfaced, was the only thing that forced the truth.

"Doctor," Mr. Moody asked, "did you at any time in the course of the morning notice anything with reference to the dress that Miss Borden had on?"

"Yes, sir."

"Will you describe it as well as you can?"

"The only time I noticed anything was when she changed it after she went up to her room. I noticed she had on a different dress when she went to her room."

"What did you notice in reference to that dress?"

"I noticed the color of it."

"What was it?"

"A pink wrapper, morning dress."

"Did you notice anything with reference to the dress she had on prior to that time?"

"No, sir."

"Did you testify on this subject at the inquest?"

"I presume I was asked questions on it."

"At that time was your memory as good as it is now or better?"

"Well, about the same, I should judge."

"Do you recall making this reply to the question that I am about to read? 'Question: Do you recall how Lizzie was dressed that morning? Answer: It is pretty hard work for me. Probably if I could see a dress something like it I could guess, but I could not describe it; it was a sort of drab, not much color to it to attract my attention—a sort of calico morning dress, I should judge.'"

"Yes, sir."

"What did you say as to the color?"

"That is very indefinite there."

"What did you say as to the drab?"

"I should say the color is very indefinite."

"I did not ask you to criticize your answer, sir?"

"I made the best answer at the time that I could."

"Do you assent at the present time to that statement of the color of the dress?"

"With the modification I make now."

"What modification do you desire to make?"

"I don't remember anything distinctly about the color."

"Do you desire to say that the dress appeared to you to be a drab dress or not?"

"I merely mean to say that the dress is a common—"

"Answer my question?"

"Wait—"

"No, answer my question, and this is the question: Did it appear to you to be a drab-colored dress?"

"It was an ordinary, unattractive, common dress that I did not notice specially."

"Will you answer my question?"

Chief Justice Mason spoke to Dr. Bowen, "Answer the question if you can. If you cannot, say so."

"I don't think I can answer it better than I did. I don't know."

Mr. Moody tried one more time, "I would like to try it once more, doctor. Did it appear to you to be a drab dress?"

"I did not pretend to describe a woman's dress, and I do not intend to now."

Regardless of the effort required, Dr. Bowen finally agreed to his initial inquest statements and conceded that the dress Lizzie had turned over to the police was hardly "drab." Couple his testimony with Mrs. Churchill's no-nonsense testimony on the same subject, and you can be sure the dress on exhibit was not the first or only dress Miss Lizzie wore the morning of that bloody Thursday. And all this, of course, proves nothing at all.

On cross-examination, the defense added or subtracted little. It established that the doctor's horse was sound and considered a fast runner and that the telegram he sent to Emma had been time-stamped by Western Union at 12:32. The telegram itself was *not* introduced, nor was it ever shown that it had been initiated at the office counter rather than called in by telephone. How shortsighted of the authorities!

At the final trial, the most important point established by Dr. Bowen for the defense was intended as an insurance policy for the most immediate future, something they might need later in the trial. The court had not yet been called upon to rule on the admissibility of Miss Lizzie's inquest testimony. Doctor Bowen began establishing doubt of that testimony by outlining his part in giving drugs to Miss Lizzie. The first was bromo caffeine for nervous excitement and headache, but the second was much more ominous: sulphate of morphine. He continued a double dosage of the latter up to and during the time she was subjected to what Mr. Jennings had called "the torture of the barbaric medieval inquisition." Based on the doctor's testimony here, the defense hoped to show that anything extracted from her had been obtained while she was drugged out of her very senses.

"I suppose physicians well understand the effect of morphine on the mind and on the recollection, don't they?" Jennings asked.

"Supposed to, yes, sir."

"Does not morphine given in double doses to allay mental distress and nervous excitement somewhat affect the memory and change and alter the view of things and give people hallucinations?"

"Yes, sir."

On redirect, Mr. Moody made no serious attempt to cancel Dr. Bowen's testimony. The prosecution's own medical advisors, waiting in the wings, could have countered Dr. Bowen in less than one sentence. [Taken *orally*, as Miss Lizzie took it, morphine in a dosage of one-eighth grain *doubled* does *not* "affect the memory and change and alter the view of things and give people hallucinations."] But the prosecution knew a counterattack would not be required. Her inquest testimony would not be admitted for several previously well-agreed-upon reasons, and "drugging" was not one of them.

The last reference to Dr. and Mrs. Bowen is the presence of their names on the guest list for the dinner party given for Lizzie on the evening she was set free by the jury. Soon after, Miss Lizzie became Lizbeth of Maplecroft, and the good doctor retired from his medical practice. He spent the rest of his life as a gentleman of leisure.

# Chapter 10

The preliminary hearing testimony of John V. Morse, unavailable until now, reveals several serious aspects of the crime and of its principals that somehow never became public at Lizzie's final trial. Many of these most fascinating elements have not been reported previously despite the totally new slant and direction they give to the whole sordid story. The hearing was open, but as far as can be determined, Mr. Jennings' copy of the transcript, the only known copy, was not available until 1970.

*John V. Morse*
Under examination by District Attorney Knowlton at the preliminary hearing, John Morse stated that on the day before the murders he had taken the 12:35 afternoon train from New Bedford, had arrived at the Borden house about 1:30, had not seen Emma or Lizzie, had been served a dinner especially prepared for him by Abby (the Bordens had finished eating a few minutes earlier, which lends credence to the unannounced "drop-in" nature of his visit), had hired a team from Kirby's stable (situated close to Dr. Bowen's house across the street), and, after inviting Andrew Borden to join him and being refused because Mr. Borden did not feel physically up to it, had journeyed to two farms, one of a Mr. Vinnicum and one owned by Andrew Borden, both located across the river in Swansea.

Mr. Morse's middle name was Vinnicum, and so it may be assumed the first farm visited was operated or owned by more than a casual friend. No such relationship was established under direct questioning, however.

Just as he had when he questioned Lizzie at the inquest, Knowlton made it unmistakably clear that the prosecution possessed full knowledge of the crime, its motive, and the persons involved. He asked his questions of Morse using the same elegant, unobtrusive technique he had followed when he asked Lizzie to name her half brother.

Since Lizzie would not testify again, John V. Morse was now the family's spokesman. He was better prepared for this than Lizzie had been. He did not become rattled as she had and he countered rather nicely, with just enough verve to announce that, yes, the message has been received—now back off.

After Mr. Morse outlined his trip to the Swansea farms, Mr. Knowlton asked, "Mr. Borden had a place over there?"

"Yes, sir."

"Did you have some business of Mr. Borden's over there?"

"Yes, sir."

"I do not care to go into the particulars of it," Knowlton interjected. "You had some business relating to Mr. Borden at the farm?"

"Yes, sir."

That last question by Mr. Knowlton is most strange. Uncle John had just admitted that his unannounced and un-scheduled visit to the Borden household was made because of or resulted in his need to go to the Borden farm on business *for Mr. Borden*, but the District Attorney *did not care to go into the particulars of it!* Anyone seeking facts would most definitely want to go into the particulars of it. Knowlton, for the prosecution, was the exception.

The particulars are of the utmost importance because, al-most unanimously, the legend contends that Lizzie com-mitted the murders because her father planned a title transfer of the farm to Abby as, five years before, he had transferred the title to the duplex. Thus, indirectly at least, the legend claims this farm was the motive for murder. Lizzie would not allow any more of her inheritance to slip away. The legend is not true, but by any and all means, Mr. Knowlton should have explored "the particulars."

In any event, Mr. Knowlton had thrown down the gauntlet

and continued by picking away at the family's as yet unlanced boil. Uncle John, however, was prepared. He conceded Knowlton's right to cast into the Borden's private fishpond, but he had his own red herring ready. When Knowlton asked if his trip to the farm pertained to "hiring a man," Uncle John replied, "I went more particularly over there that day to see about some cattle I bought from him. I thought I would make arrangements to take them."

Uncle John felt that follow-up questions about a man who might be considered for hire on the Borden farm was much too close to the truth and might evoke door-opening questions. In his answer, therefore, he politely conveyed this to Knowlton while countering with a cattle purchase. This was safe and easily accepted as truth. After all, there was nothing questionable about taking a shipment of cattle back to Fall River in a hired rig and then transferring them to the New Bedford train. If it was questionable, no one questioned it. Neither side cared about the truth at this juncture; they were more concerned with the necessary establishment of power bases, the jousting this required, and the provisions of the agreement made with the silent government at the Mellen House.

Knowlton backed off and asked Morse safe questions about his opinion of the Bordens' health, the fact that Miss Emma was not at home, the fact he had not seen Miss Lizzie until, as Mr. Morse answered, "the time of the tragedy." Knowlton quickly rectified this poor choice of words for him to "after they were killed" since the "time" had not yet been established and Mr. Morse's knowledge of it could have proved embarrassing to the prosecution and the acquittal that had been promised.

After reviewing the layout of the house and stating he had slept the night before the murder in the bedroom in which Mrs. Borden's body would be found, Mr. Knowlton asked Morse to outline his version of the murder morning.

"What time did you get up in the morning?"

"About six," Uncle John replied, "if I recollect right."

"What time did you come downstairs?"

"I came down a few minutes afterwards. I made my toilet and came downstairs maybe twenty minutes."

"When you came downstairs, who did you find there?"

"Not anyone."

"Did you see the servant?"

"Not until about breakfast time."

"Who did you first see after you got down?"

"Mr. Borden."

"When did Mrs. Borden appear?"

"Fifteen or twenty minutes after Mr. Borden came down."

These various arrival times do not agree with Bridget's account of what happened that morning. This conflict with Bridget's testimony has no worthwhile significance other than for the reinforcement it gives to the size and layout of the house. Lizzie and Bridget both avowed they had little contact with each other on the murder morning, and this has not been accepted as feasible. Here Uncle John proves that four or more people could be on the same floor in the house at the same time and not have any contact, visual or otherwise.

Mr. Morse next told of the after-breakfast movements of Mr. and Mrs. Borden in and out of the rooms he was in as they prepared for their day or began some of the day's activity. When Knowlton asked him about what time he left the house, John replied, "I think about quarter to nine."

He and Bridget agree to the minute on this count. He repeated he had not seen Lizzie and stated that when he left, Mr. Borden ". . . unhooked the door, and he hooked it, and the last words I heard him say was, 'John, come back to dinner with us.'" Strangely, his reply to this invitation was not asked nor was it offered. All accounts of the murder have stated that he accepted the invitation.

Uncle John next outlined his travels after leaving the Borden house. Each step is clear and concise, and the newspapers checked well beyond the limits of his testimony.

From the house he went "to the post office and wrote a card to William Vinnicum of Swansea, and went from there out to the north door, and went up Third Street; from there to Pleasant Street, up Pleasant Street to Weybosset Street, Number 4, to Daniel Emery's."

"That is way up to the eastward?" Knowlton asked.

"Perhaps a good mile up there," Morse replied.

"You have some friends up there that you went to visit?"

"A niece and a nephew from the West—my brother's children."

"What time did you start to come away from there?"

"I think about twenty minutes past eleven."

Note that Mr. Morse was not asked what time he arrived at his niece and nephew's house, only what time he left it. His departure time from that house, so few minutes after the initial telephone call to the police, is noteworthy.

Uncle John's alibi is solid for the time when the murders were committed, but *only* for the *exact times when they took place*. For at least forty-five minutes *before* the first murder, he had no substantiated alibi. No one could be found who witnessed any of his movements from the time he left the Borden house (or, in fact, *of* his leaving the Borden house, except Bridget), went to the post office, wrote and mailed a card, walked more than a mile on the second busiest street of the city, and arrived at the Emery house. On the other hand, every step of his travels *back* from the Emery house could be checked inch by inch, and all were beyond any hint of doubt and had been sworn to by uninvolved (and nonrelated) solid citizens.

His alibi began about the instant Abby was killed and continued until well after Lizzie discovered her father's death. The next gap in it occurred when he walked from the horse-car stop on Pleasant Street at the corner of Second Street to the Borden house, two short city blocks. Although no one came forward to claim having seen him, this lack has never been questioned because it occurred so obviously after the fact.

The striking difference between his having no substantiated alibi for his travels *to* the Emery house as compared to his having a well-above-normal oversupply for his travels *from* there makes good sense if his need for an alibi was called to his attention *while he was visiting the Emerys*. It was. In other words, he knew the Bordens had been murdered *before* he journeyed back to the house allegedly for the sole purpose of accepting Mr. Borden's invitation to join them for dinner.

Evidence of this was provided by the *Herald* in its follow-up account of Officer Medley's interrogation of Mrs. Emery and Morse's niece Annie. After affirming that Uncle John Morse had been at her home, she said, "He left here at 11:30 o'clock this morning."

"Then you noticed the time?" she was asked.

"Oh, yes."

After she was asked how she "fixed" the time, she hesitated, replied that her niece Annie was sick and Dr. Bowen was her physician (as if he would be making house calls in the middle of the emergency), and said, "Dr. Bowen came in just as Mr. Morse left." She obviously had been coached at how to explain his appearance at her home.

Neither Mrs. Emery nor her niece was called for questioning at any of the hearings or at the trial. An oversight, of course.

All accounts of the Borden murders claim that Dr. Bowen left the murder house to send a telegram to Miss Emma, and there is plenty of evidence that he did cause one to be sent. At the best, however, the telegram was of secondary importance.

The primary reason for Bowen's headlong dash out of the house within seconds of his arrival was Miss Lizzie's fervent plea for him to find John Morse and tell him that Andrew Borden had been murdered. She convinced Bowen that this must be done as quickly as possible. According to the *Globe*, he called Morse on the telephone; according to the *Herald*, he went in person.

The reason Lizzie sent Dr. Bowen to find John Morse was that he had declined Andrew's invitation to return for dinner. He had stopped at Mrs. Emery's house on his way to the railroad station, and Lizzie was desperate for him to return to the Borden house. The meeting Uncle John had planned had gone wrong, and Lizzie was desperate for him to know that Andrew had been murdered. She knew who had killed her father (she didn't know yet that Abby had been murdered, too), and she knew that if he was caught by the police or surrendered himself to them, he would be a danger to all she held dear. The murderer must not be caught. The sooner that Uncle John knew, the sooner the proper measures could begin.

Mr. Knowlton attempted to substantiate the critical timing portions of Mr. Morse's alibi: "You think you left [the Emerys'] about twenty minutes past eleven?"

"Yes, sir," John replied. "I looked at my watch about going back to dinner."

Mr. Borden's invitation to John takes on great importance. For what other reason would he be going back to the house?

"How did you come back?" Knowlton asked.

"From Mr. Emery's? On the car that comes down Pleasant Street, and I got off at the corner of Pleasant and Second Street."

"You went right up home?"

"Yes, sir."

"Did you see any crowds upon the street when you came up?"

"Nothing that attracted my attention."

This answer is unbelievable, and yet *no one has ever questioned it*. By his own testimony, when Mr. Morse arrived at the Borden house that morning no earlier than 11:45, the alarm had been sounded at least thirty minutes earlier. He would have arrived with:

1) Bridget and Lizzie inside the house;

2) Mrs. Churchill, Miss Russell, and Mrs. Bowen in the house comforting Lizzie;

3) Two medical examiners (Dr. Bowen and Dr. Dolan) and perhaps three other doctors;

4) Citizen Charles S. Sawyer on guard at the side door (Pressed into service by the Fall River police, he had a physique that any NFL defensive lineman would covet. He had orders to stop unauthorized persons from entering, and he did not know John Morse.);

5) Between six and ten policemen;

6) A minimum of three reporters and any entourage they may have had;

7) Several *hundred* citizens who appeared on the scene within minutes; and

8) Dozens and dozens of horses and wagon teams that had to have been in the street in front of or near the house.

Other than these few people and things, it must be agreed that nothing happening around the Borden house when Mr. Morse arrived could possibly have attracted his attention.

As improbable as it may sound, there is a distinct possibility

181

that Morse *did not* see anything. In cross-examination, Jennings questioned Uncle John about his arrival at the Borden house. "When you came up the street, who, if anybody, did you see before you went into the yard, as you came up Second Street?"

"No one that I could recognize," Uncle John replied. "There might have been a few men along, the same as generally. I did not see anything unusual about it."

"Which gate did you go into?"

"Into the north small gate."

"Where did you go?"

"I went around to the pear tree."

"But you did not have to go by the screen door to get to the pear tree?" Jennings inquired.

"Yes, sir."

"Did you not see anyone in the entryway then?"

"No, sir."

"Neither Bridget nor Mr. Sawyer?"

"No, sir."

Other than his having gone to the pear tree, not a word of what Uncle John said is true.

Mr. Morse alighted from the west-bound Pleasant Street horsecar (he gave the car's number) driven by conductor (badge number given) at its arrival time (also given) at the corner of Second Street and proceeded up the hill to the first cross street (Borden Street, named for a past Borden, not Andrew) and walked east to Fourth Street to Mr. Harrington's (Lizzie's other uncle) cartage and blacksmith shop. After a wild and panic-filled discussion with Mr. Harrington, a meeting with the murderer, or both, he retraced a few steps, traveled up Third Street to the *rear* of the Borden lot line, went through a fence opening prepared the night before, secured the opening, and proceeded to the same pear tree Lizzie had visited only a few minutes earlier. No one reported seeing him, and as he testified so classically, he "saw no one he recognized."

What I have written, of course, is not testimony, it is reconstructed fact based on common sense—and much more believable than the story that has been accepted all these years.

*Borden House Side entrance, 1892*

Mr. Jennings continued, "How long did you stay out there under the pear tree?"

"I might have been there two or three minutes," Uncle John replied.

"Did you see anybody in the yard at that time?"

"I do not think I did."

"Then you came back to the screen door, and there you found Bridget?"

"Yes, sir."

"She said what to you?"

"She said Mr. and Mrs. Borden had both been murdered."

"Was Mr. Sawyer there at the time?"

"Yes, sir."

"Was that after you had gone inside, or was it while you were standing on the steps?"

"I was standing on the steps then."

It may be necessary for you to take a quick look at the lot plan of the Borden house to realize how improbable Mr. Morse's testimony is. He said he passed the side door where Bridget and Mr. Sawyer were without seeing them or being seen, went into the back yard, stayed there two or three minutes, came back to the side door, saw Bridget and Mr. Sawyer for the first time, and finally talked to them. This is physically impossible, but, like so much else, it was never questioned.

Under direct examination by the district attorney, Morse repeated the tale of his arrival at the Borden house after the murders and his first news of the tragedy. Knowlton asked, "When did you first learn anything had happened?"

"At the door."

"Who told you?"

"I think the servant girl."

"Did you see Miss Lizzie when you got there?"

"After I had been in the house two or three minutes, I saw her."

"Did you have any talk with her then?"

"A very little—just spoke to her, and that was all."

"What did you say to her?"

"I cannot tell. I might have said, 'For God's sake, how did this happen?' Or something like that."

In all likelihood, that is *exactly* what Uncle John asked his niece. Something had gone awry, so *very* wrong that he must have had a most sincere desire, plus a need, to know *how* it could have happened.

Everyone who had the slightest contact whatsoever with Lizzie was asked, in detail, about every word passed between them. This is true of the police, the medical personnel, and every neighbor or casual acquaintance, but it is *not* true of Uncle John. The two questions just asked by Hosea Knowlton are the only times in *any* of the legal proceedings when John Morse was asked about any conversation he may have had with Lizzie. It is strange how *his* conversations, which should have been most revealing, were overlooked by both sides, even though both he and Lizzie professed not to speak with each other. We know they did.

Mr. Morse could not give clear-cut answers to just who was in the house or just where the nameless people were located when he entered. He excused his inability to do this by saying, "I was so excited at that time I could not tell you who they were. I was nervous, to tell the truth about it."

This statement, too, is most telling. Reflect on the horror of the crime, and it is easy to believe he could be excited, shocked, upset, stunned, incredulous, quizzical, and even angry; but there is no possible way to justify "nervous" unless he feared the immediate exposure of his personal involvement.

The image Morse creates is one of his arriving at the Borden house expecting a leisurely dinner with Mr. and Mrs. Borden and blindly rushing into a horror waiting to envelop him. This misses the mark by at least a mile and a half.

In his cross-examination of Mr. Morse, Jennings attempted to reinforce Lizzie's sharing of Mrs. Borden's "poisoning" symptoms. He had Mr. Morse confirm Mrs. Borden's supposed testimony that Lizzie was at home at the time three people accused her of attempting to purchase cyanide. He asked, "Did she [Mrs. Borden] say whether Lizzie had been up there [in her room] all the morning or not?"

"I understood her that she had."

"You understood Mrs. Borden to say that she had?"

"Yes, sir."

"Been up there sick?"

"Yes, sir."

At Mr. Jennings' direction, John Morse then gave his version of Bridget's window washing assignment. Bridget had insisted Mr. Morse left the house minutes before Mrs. Borden issued her instructions for the day. Not so, said Mr. Morse. He was asked, "Do you recollect whether there were any directions given by Mrs. Borden to Bridget about what she should do that day?"

"Yes, sir."

"When was that?"

"While we were at breakfast."

"What was it?"

"That she was to wash the windows."

"Can you recollect the conversation, the substance of it, between the two, when she gave the order?"

"I think in the first place," Uncle John began, "she asked her what she was going to do, or something of that kind."

"Who was that?"

"Mrs. Borden asked Bridget what she had got to do. Bridget said I have nothing more than common work; I think something [like] them words."

"Then what did she say?"

"Well, she says, will you wash windows? She said that she would."

Bridget's testimony is in direct conflict with Uncle John's. It seems such a simple point, one that should be accepted as an honest difference of opinion between two witnesses. This is not the case, however, because only Bridget can be wrong, but why she could be correct in everything else to which she testified *except* this point forces exploration.

She was adamant in her claim that Uncle John left the house that morning before Mrs. Borden discussed the subject of window washing with her. If she is correct, Uncle John had no knowledge of Mrs. Borden's orders.

This discrepancy has been exploited in some reviews of the crimes to prove that, in concert with his total lack of alibi for the morning before his visit to the Emery house, he did *not* leave the Borden house as early as he claimed and thus could have had an active part in Mrs. Borden's death. This is possible, but there is a simpler explanation.

Lizzie Borden and John Morse had programmed an event to take place within the Borden house the morning of August 4. Emma Borden knew the particulars, and Bridget Sullivan did not, but neither had roles to play other than *not* to be there. Their absence from inside the house was mandatory. Emma was no problem; she was easily convinced to take her first extended visit away from the house since becoming an adult.

Bridget presented no problem either. If the window assignment had not come about, she would have been ordered out on an errand or a shopping trip. As it was, when Lizzie came down from her bedroom that morning in synchrony with Uncle John's departure, she simply called her stepmother's attention to the "very dirty windows." It was more than likely that Abby would agree and, after determining that Bridget did not have a scheduled workload that morning, would assign the task to her. Hence, Bridget was correct when she testified that Abby told her to go outside and wash the windows and gave the time when she was so ordered, a time after Uncle John had left and Lizzie had come down from her bedroom. Lizzie, however, had indirectly assigned the task by simple suggestion.

Uncle John knew that Bridget would not be in the house during the critical time, and it made sense for him to reinforce Abby's having sent her outside. Actually, he confused the script with fact.

On redirect Mr. Knowlton uncovered some most telling evidence, and since it was not offered at the final trial, it has never been told before. At the inquest, Lizzie had blurted out that her Uncle John (the man to whom she never spoke) was the one who had discussed her father's will with her. No follow-up was asked of Lizzie. Uncle John may have discussed the will at length in his inquest testimony; we do not know. At Lizzie's final trial, he was *not* asked about it, and he volunteered nothing. At the preliminary hearing he said too much, and his *only* pauses or hesitations in answering any questions during the entire hearing proceedings occurred here.

Mr. Knowlton asked him, "I also meant to have asked you whether at any time you had any talk with Mr. Borden about a will, about his making a will?"

"He told me that he had a will once," Uncle John answered.

"Did you ever have any talk about it?"

"No, sir."

"Did he ever say anything to you about a will, or anything that he proposed to do? I do not ask you what yet?"

"He told me that he had a will."

Mr. Morse stood alone in stating that Andrew Borden had a will. He also stood alone as Mr. Borden's only acknowledged confidant.

At the final trial we will be asked to believe that Andrew J. Borden—who knew trusts and made part of his latter day fortune in their formation, whose only joy in life was the tight-fisted control of money, who knew he had a daughter with no respect for a penny earned and less for a penny saved, who knew his two daughters had no love for his wife who, in her own right, was virtually penniless with no means of self-support, who knew from his days as an undertaker how chaotic death could be when money affairs were not premanaged and prearranged—we will be asked to believe that this very same Andrew Jackson Borden *died without leaving a will.* In addition, we will be asked to believe that the testimony *to the contrary* by Andrew's only friend and confidant *simply did not exist.*

No other analysis of the Borden murders mentions John Morse's testimony concerning the existence of Andrew Borden's will. Undoubtedly, this is one reason the preliminary hearing transcript was sequestered by Andrew Jennings. It was Jennings, Andrew Borden's lawyer, who said shortly after the murders, "I do not know that there is a will; and I might add that, if I did know, I do not think I would be at liberty to tell. That would be a matter of trust with me."

Mr. Morse not only said under oath that a will existed, he went on to explain some of its features.

Knowlton asked him, "Did he (Andrew Borden) ever tell you about any bequests that he had a notion of making?"

"I think he said something about making . . . he did not say how or anything like that."

That was pause number one, the very first time Mr. Morse was at a loss for how to say something. We will forever wonder what Mr. Borden said about "making . . . ."

"Whether he ever did say anything to you about any purpose?" Knowlton prodded him.

"I think sometime he made a remark about a bequest."

"When was that?"

"I think somewhere within a year."

"Where were you and he at the time?"

"I think on South Main Street."

"What was it he said?"

"That is all he said."

"What?"

"Something about some bequests that he would make," John Morse explained. "He did not say what they were, or anything about it; something about giving something away, bequest to somebody, he did not say who; something about these bequests that he . . . he did not say anything more about it."

"What did he say?" Knowlton inquired.

"He did not know but what he might make some public bequests—words to that effect."

"Won't you tell me what he said?"

"He talked like he was going to make some public bequests—just in that way."

"That was sometime within a year?"

"Yes, sir."

"Can you fix the time any better than that?"

"I could not."

"Did he say anything more specific than that?"

"No, sir."

"Did he say anything about his farm, about giving that away?"

"We were going over . . ."

"Was that another talk?"

"Yes, sir."

"I will ask you when that was, too."

"That was sometime in May of this year."

"What was it he said about it?"

"We were riding over to his place," John began. "We got to speaking about the old ladies' home, you know. He says, 'I would give them some land here, if I thought they would accept it.' Something to that effect."

"Nothing about a will then?"

"No, sir."

"About giving it to them?"

"Yes, sir, that is all."

That Andrew Borden would even consider making a donation of land to any charity is beyond belief. He most certainly would have considered *selling* land to them, but only at a price he would dictate. To Morse's credit, his exact words contain disclaimers and good-sized loopholes in which his credibility can hide. Actually Morse was near the truth. Mr. Borden was planning something akin to the action to which Morse alluded; Uncle John was well aware of it and had discussed it with Lizzie.

Mr. Morse was a reluctant witness during this portion of this most difficult questioning, and there can be just one reason he volunteered as much as he did. It is a safe bet that the same subject had been broached at the inquest, and he was forced to follow through at this hearing.

Legend says Andrew planned to sign over the farm to his

wife, and before he could consummate such a horrifyingly, shameful depletion of his daughter's birthright, Lizzie killed them. The basis for this foolish speculation may easily have come from John Morse's testimony when it was given here.

Knowlton's direct question, "Did he say anything about his farm, about giving it away?" was not answered by Mr. Morse because Mr. Knowlton interrupted immediately. That interruption and the evasion it evoked is enough to make a parson cuss. Knowlton must have realized that he himself had overstepped the limits and, by way of an apology, interrupted Mr. Morse before he, too, said too much.

However exasperating this incomplete testimony is, we are grateful for the information it *does* give us. Because it was excluded from the final trial ten months later, this testimony takes on added importance.

The way this testimony was reported in the newspapers is another outstanding example of how the public was misguided. The *Globe*'s same-day coverage of Mr. Morse's testimony about Mr. Borden's will is produced here in its entirety.

The Fall River Daily *Globe*
August 27, 1892

Borden told Morse he had made a will. They were on South Main Street at the time. He said something about some bequests. Witness did not know what they were but understood he would make a public bequest.

Some time in May of this year while riding over toward the farm in Swansea, he said he would give the girls some land if he thought they would accept it.

Check this against the actual preliminary hearing testimony. Both are presented *exactly* as they were written. Mr. Borden's alleged (by Morse) gift of land for the charitable purpose of building an old ladies home became a gift, not to the old ladies but *to his own daughters!*

Mr. Knowlton next attempted to clarify the amount of contact and communication between Lizzie and Uncle John, perhaps as a follow-up to Lizzie's profession of non-contact.

Uncle John agreed with Lizzie, even to the extent of not com-
municating with her through letters. Knowlton asked, "Were
you on corresponding terms, I mean terms to write letters
back and forth—that is pretty bad English I guess—with any
member of the family?"

"Yes, sir," Uncle John replied, "Mr. Borden and Miss
Emma."

"Did you with Lizzie?"

"I do not think I ever had a letter from Lizzie in my life."

"And never wrote to her?"

"I do not think I did, only through the other letters."

It would seem that at every chance, both Uncle John and
his niece swear they never communicated with each other.
Yet at the inquest, Lizzie had admitted she had discussed her
father's will with her uncle. When Knowlton had the opportunity to ask each, in turn, pointblank to explain how this was
possible, he did not.

District Attorney Knowlton was an intelligent man. This
omission was not an oversight. It was the necessary avoidance of a dangerous subject. The danger threatened *both
sides* and formed the coercive bond between Lizzie Borden
and the Silent Government. For Lizzie, the danger was in laying
bare the fact that she and Uncle John *had* communicated and
thus both had lied.

As part of the Mellen House agreement, the Silent Government had agreed that Andrew Borden's last will and testa-
ment would never see probate. They had the power to make
this guarantee, and they conspired and agreed to commit an
illegal act and a felony. This was no problem for them. They
were the law.

*George W. Allen*

Officer George Allen's testimony is overlooked in all past
accounts because it contradicts the humorous image the legend has made of a mere clerk (Allen was the committing officer) being pressed into service as a "real" policeman and
sent in response to the most important report of a crime ever
received by the Fall River police. This, says the legend, was
necessary because on the murder day the police had declared
themselves an unauthorized holiday and had all gone on a

clambake (the fact of the clambake is true). According to the legend, this "clerk" was the only person available. Not only did it take him half an hour to get there (legend confuses Allen with Officer Patrick Doherty), the "clerk" proved his incompetency by, not once, but twice, running away from the horror of the scene screaming bloody murder. And, as if that isn't enough, on his way to the Borden house the first time, he was so afraid of what he would find there that, for his own protection, he pressed into service the biggest and strongest citizen he could find.

The legend is much more fun than Officer Allen's sworn testimony, and so the truth is sacrificed for a most welcome laugh. One early report that promoted the legend was *Trial of Lizzie Borden* by Edward Pearson:

> An unofficial but reliable account of Allen's visits, received from two newspaper reporters, says that the sight of Mr. Borden's body nearly scared the officer "out of his wits." He ran back to the station, and to his chief gasped out: "He's dead!" The unperturbed marshal replied: "Who's dead, you fool?" Allen managed to say: "Old Mr. Borden!" The marshal could not leave his post, but ordered Allen back to the house of death. In ten minutes, however, Officer Allen came panting back again, this time croaking: "*She's* dead!" (page 165).

This image of the Fall River police actually was fostered by the testimony of Officer Patrick H. Doherty, the first policeman to testify at the first open hearing. He was therefore presented to the public as the first policeman on the scene, more than twenty minutes after the marshal received the call from Mr. Cunningham.

Doherty's report of the first person he found when he arrived at the scene produced the most hearty belly laugh of the whole tragic affair. Doherty stated, ". . . I went up to the [Borden] house. I walked as far as the Post Office, and I ran. I met Mr. [Deputy Sheriff] Wixon near Mrs. Buffington's. I brought him in there with me. I went in first."

Mr. Knowlton then asked Doherty, "How many people were there when you got there?"

"There was a reporter sitting on the steps."

To add insult to this injury, the reporter, John J. Manning, would testify at the trial he had been waiting *for several minutes* before Doherty arrived. The legend has loved it for decades.

Admittedly, the Fall River police force was not overstaffed on the day of their clambake. Not only was the date of the murders an unfortunate one for the reputation of the force, but at the *time* the murders were reported, most of those on duty were beginning to get ready for dinner.

Officer Allen was a five-year veteran and held the position of committing officer. He was on duty in the central station when Marshal Hilliard took the telephone call from Mr. Cunningham. As the person responsible for receiving prisoners committed to jail, Officer Allen was awaiting a prisoner scheduled to be admitted at 11:30. After his telephone call from Mr. Cunningham, the marshal ordered Allen to investigate immediately a reported "row" at 92 Second Street.

From the instant Allen was given this order to the time he arrived on the scene was four minutes. He arrived there no later than 11:20. He knew the exact minute because he looked at the station house clock before leaving to make sure he had time enough to investigate and return for his committing duties. He verified the time shown on the station house clock with his own watch. Both read 11:15.

He knew it took him four minutes to get to the Borden house because he retraced his steps on several occasions at the half-walk, half-run pace he used on the murder day. He had a sense of urgency that caused him to run part of the way, he confessed, because he felt that at 11:30 he should be back at the station for his duties there.

On his run to the murder scene, Allen met Charles S. Sawyer, and because he knew he needed to return to the station house as soon as possible, he had taken Sawyer along with him, should the still unknown "trouble" require muscle. Sawyer had been on the fringe of the group Mrs. Churchill approached in her search for her manservant, and her actions and words had alerted him to "something going on" at the Borden house. He was overflowing with natural curiosity. When they arrived at the house, Allen stationed Sawyer outside the side door with instructions to allow no one in or out other than police officers.

Allen testified that on his first visit to the house, he saw Miss Lizzie, Mrs. Churchill, Miss Russell, and Bridget Sullivan. Dr. Bowen, he tells us, was leaving the house to send Miss Lizzie's requested telegram. He knew Dr. Bowen and allowed him to pass. Allen looked at Mr. Borden's body, checked the front door (it was securely locked), and checked several first-floor closets large enough to afford a killer a suitable hiding place (he found no one hiding in them). He did not check the second floor or the cellar. He announced he would "go down and get some officers up there to investigate the case," told Sawyer "to stay there until I get back," and returned to the station house where he reported his findings to the marshal. The marshal then ordered Allen to find Officer Mullaly, who was close by, apprise him of the situation, and return to the Borden house with Mullaly.

Allen did exactly as the marshal ordered and, upon his return to the house, found the murder scene overrun with other officers, most of whom had been interrupted at dinner when the marshal contacted them by one means or another. We are never told who admitted the prisoner Allen was supposed to commit that day.

On this second visit to the house, Allen learned that Mrs. Borden had been found murdered, viewed her body, saw Mr. Morse in the house, and, after a trip to the basement, could attest that the basement door was bolted on the inside.

The significant part of Allen's testimony came when he was questioned about his viewing of Mr. Borden's body—although this significance has never been recognized. While reviewing Allen's testimony, we shall also examine the issue of the position of Andrew Borden's body. Allen was the first uninvolved person with knowledge, training, and authority to view it. He was asked by Mr. Moody, "Did you notice anything about the sofa and the furniture on the first time that you went into the sitting room?"

"I noticed how Mr. Borden sat on the sofa," he began, "or laid on the sofa, at least."

"Will you take that photograph [photograph Number 5] and tell me if you noticed anything else?"

"I noticed the shoes were on, and how small the ankles was for the shoes."

*Andrew Borden in death; the famous photograph No. 5.*

Lizzie Borden testified that her father had removed his shoes before lying down for his nap. Officer Allen and photograph Number 5 contradict Miss Lizzie. Moreover, Lizzie said her father was napping. Officer Allen's first impression when he was confronted with Mr. Borden's body was, "*I noticed how Mr. Borden sat on the sofa.*" Mr. Borden's position shown in the photograph is not a comfortable one for napping.

Only a few hours after the murders, Andrew Jennings said, "The theories advanced are simply ridiculous. They do not offer a motive. If it was shown that the thing was done during a quarrel, in the heat of passion, it would be different; but to suppose that for such a matter a man will lie in wait or steal upon his victim while asleep and hack him to death is preposterous. Even with revenge in his heart, the sight of his victim asleep would disarm most any man."

Andrew Borden was not sleeping when he was murdered.

He was engaged in conversation with his murderer. The first blow of the blunt side of the murder weapon killed him while he was sitting up. Subsequent blows were delivered in uncontrolled rage.

Officer Allen was not the first to hint that Mr. Borden's position on the sofa was unusual. At the preliminary hearing, Dr. Bowen had been asked the following questions by Mr. Adams: "What was the position of Mr. Borden on the sofa at this time when you saw him, because, as I understand it, you were the first person who came in there?"

"He was lying on the right side of his face," Dr. Bowen answered. "The head of the lounge or sofa was near the door leading from the dining room to the sitting room."

"Calling your attention to Photograph Number 5, and the position there, I ask you how the position which you saw him in varies from that, if it does at all?"

"The only difference I can see, I think the whole form has sunk down, has slipped down. I do not think the head is quite as high now as it was when I first saw him. The only way I can explain that is that by walking through the room, he may have settled down some way."

"Settled down into the sofa, up towards the foot of the sofa a little?"

"I thought the head was a little higher up on the arm."

The doctor's observation was that initially Mr. Borden's head and body had been higher on the sofa. Officer Allen, who saw Mr. Borden's body just a very few minutes after Dr. Bowen, also had the first impression that Mr. Borden was sitting.

The legend has always claimed that Mr. Borden was murdered while he napped, and ten or more blows were rained onto his head while he was lying down with his head on the sofa's arm. If this is true, it would seem logical that the hammerlike blows his head received would have driven it into the sofa, and a photograph taken later could possibly show a spring-back action with the head *higher* rather than lower than first observed. But Dr. Bowen stated that when he first viewed the body, "the head was a little higher on the arm" than it was in the picture.

There are three other observations to be made about the

picture of Andrew Borden's body that was entered as evidence. First, at the final trial, George A. Pettee, a civilian spectator who was shown the body of Mr. Borden by Dr. Bowen just after Dr. Bowen returned to the house, said Andrew Borden's feet were crossed. They are obviously not crossed in the photograph. This discrepancy was never questioned, even though it seems significant since a sitting person crossed his legs, not a reclining one. The unprovable conclusion is that Andrew Borden was sitting up when he was killed and was later lowered into the position shown in the photograph.

Second, Mr. Borden's hands in the photograph are made into fists. I do not know of anyone not physically deformed who sleeps with his hands clinched into fists. Fists more generally connote aggression or are the first reflex action of defense.

Finally, photograph Number 5 gives us a chance to consider the blood spots. Granted, the photograph is high-grained, poor quality, and reproduced badly, and the wallpaper pattern is confusing. Moreover, because the spots were small—ranging from pinhead size to peasize—they did not photograph well. What stains were there disappeared fast because Emma washed them away the third day after the crime, but they would have been there when the photograph was taken,

A record of the blood spots was not lost, however, because Dr. William A. Dolan, the county's medical examiner, was one of the earliest arrivals at the Borden house. At the preliminary hearing, he testified with boring detail as to the number, size, and location of blood spots. For instance, on the wallpaper above the position where Mr. Borden's head is shown in photograph Number 5, were eighty-six spots, the highest of which was three feet, seven inches from the floor. Dr. Dolan enumerated, described, and located each spot, no matter how small and seemingly unimportant. *If* Andrew was seated on the sofa when he was first struck, rather than reclined as he was found, his head would have been in the general area of the lower edge of the picture on the wall, closer to the white door to the dining room, which is shown closed.

In detailing the individual blood spots, Dr. Dolan said, "On that picture and frame were in all forty spots. The highest spot there was fifty-eight inches from the floor."

Mr. Knowlton then asked him, "How were those distributed, with any sort of regularity?"

"No, sir," Dr. Dolan replied. "They were more as though shooting directly upward."

Amazingly, Dr. Dolan was *not* asked how this pattern could have possibly occurred if Mr. Borden was killed while his head was on the arm of the sofa in sleep. There was no follow-up at all.

On August *16*, an architect-engineer, Thomas Kieran, was sent by the government to draw house plans and lot outlines and to take full and complete measurements of all evidence germane to the crime scene. He testified he found *a* blood spot on the picture frame. (Poor Emma had missed one when she cleaned up.) This one blood spot is of no consequence in relation to Dr. Dolan's revelation of thirty-nine others. However, Mr. Porter, in his 1893 book, *The Fall River Tragedy*, accounted for the evidence of the preliminary hearing, overlooked the forty spots mentioned by the doctor, and reported just the one mentioned by Mr. Kieran. Since Porter's account was the sole source of meaningful information about the preliminary hearing until the Jennings transcript came to light, this misrepresentation of evidence has seriously handicapped those who have searched for the truth. Therefore Dr. Dolan's actual disclosure has never been considered until now.

At the final trial, Dr. Dolan's testimony on blood spots covered page after page. The defense insisted on covering it in "tedious repetition" to guarantee that no one would listen because it was so boring. Dr. Dolan outlined in detail each isolated spot and each cluster. In every instance, he was asked direct questions about each spot, each cluster, each pool, and each puddle *except for one cluster*. The exception followed the doctor's statement that "There were forty spots on the picture and frame that hung over the lounge sofa, the highest being fifty-eight inches." No questions. No explanation. No follow-up ensued either in direct questioning or under cross-examination by Mr. Adams. What was not asked tells us more than what was asked.

\*     \*     \*

## Charles S. Sawyer

Charles S. Sawyer testified at both the preliminary hearing and the final trial. He did not contribute much new information, but he fully enjoyed his day in the sun.

Sawyer was one of the group of men Mrs. Churchill approached when, at Lizzie's request, she sought medical assistance. His curiosity was also piqued when he saw Miss Russell, whom he knew, coming up the hill. He crossed the street, fell in step with her, and walked with her to the Borden gate. However, he did not enter. He turned, saw Officer Allen running toward him, and hurried to meet him in front of the Churchill house. Sawyer then returned with Allen, entered the Borden gate, and took up his assigned guard post at the side door. Sawyer said Dr. Bowen left the house almost at the same instant he took up his post.

Sawyer affirmed that Deputy Sheriff Wixon and Officer Doherty were the next policemen on the scene and that they did not arrive until ten or fifteen minutes after Officer Allen had left.

John J. Manning, a newspaper reporter, arrived after Sawyer had been on duty for at least ten minutes. Sawyer would not let Manning enter the house, and when Dr. Bowen arrived back after his errand to send the telegraph, he, too, refused entry to Manning. But when Officer Doherty arrived, he quickly invited Manning to enter with him. Other than reinforcing most people's opinion as to the lack of competence of the police force, the only thing we learn from this is that Dr. Bowen returned to the house before Officer Doherty arrived.

At approximately six o'clock that evening, Sawyer located someone with authority, mentioned he had not had his noon dinner and was growing hungry, and asked if he could leave his post. He was excused. He had been forgotten.

# Chapter 11

**D**eputy Francis Wixon and Officer Patrick H. Doherty, the second representatives of the police force at the Borden house, arrived at about 11:35 A.M. on August 4.

*Francis H. Wixon*

At both the hearing and the trial, Wixon stated that after looking at the crime scene, he left the Borden property by scaling the six-foot-high barbed-wired fence separating the Borden back yard from Dr. Chagnon's side yard: He ran up on a pile of lumber stacked against it, stepped on the fence's stringer, and jumped to the soft grass on the other side. While this required some energy, it was not an Olympian feat performed by an athletically active young man. Although Wixon did not state his age, he was a twenty-year veteran of the sheriff's department and had served in the Civil War thirty years earlier. Within two hours of the crime, before it could be sketched or photographed, this fence-stile lumber pile disappeared. In their hunt for a murder weapon, the police moved it, board by board. They found no weapon, but they did destroy an escape route the murderer might have taken.

Deputy Wixon's testimony of how he left the Borden property was welcome at the preliminary hearing because it could be used to show that another person *could* have committed the murders. At the preliminary hearing the defense needed to prove reasonable doubt: anyone could have been the murderer, with Lizzie as one possibility. At the final trial, however, Lizzie *alone* must be the only suggested suspect, and she must be found not guilty by reasonable doubt or by any means available short of naming someone else as the murderer. In most trials, proving that someone other than the accused committed the crime is a valid defense. In this case, however, Lizzie's purpose was not only to show she was not guilty of the murders, but also to prevent the identification of the real murderer from being revealed. Thus, at the final trial, Wixon's testimony of how he left the property was of no interest. There was no desire to show that someone else may have been involved.

The second interesting part of Wixon's testimonies occurred at the final trial and is of no importance at all for the direct information given. It is priceless, however, for the unintended insight it gives to the close cooperation among the prosecution, the defense, and the court to ensure the successful achievement of the objective that had been purchased. The defense was in control of the entire proceeding.

For inheritance reasons, it was important to determine which Borden died first. Had Andrew died first, even without a will, Abby would have inherited a minimum of one-third of Andrew's wealth. If Andrew had left a will in which he left everything to Abby, his entire estate would have been hers. At her death there would have been no reason whatsoever for *any part* of it to go to Andrew's daughters, unless she had so stipulated in a will of her own. If Abby died first and Andrew had no will, all of his wealth would go to his children who, as far as most people knew, were only Emma and Lizzie since Andrew did not publicly acknowledge his illegitimate son, William.

Within hours of the crime, it was general knowledge that Abby had been murdered long before her husband. No one ever hinted that this was anything but the truth. At the trial, all medical testimony was in full accord on this point. It was safe ground, totally unquestionable.

In his final trial testimony, Wixon stated that before he went outside to engage in fence jumping, he had viewed the bodies of both Bordens. In response to a question by the defense, he replied he had seen many wounded bodies during his war service and that he "had had occasion to see wounds,

201

fresh and otherwise." Mr. Borden's wounds "looked to me like quite fresh wounds, . . . bright color, the same as I had seen in army wounds." He saw no coagulation.

The condition of Mrs. Borden's wounds was different. On these the blood "was very dark and coagulated." With regard to relative thickening and clotting, "I didn't see any thick blood on Mr. Borden at all," but on Mrs. Borden, "it looked as though it was thick."

Nothing Wixon had said to this point was beyond his limited field of expertise gained by his wartime exposure to freshly butchered human remains. Mr. Moody then asked him a question in which he included a plea for an objection; he got one, quite naturally, and what followed was nothing less than ludicrous.

Mr. Robinson was an attorney for the defense, but he was in full charge at Lizzie's final trial, not only of the defense but also of the tribunal of judges who were the court. The exchange here is a demonstration of his unquestioned authority.

When Mr. Moody, for the prosecution, asked, "You needn't answer this question, Mr. Wixon, if you please, until it is passed by the court. Did you form an opinion at the time as to which of the two had come to their death first?"

Mr. Robinson quickly responded, "I object to that."

"I thought we would at least submit it to Your Honor's consideration," Moody apologized.

"I think I won't insist on the objection; he may answer it," Robinson retorted.

Judge Mason dutifully agreed. "It is excluded."

In response, Moody addressed the judge, "I don't know that your Honor knew that the objection was withdrawn."

"I understood it to be insisted upon," Mason answered.

Mr. Robinson quickly came to the judge's rescue, "Your Honor did not hear me. I said I would withdraw the objection, and he might answer it."

"If the objection is withdrawn, it may be answered," Mason replied. "I understood you to insist upon the objection."

"No, Your Honor misunderstood me; but I want to say that I don't suppose it will be followed up by an attempt at expert knowledge on the part of this witness."

*Abby Borden in death. The bed that blocked view of her body through the doorway has been removed.*

Prosecution Attorney Mr. Knowlton's reply was dutifully compliant: "Not as to the relative length of time."

So, Mr. Moody finally asked his question of Wixon, "Did you form such an opinion?"

"No, sir; I did not," Wixon answered. "I don't consider myself competent."

On the surface it may appear that Mr. Wixon was being asked to establish the time between the two deaths. He was not. Actually, there was no reason for this question, but there was even less reason for Mr. Moody's telling Mr. Wixon not to answer until the court ruled on the objection the defense would make. In his phrasing of the question, he by-passed the objection by the defense and jumped right to the ruling by the court, but the defense came in on cue and objected. The prosecutor appealed for the court to at least consider the question before throwing it out, and the defense, realizing there was no reason for its objection, withdrew it.

It was too late. The court, hearing its patron utter the magic word *insist*, had ruled with its rubber stamp of exclusion rather than considering the question based on law, procedure, or merit. It fell on Moody to tell Judge Mason he had made an error, on Robinson to chastise his old buddy, on the judge to tell Robinson to use more care in the future when he used the word *insist*, back to Robinson to save face for everyone by qualifying his original objection, which by now had been disallowed, and on Deputy Wixon to tell them all the whole brouhaha was unnecessary in the first place. No wonder reporters from out-of-town newspapers called the final trial the "Carnival in New Bedford."

### Patrick J. Doherty

Officer Patrick H. Doherty testified that Officer Mullaly and he began a search of the house minutes after they arrived. They started in Bridget's room in the attic and included her clothes "presses" in their search. They checked all of the attic, worked their way down to the second floor, and finished in the cellar. Doherty questioned Lizzie: "'Miss Borden, where were you when your father was killed?' She said, 'I was in the barn.' I said, 'Is there any Portuguese working on the farm over the river for your father?' She said, 'No, sir.' 'Who works for your father?' She says, 'Mr. Eddy and Mr. Johnson; and Mr. Eddy has been sick.' I asked her if either Mr. Eddy or Mr. Johnson were in town this morning. She said, 'No, sir. Neither Mr. Eddy nor Mr. Johnson would hurt my father.'

All the things that have been said about Lizzie Borden and her immediate reaction to her father's death depict her as hard-hearted and unfeeling. This short exchange does not support those opinions. There is genuine tenderness and affection in these words she used in her defense of Mr. Eddy and Mr. Johnson.

### John J. Manning

Mr. Adams seemed to relish asking Officer Doherty to identify the "enterprising reporter who was sitting on the doorstep" patiently awaiting the arrival of the police. Doherty identified the reporter as John J. Manning.

Manning did not testify at the hearing. At the final trial Mr. Jennings asked him, "Well, did you look through the house, more or less?" This question evoked a reporter-type rundown on his observations and ended with the statement that neither Borden had shed as much blood as "would be in an ordinary killing." After looking through the house for about ten minutes, Manning went outside where he "went around the house and around the yard a great deal; walked along the flower garden on the south side of the building; walked along the Kelly fence; went around a pile of lumber that was in the back yard and also along the fence in the back. Then I went to the barn door; it was open; I went in there a moment."

"Did you see anyone in there?" Jennings asked.

"I think there were two or three persons in there at the time, yes, sir; I do not recall who they were."

"Were there any other people in the yard at that time?"

"I think there were, yes, sir. I don't recall who they were."

Charles Sawyer had earlier testified that there were "a great many" people in the yard, including "lots of" boys. In fact, the back yard was a mob scene. Jennings next asked Manning, "What did you do after you came out of the barn?"

"Walter Stevens [another reporter] and myself went to the back door and looked around for footprints that might lead from the back cellar door outward," Manning replied. "He tried the door and said it was fastened."

This testimony was given at the final trial where, unlike the earlier hearing, the *last* thing Jennings wanted was a suspect *other* than Miss Lizzie. Manning was his witness, carefully coached and nurtured to report ground trampling and footprint obliteration should anyone even suggest that someone else had killed the Bordens and escaped by the obvious route.

At the preliminary hearing defense attorney Jennings had questioned John Morse at great length to establish that the cellar door was open. Here at the final trial, he did not question Manning's statement that Mr. Stevens tried the door and said it was fastened. Working as a well oiled team, District Attorney Knowlton removed the door from consideration once and for all. He made sure it was firmly shut, then continued his cross-examination of Manning.

"You said you tried the back [cellar] door, did you?" he asked.

"No, sir; Mr. Stevens tried it."

"The cellar door. Did you at any time try the front door?"

"No, sir; but I went to the front steps and looked all over them."

"And what were you looking for on the [front] steps?"

"Well, traces of blood, that it was supposed might come from a person coming from the house."

"Did you find any?"

"No, sir."

Mr. Knowlton had Manning confirm there was no blood on the *front* steps, and then he had him repeat his "lack of blood" observation he had made in the house.

"Did you see any blood spots in the sitting room where Mr. Borden was?"

"Yes, sir," Manning replied.

"Where did you see them?"

"On the door, back of his head, back of the sofa."

"They were not easily visible, were they, unless you looked for them?"

"Not unless you looked for them, no, sir."

*Walter P. Stevens*

Walter Stevens was a reporter for the *News* who arrived at the Borden house at the same time as Officer Mullaly, which, Mullaly testified, was "twenty-three minutes to twelve." At the final trial he said people had already begun to gather.

Stevens met Manning in front of the house, and at Manning's suggestion, they walked together through the yard looking for whatever they could find.

During examination, Knowlton asked Stevens, "What were you doing in the yard?"

"Looking around."

"Looking around where in the yard?"

"Well, we looked in the grass as we walked through it, looked to the other side of the fence, looked at the fence."

"Did you see any tracks or traces of a person there?"

"Well, there was a break in the fence, but it wasn't a new one."

"Besides that did you find any traces?"

"No," Stevens replied. "The grass was trampled considerably; it was quite long."

"That is, as by a good many people?"

"It might have been."

At the preliminary hearing, this testimony would have been an unbelievable windfall for the defense: trampled grass and a hole in the fence (not a "new" one, mind you, but nevertheless another clear-cut escape route). But at the final trial it was the prosecution that brought out Stevens' testimony. Jennings did not pursue this testimony at all.

Knowlton next asked Stevens about the cellar door. He did not claim the door was locked. He was on the outside and stated that he ". . . tried the door, but couldn't open it."

"And you got the impression from trying it that it was fastened?" Knowlton asked.

"Yes, sir."

Walter Stevens was correct. The door was shut, and he could not open it because it was bolted on the inside just as Officer Allen saw it minutes later and so testified. All of this contradicts John Morse's testimony that Miss Lizzie had followed the script and left it open as the obvious escape route for the killer. She had not.

For whatever reason, when Lizzie returned to the house by the same route she used for leaving it, she shut the cellar door and locked it. Whether it was a simple reflex action or shrewdly calculated is unknown.

Knowing her father had time to nap before dinner and with the innocent intent of seeing to his comfort now that his guest had left, after checking her flats she looked in on him and found him as he is shown in photograph No. 5 (see page 195). Her panic and her shock were not feigned.

*Michael Mullaly*

At the preliminary hearing, Officer Michael Mullaly said that, according to his pocket watch, he arrived on the scene at twenty-three minutes before twelve and that Dr. Bowen had just returned when he arrived. We can now determine that Dr. Bowen was away from the house for seventeen minutes.

Mullaly told Lizzie he had been sent there to get a report of what had happened. He said, "She told me she had been out of doors and when she came in she found her father dead on the sofa." These are Lizzie's first words to a trained, uniformed representative of authority. They have the ring of simple truth.

Mullaly joined with Officer Doherty in searching all levels of the house. He then had a second conversation with Miss Lizzie, and "I inquired of her if she had seen anyone around on the premises. She told me she had seen a man there in the morning."

Knowlton quickly replied, "That morning?"

"That morning, and that this man had on dark clothes; and that was all. She told me he was a man about Officer Hyde—about as large as Officer Hyde."

"Did she say where she saw him?"

"I do not think she did."

At the inquest five days after the murders, Lizzie alluded to a man or two sneaking around the premises in time past, but she made no reference to anyone on or near the property on the murder day. Lizzie was not alone in reporting a man lazing around the Borden front gate, but this report credited to her by Officer Mullaly is the only time we will hear of Lizzie mentioning such a person. When she spoke of him to Mullaly, she did not know the identity of the man outside the house. Within a few hours of the crime, however, she learned who he was and realized he could not be exposed without also exposing the murderer. Therefore she did not mention him again.

Henry Hawthorne said the man Lizzie and other witnesses saw that morning was William L. Bassett and that he lived in nearby Westport. While Lizzie Borden may have known *of* him, she had no reason to *know* him. He did not kill either Borden. But he did deliver the note to Abby that was to have caused her to leave the house.

*John Fleet*

The first police supervisor on the scene was Assistant Marshal John Fleet. He stated his arrival time as "something between quarter to twelve and twelve o'clock."

Mr. Fleet was not a polished narrator. When he was asked

by Knowlton for any conversation he had had with Miss Borden he set off on a seemingly endless account:

"I asked her if she knew anything about who had killed her father and mother. She said it was not her mother, that her mother was dead. She said it was not her mother, it was her stepmother. I asked her if she had seen anyone around the premises that she—or seen anyone around the premises this morning. She said she had not; and then she said she had heard a man at the front door talking to her father about nine o'clock, or thereabouts, nine or a little before nine. I asked her what they were talking about, and she said she did not know, but she thought he was talking about some store. I asked her then if she thought that man would be the one to do him an injury, or to kill him. She said no, she did not know. I asked her if she knew who he was. She said she did not know, she did not see him, but heard them talking. She said that he spoke like an Englishman, and she thought he was there after a store, something about a store. I asked her if she knew anyone that had ever threatened her father, or suspected anyone that would do such a thing as kill him, and she said, 'No, I did not know that he had an enemy in the world.' Then Miss Russell said, 'Tell him all, Lizzie, tell him about that man you was telling me about.' So then she says that about two weeks ago a man came to the door and they had some loud talk, and the man seemed to be mad or angry. I asked her what he was talking about. She said he was talking about a store, and wanted Mr. Borden, she should judge, to let him the store; and he would not, saying that he would not let it for that purpose. I asked her if she knew who he was. She said she did not, but supposed he was a stranger, someone out of Fall River. I asked who else was in the house during the day or last night. She said Bridget, the work girl, she did not say Bridget, she said Maggie, the work girl, was there this forenoon. She said that Bridget had been in the house in the forenoon. Well, I says, 'Do you suspect Bridget?' She says, 'No, I don't.' I says, 'Where was Bridget during the time that your father—that is, at any time this morning?' She said she had been outside washing windows, and that she came in, and after her father came in, she went upstairs, as she thought, to fix her room or make her bed; but she did not think that Bridget had anything to do with it. She said that after she went upstairs, that she went up to the barn."

Not to miss commenting on the monologue, Knowlton observed, "You have got some 'shes' there."

Fleet continued, "When Bridget went upstairs she said that she, meaning Lizzie, went up in the barn. I says, 'up in the barn?' She says, 'Yes.' 'What do you mean by *up*?' 'Upstairs in the barn.' 'How long did you remain in the barn?' She says, 'About a half an hour. When I went out, my father was laid on the lounge. When I came back I found him killed, or cut up, in the same position as I left him.' She also said that John V. Morse, her uncle, came there the day before, and he slept in the room where Mrs. Borden was found killed. I asked her if she thought that John V. Morse could have had anything to do with this. She said that it was impossible, because Mr. Morse went away before nine o'clock this morning and did not come back until after the murder. I then had a conversation with Morse."

Knowlton's reply was terse, "That I do not care for."

Once again, *any* conversation with Uncle John is squelched!

Mr. Fleet exhibited an amazing power of recall, and there is no reason to doubt any of it. Fleet is called an important witness by most accounts because of the way he reported the indignant rebuff Lizzie spat back at him when he referred to Abby as Lizzie's mother. This indicator of her vicious attitude and demeanor during what should have been a moment of deep grief, say some commentators, proves she hated Abby enough to kill her. This has been stated and accepted as fact for so long, it would be all but impossible for anyone to accept it as anything but the truth.

When Lizzie Borden said this to Fleet, she did, beyond any doubt, feel hatred for her stepmother. But this is a "new" emotion. There are no serious reports of overt manifestations of hatred beyond normal resentment.

Lizzie did not care that her stepmother had been murdered; secretly that may have pleased her. She *did* care that her father was dead and, in her mind, *Abby had caused his death*. She masked her grief for her father with hatred, not directed toward the murderer but toward the reason the murderer had killed. To Lizzie, that reason was Abby.

Her emotions caused her to make some strange self-contradictions during those early minutes of the investigation. She told Mullaly she had seen someone outside the house that morning. She did not repeat this to Fleet, but she did tell Fleet of someone who came to the door and spoke to her father that morning. She told this to no one else. She refused to point a finger at anyone. Just as she had defended her father's farm hands, she defended Bridget and Uncle John.

## James Winwood

James Winwood testified in his capacity as the undertaker who had prepared the bodies of Abby and Andrew Borden for burial. He testified freely, without challenge, to the nature of the wounds he found on each body.

He stated that the bodies were released to him for preparation for burial at "about half past five" of the murder day, little more than six hours after the crime. Admittedly, more than half a dozen medical experts had joined in performing an autopsy (using the Borden dining room table as their laboratory), and the excessive heat of the day forced taking immediate measures, but it was still a very quick disposal of critical evidence.

Someone with authority had second thoughts because Winwood was notified about nine o'clock on Saturday morning, the day of the funeral, that the bodies should not be buried. After the grave side service at Oak Grove Cemetery and, without notification of the family until much later, both bodies were placed in a holding vault pending another autopsy planned for the following week. At the second autopsy, each skull was removed from its body, cleaned, and later presented as an exhibit at the trial. Authoritative reports state that each skull was eventually replaced and both Bordens, disjoined as they may be, now rest whole in eternal slumber.

## Medical Witnesses (Preliminary Hearing)

Along with Medical Examiner Dr. William A. Dolan, Professor Edward S. Wood, physician, chemist, and then holder of the chair in chemistry at Harvard University, testified extensively at both the hearing and the trial. Unfortunately, legal chemistry and medical jurisprudence were not as far advanced in 1892 as they are today. Given a drop of dried blood today, a forensic laboratory with Harvard's capabilities would determine from what species it came and, if human, the sex, age, height, weight, and hair and eye color.

Professor Wood had full access to Harvard's 1892 laboratory and he admitted that he could not state with certainty whether one dried blood spot found on Lizzie's clothing was human blood or not.

Professor Wood also testified he checked the stomach contents of each Borden (their stomachs had been removed at the first autopsy and sent to him) and, knowing what was eaten for breakfast and the fact that each had eaten the meal at the same time, he was able to determine the relative time of death.

He further testified, "I tested Mr. Borden's stomach also for prussic acid, with a negative result. There was no evidence of any irritant poison having been in the stomach at all, no irritation. There is no other ordinary poison which would prove fatal immediately; that was the only one I considered it necessary to test for, under the circumstances." This finding proves nothing. A minuscule oral dosage of prussic acid (cyanide) is instantly fatal. The only way it could get to the stomach would be by direct injection or ingestion in a slow-dissolving capsule. Had Mr. Borden been given as little as one grain in, say, a swallow of tea, death would have been instantaneous, and no trace would have been found in the stomach.

Dr. Dolan had sent two axes and two hatchets found in the Borden cellar to Harvard for forensic examination by Professor Wood. The testimony of all the policemen who handled these tools said all four had spots on them that looked suspiciously like blood, and one or more had hair clinging to it that looked suspiciously like human hair. The policemen were sure that one or more of the four had to be the murder weapon. None was the murder weapon.

At the preliminary hearing, Professor Wood testified that all the spots he found were either rust, paint, or water stains, and any hair he found had once graced a cow, not a human head. In addition, none of the four tools fit the holes in either Abby's or Andrew's carefully preserved skulls.

There was no murder weapon. Neither was there any hint of one.

The government's case was shattered. The defense was elated.

It is difficult to explain why so many pages of testimony were extracted from the medical witnesses. Each blow each Borden received was described as to location, depth, and damage wrought. In any search for truth, the descriptions added nothing. When the witnesses were finished, the Bordens were still dead and had been rendered in that condition by a person either male or female, either sane or insane, either right- or left-handed, either tall, medium, or short, of greater, lesser, or medium strength, who would or would not have been blood spattered. The medical witnesses must have been retained on an hourly basis, for each wanted to spend as much time as possible saying his piece.

*Phillip Harrington*

At the hearing, Officer Phillip Harrington was the last witness for the prosecution. He guessed he arrived on the scene at 12:20, which would make him the last of the early arrivals. Harrington showed expertise in observation and tact, two characteristics normally lacking in the rest of the force. Perhaps for this reason, his testimony is particularly interesting.

Harrington, as had almost everyone who arrived before him, interrogated Miss Lizzie. "I asked her if she could tell me anything about the crime. She said, 'Nothing at all.' She was cool and collected and stood erect without any support at all. Then I asked her who was in the house at the time she saw him murdered. She said there was no one there that she knew of but the girl, Maggie, and herself. I asked her where she was at the time the murder was committed. She said in the barn."

Harrington then told her, "I thought it would be well for her to be careful what she said at this time, owing to the excitement. I said that perhaps on the morrow she would be in a better frame of mind to give a more clear statement of the facts as she knew them. She made a curtsy, and said, 'No, I can tell you all I know now just as well as at any other time.'"

He then asked her if, when she was going to or from the barn, she saw anyone in or around the yard. She said, "No, I did not." When he reminded her it was but a short distance from the barn to the house, she said, "Well, I was up in the loft."

Harrington then asked her to mention anybody, "no matter how insignificant it may appear to you or how remote it may be at the present time." He quoted Lizzie as saying, "'Several weeks ago there was a man called to see father, and before parting they had very angry words, the conversation became very animated. He went away.' She said, 'He came back here two weeks ago, and they had another conversation,' a part of which she overheard. Before they got through, she said they got quite angry again; but finally before they finished, her father said, 'When you are in town again, come and I will let you know more about it.' So they parted. She did not see them part, but it was the last she heard, she said. Then said I, 'He must be a man from out of town.' 'Well,' she says, 'I should judge so.' 'Then you do not know?' She said, 'No.'"

Officer Harrington then urged Lizzie "not to submit to any further interview today, and tomorrow you may recollect of having seen this man, having heard his name, or of having heard your father say something about it."

Miss Lizzie heeded Harrington's advice. Before the afternoon was over, she was characterized as being "uncooperative and interfering."

If this testimony is correct in the words credited to Mr. Borden through two intermediaries, the man he was speaking to was the murderer. Had Lizzie not been hushed when she was reeling from the shock of the crime and had not had time to form her later resolute stand, she might have been persuaded to tell Harrington enough more to cause the investigation to follow the path to the killer.

Harrington's words allowed Lizzie time to consider her choices. She did, and that evening the clan gathered: sister Emma, Uncle John Morse, and Uncle Hiram Harrington (no relation to Officer Harrington). By Friday evening, she and the family had consulted with each other and Attorney Jennings, and he outlined their options. Lizzie, who had the most votes because she had the most to lose, elected to stone-wall the police. Officer Harrington's powers of persuasion did not prevail; Uncle John was sent to the post office and later went to Turner Street to speak with Uncle Hiram Harrington, and Andrew Jennings was given *carte blanche* and sent to the Mellen House.

The next incident Officer Harrington outlined is treasured by the legend because it allows the most conservative imagination to see the wildest images. After his interview with Lizzie, he came downstairs to the kitchen where he saw Dr. Bowen standing by the kitchen stove.

During his questioning, Knowlton asked, "This does not in any way affect Dr. Bowen. For any reason did you look in the stove?"

"I was going to tell you what he had in his hand. When he took the cover off the stove, the fire was very low, and there appeared to be, or there was, rather larger coal, or larger remains of something that appeared to be burnt paper, and it was quite large. I should say quite large judging from the size of the stove, comparatively speaking."

"Why did you say it looked like burnt paper?"

"Because I have seen burnt paper before, that is all the reason."

"What sort of fire was it that there was there?"

"I could not swear that, but there was a small red spot down in the center."

On this point we gain further information at the final trial. The fact that the subject was allowed to surface at all at the trial is reason enough to know that, as intriguing as the burning papers in the stove may be, they had nothing to do with the case. For ten months before the trial, however, those who heard these words speculated on just what that "burnt paper" could have been. The guesses were boundless: the deed to a Borden property, Andrew's will, the note Abby claimed she received. There were those who claimed that what Officer Harrington thought was paper ash was really wood ash and that what he saw was the remains of a hatchet. The ashes were anything anyone wanted them to be.

At the final trial, Mr. Moody's questioning disclosed that Harrington had been on the force for ten years, had known

Andrew Borden for twenty to twenty-five years, and had worked for him as a carpenter for three of those years. He added to his conversation with Lizzie that she said when her father came home that morning he had a small package in his hand. (Others had testified to this, but Lizzie had not mentioned it before.) Her curtsy to him became a "stiff" curtsy, which lend it an air of defiance.

Moody asked, "Did anything occur with reference to the stove in the kitchen?"

"Yes, sir," Harrington replied. "Just as I went to pass by Dr. Bowen, between him and the stove, I saw some scraps of note paper in his hand. I asked him what they were."

"You say you saw Dr. Bowen with some scraps of note paper in his hand?"

"Yes, sir. I asked him what they were, referring to the pieces of paper, and he said, 'Oh, I guess it is nothing.'"

Mr. Moody's repeating of Harrington's answer denotes his surprise that there had been no objection by the defense, and it was intended to provide the defense with a second chance to speak up. It worked.

Mr. Robinson rose to object: "I cannot let this go in unless you give me an assurance that it has nothing whatever to do with it."

This is an unusual demand that should have been greeted with a hearty laugh. *Anything* on the murder scene "had something to do with it" until proved otherwise, and the prosecution had every right to develop the relevance of any scraps of note paper. The court might have so ruled, but Mr. Knowlton saved them the decision.

"It has nothing to do with the case at all," he replied.

"You claim the paper had no significance?" Robinson asked again with what must have been surprise in his voice.

"Well," Knowlton replied, "He said it had no significance."

The defense (Robinson) now had the prosecution (Knowlton) proclaiming the unknown paper scraps in Dr. Bowen's hand *were not evidence* because *he* said so, with the "he" not defined. These early insights into how the final trial was conducted begin to reveal just how important the unfettered information gleaned from the preliminary hearing really is.

Officer Harrington continued with his explanation: "So he

started to arrange them so as to determine what was on them, or to learn their contents. They were very small and it was rather difficult, but on one piece, on the upper left-hand corner, was the word "Emma." And it was written in lead pencil, as well as other pieces I saw."

"Now then, what did you do with the paper?" Moody asked.

"I asked him again what they contained, and he said, 'Oh, I think it is nothing. It is something, I think, about my daughter going through somewhere.' He then turned slightly to his left and took the lid from the stove and threw the papers in— or the pieces in."

"Now then, did you observe anything as he lifted the lid from the stove?"

"Yes, sir."

"Go on and state what you did and what you noticed."

"I noticed the firebox," Harrington continued. "The fire was very nearly extinguished. There was a small fire, which I judged was a coal fire. The embers were about dying. It was about as large as the palm of your hand. There had been some paper burned in there before, which was rolled up and still held a cylindrical form."

"Now would you describe that roll of burned paper by measuring it with your hands, please?"

"Well, I should say it was about this long. [Indicating] Twelve inches, I would say."

"And how large in diameter?"

"Well, not over two inches."

"Could you tell anything about what sort of paper it was from the ember? If you can, say so."

"I can tell the impression I had."

Moody saved him the effort. "I don't think I will ask for that."

One must never cease wondering how they got away with it. Harrington's "impression" could have proved embarrassing to the defense, so the prosecution did not ask for it. In fact, Dr. Bowen himself could have been asked about the scraps of note paper. He never was.

The kitchen of a hundred years ago always sported a wood-bin and a coal hod, and it seldom needed anything similar to a modern waste basket. If what you had to throw away was flammable, it went into the woodbin or the coal hod or directly into the firebox. Dr. Bowen was never asked what he had to dispose of. It may have been Uncle John's copy of the murder plan in his own handwriting, but it also may have been an unrelated torn-up note that referred to some travel plans made by Dr. Bowen's daughter (whose name, by the way, was *not* Emma). In 1892 the most acceptable way to dispose of scraps of paper would be to put them in the kitchen stove.

Admittedly, in this instance the wild conjectures of the legend are much more fun than the rational probabilities.

*William Medley*

It is generally reported that Lizzie answered each person who asked where she was while her father was being butchered with a different location. In fact, she undoubtedly saw the murderer when he left the house. It is likely that they spoke to each other. They may even have had a long chat, but at that point Lizzie had no idea he was a murderer. She learned that when she returned to the house from the yard.

As the initial shock of what she found wore off, Lizzie began to realize the staggering enormity of the situation, but she had no firm direction as to what to do or say. She knew she must find Uncle John and talk to him, and she had to improvise until he got there.

Lizzie could do nothing about the escape route the murderer had taken, but she could remove herself from being in the line of sight. She did this by what she told people, given here in the order she talked to them:

> To Bridget: "I was in the back yard. . . ." (the truth)
> To Mrs. Churchill: "I went to the barn. . . ."
> To Dr. Bowen: "I was in the barn. . . ."
> To Miss Russell: "I was out in the barn. . . ."
> To Officer Mullaly: "I was outside. . . ."
> To Officer Doherty: "I was in the barn. . . ."
> To Officer Medley: "I was in the barn. . . ."
> To Marshal Fleet: "I was up in the barn. . . ."
> To Officer Harrington: "I was up in the loft of the barn. . ."

To the first two who asked, she mentioned hearing an associated noise that caught her attention (to Bridget a groan, to Mrs. Churchill a distressing noise); and to Officer Doherty she added that she heard no screams, but she did hear some noise like "scraping." She may have realized that her barn location was too far removed from the murder scene for her to hear anything, and she stopped mentioning any noise.

There is no other logical explanation for Miss Lizzie to have changed her location as she did. If she had killed her father, what difference would it make *where* she claimed she was other than out of the house? The progression away from the pear trees, where she had been, to the loft of the barn is pure genius on her part. Each step away from the trees shows logical thinking under pressure.

Officer William H. Medley did not testify at the preliminary hearing, but he was a star witness for the prosecution at the final trial on two counts: he told of the finding of five hatchets or axes, and he claimed to be the first person to enter the barn and climb up to its loft after the murder. He detailed how he checked the dust on the loft floor, and he swore *no one* had walked on that floor for weeks prior to his examination. This had to include Miss Lizzie.

Officer Medley stated he had been a patrolman at the time the crime was committed, but by the time of the trial, he had been made an inspector. Medley claimed he arrived at the Borden house a minute or two before Marshal Fleet, waited outside for Fleet's arrival and his instructions, walked around the house, entered it, talked to Lizzie, and left the house to check the barn.

"When you got to the barn," Moody asked him, "how did you find the door?"

"The door was fast with a hasp over a staple and an iron pin in it."

". . . did you see anyone else out or about there?"

"Yes, sir. There were quite a number outside in the yard."

"After you went into the barn, what did you do? Describe in detail."

"I went upstairs," Medley began, "until I reached about three or four steps from the top, and while there part of my body was above the floor, above the level of the floor, and I looked around [the loft floor] to see if there was any evidence of anything having been disturbed, and I didn't notice that anything had or seemed to have been disturbed, and I stooped down low to see if I could discern any marks on the floor of the barn having been made there. I didn't see any, and I reached out my hand to see if I could make an impression on the floor, and I did by putting my hand down so fashion [illustrating] and found I had made an impression on the floor."

Asked to describe what was on or about the floor, Medley replied, "Seemed to be accumulated hay dust and other dust." Medley went on to state he then climbed the rest of the steps to the loft and saw no footprints in the dust other than his own as he made them, and they were easily discernible. His best judgment as to the time he made this inspection was eight to ten minutes after his arrival. Fleet testified to arriving between 11:45 and 12:00 noon, and Medley said he was there a minute or two before Fleet. He investigated the barn close to noon.

Medley's testimony here was given at the final trial where it was countered by the defense with a parade of small boys and grown men who swore they romped and tread on the loft's boards long before Medley arrived on the scene. There is little reason to think Medley was lying or mistaken in his testimony, but no one could swear to the actual timing of any of the noon-time activities on the Borden property.

Medley's testimony negates Lizzie's claim to be "upstairs in the barn," but it had been a good gamble on her part. Since Medley was not heard at the preliminary hearing, she was still safely cloistered in the barn when the grand jury heard testimony.

### Rufus R. Hilliard

Marshal Rufus R. Hilliard stated that he did not appear at the Borden house until between two and three in the afternoon and that he personally organized and assisted in searching the barn, the yard, and the neighboring yards.

Marshal Hilliard outlined the searches made that day, those made on Friday, two made on Saturday, and the last major effort made on Monday morning. Each of these was an organized, orderly, formal search by a group of policemen. He admitted that most of his men had also conducted selective hunts of their own. He reported that the household was fully cooperative, helpful in many ways, that they assisted when asked and answered all questions. This applied to Bridget, Miss Emma, Miss Lizzie, and starting with the search on Saturday after the funeral, Mr. Jennings. Each search was "full, thorough, and complete."

### George F. Seaver

George F. Seaver was a member of the Mellen House Task Force, and he listed himself as a member of the Massachusetts District Police. He arrived after 5:00 on the afternoon of the murder, and Marshal Hilliard acted as his tour guide. He questioned most of the marshal's men, but he did not have an interview with Miss Lizzie. He assisted in searches, looked at blood spots, saw axes and hatchets, walked the yard, looked over the fence, personally checked the cellar, and saw nothing. He returned the next day and joined in the search that extended from top to bottom and back again, including every box, crate, barrel, trunk, chest of drawers, closet, and every dress in every closet. He said it was a thorough search.

### John Donnelly

John Donnelly was a hack driver by trade and a curious man by nature.

Defense Attorney Jennings was questioning him at the point we pick up his testimony. "Did you go up to the Borden house on the morning of the murder?"

"Yes, sir."

"About what time did you get there?"

"I could not just give you the time. I think somewhere about twelve o'clock."

"What is your best recollection?"

"I should not want to make it much after twelve."

"Did you go into the barn at all?"

"Yes, sir."

"Do you know whether Officer Medley was there at the time or not?"

"I did not see Officer Medley there nowhere."

"Did you notice anything about the hay?"

"Yes, sir."

"What did you see in the hay?" Jennings prompted. "Anything about the hay that indicated anything, except the usual condition of hay piled up there?"

"It looked so to me as though there had been somebody laying on it, Donnelly replied. "I do not know whether there had or not."

On cross-examination, Knowlton asked, "What was it that looked as though somebody had been lying there?"

"It looked as though there was a form of a body on there, that had been sleeping on there, or something."

Mr. Donnelly added that "Charlie Cook, who works for the telephone company" was with him at the time, and both saw the depression in the hay and remarked about it. Charlie Cook was not called as a witness. When Knowlton asked if they had reported their find to the police, Donnelly answered, "No, sir. As I did not disturb the hay at all, I thought let them see it themselves."

*Benjamin J. Handy*

Dr. Benjamin J. Handy is famed in the legend for having seen a "wild-eyed man" in the vicinity of the Borden house on the murder morning. However, the description of the man's eyes came from a newspaper reporter, not from Dr. Handy.

The doctor reported he drove his carriage past the Borden house twice on the morning of the murder, first about nine and later "between twenty minutes past ten and twenty minutes of eleven; that is as near as I can calculate."

Jennings asked him, "Did you see any person in the vicinity of the Borden house at that time?"

"I did. A stranger."

"What attracted your attention to him?"

"I noticed a very pale, exceedingly pale individual, and he was passing very slowly up the street, south."

"Describe his appearance as near as you can."

"He was a young man of medium height, dressed in a light suit of clothes," Handy began. "I was struck by his peculiar appearance. I could not define what I saw about him. There was something about him that attracted my attention so that

I turned and looked at him the second time as I went by him."
"Can you describe him any further than you have?"
"I have the impression that he had a mustache. He was a small man; five feet three or four. He had a very full and a very white forehead, full face."

Dr. Handy said he had seen the same man a week or two before in the same vicinity, that he was familiar with and knew the neighborhood drunk and the one or two other characters who often passed by and acted "strange." This man was a stranger.

Under Knowlton's cross-examination, the doctor told of reporting this sighting to the police around six o'clock that day and that "quite active efforts have been made by the police to find the man." He added that the man was pacing between the Borden house and Dr. Kelly's house, taking a few steps in one direction and then turning and taking a step or two in the other. The man did not act drunk, but he acted as if he was waiting for someone and was agitated and growing impatient.

*Delia S. Manley*

Mrs. Delia S. Manley lived on Second Street two blocks south of the Bordens. She knew all of the people who regularly frequented the neighborhood. About quarter to ten on the morning of the murder, she was shopping "in the vicinity" and stopped to speak with an acquaintance on the sidewalk on the same side of the street as the Borden house and between the Borden house and Mrs. Churchill's house. She, too, saw a young man standing by the Borden gate.

"What was this man doing?" Attorney Jennings asked.

"He did not seem to be doing anything, only standing in the gateway, leaning against the south gatepost; standing something like that."

She could not describe the man. She could not say how he was dressed. She could not say she had never seen him before that day.

On cross-examination, Knowlton discovered that there were three people in the carriage with whom Mrs. Manley was speaking. One of them, Sarah Hart, and Mrs. Manley both testified at the final trial.

*Marienne Chagnon and Martha Chagnon*

Dr. and Mrs. Chagnon were back-yard neighbors of the Bordens. Both Mrs. Marienne Chagnon and her stepdaughter Martha testified that at some time between 11:00 and 11:30 on the evening before the murders, they were home alone and were frightened by a pounding noise that came from the back yard in the vicinity of the Borden fence. The noise lasted about five minutes.

"What did it sound like?" Jennings asked. "What did it appear to be?"

"It seemed to me it was like someone jumping on the fence," Mrs. Chagnon replied.

They had not investigated because they were afraid.

*Alfred Clarkson*

Alfred Clarkson went trespassing on the Borden property at 11:40 on the morning of the murders. He had been there about seven or eight minutes when he went into the barn and immediately to the loft. At the preliminary hearing, Mr. Jennings asked him, "Did you notice anything about the hay, whether it appeared to have been disturbed at all, or not?"

"In two or three places it looked as though it had been stepped in," Clarkson answered. "In one place it looked as though a man had laid there."

"Was anyone up there at the time that you recollect?"

"Yes, sir."

"Who?"

"There were three gentlemen that I did not know."

"Do you know Officer Medley?"

"I think I do."

"Did you see him up there in the barn?"

"No, sir."

"Did you see him up there around the premises when you first got there?"

"No, sir."

"Did you see him afterwards?"

"In the afternoon."

"You did not see him until afternoon?"

"No, sir."

On cross-examination, Knowlton, once again, aided the defense. "Did these three men go up before or after you?" he asked.

"Before me."

"What officers did you see when you got there?"

"Officer Allen."

"How did you fix the time when you got there?"

"Simply because I looked at my watch."

Here we have the testimony of a reliable witness who, if correct in time and movements, totally cancels Officer Medley's report given ten months later.

Did Miss Lizzie go into the barn and up to the loft? In truth, we do not know. *All* police testimony in the Borden case is viewed with open suspicion, but why would Medley lie to *hurt* Lizzie's cause? It makes no sense. In his summary at the final trial, Knowlton defended Medley, while Lizzie's own attorney insisted Lizzie had been under the pear trees and not in the barn.

All logic dictates that Miss Lizzie was under the pear trees when the murderer left the house and the property. Proof? There are times when logic is its own proof!

# Chapter 12

Step one of the Mellen House agreement was completed perfectly; everyone was pleased. The inquest into the murder of Andrew and Abby Borden resulted, on August 12, 1892, in the arrest and arraignment of Lizzie Borden, who was ordered to be held in the county jail. Lizzie's demand that the murderer remain anonymous had been complied with, and her arraignment all but guaranteed the murderer's continued anonymity.

Step two was for the judge at the preliminary hearing, which was held August 25–September 1, to find probable cause for the case against Lizzie to be presented to the grand jury. This would lead to the third step of the Mellen House agreement: the dismissal of the case against Lizzie in the privacy of the grand jury hearing. The preliminary hearing would be public. It would be easier to explain the dismissal of the case against Lizzie to the press if Lizzie's legal proceedings ended in a private venue. In the original agreement, no final trial was foreseen, so what was said at the open hearing would be significant. It would be the only time the press could hear witnesses.

Mr. Jennings had much to do in the two weeks between the inquest and the preliminary hearing. It was no coincidence that during this time—on August 17 and 18—the articles about Andrew's will appeared in the *Globe* (see pages 112 and 114). The prosecution was trying to establish the will as Lizzie's motive for the murders; the defense was trying to deny the truthfulness of testimony about the will before the testimony was given.

During the dinner recess on the first day of the hearing, Melvin Adams issued the equivalent of a modern press release. Miss Emma Borden, he said, had received a letter from a Samuel Robinsky. It is reproduced here exactly as it was printed in the *Globe*.

Waltham, Massachusetts
August 27, 92

Miss Emma Borden:—Dear Madam.—You must excuse that I take the liberty of sending you these few lines. I ought to have written to you before but I was unable to do so as I was travelling every day. My name is Samuel Robinsky, I am a Russian peddler when the fatal murder in Fall River occurred I was only a few miles from Fall River that day while sitting on the roadside towards New Bedford, I met a man who was covered with blood he told me that he worked on a farm that he never could get his wages so he had a fight with the farmer he said he ran away and did not get any money after all he had was a 5 doll bill he bought from me four handerchiefs 1 looking glass 1 necktie collar and shoe blacking his boots was covered with blood and he puts lots of blacking on it.

I helped him to fix up again and get cleaned but by this time I did not know anything about the murder. I felt sorry for him and thought only he give the farmer a good licking. I advised him to travel at night which he said he would do, as he feared arrest during the day. I gave him my lunch and he gave me a quarter and told me not to say anything that I met him he asked me what time the train left for Boston after 8 o'clock at night and I told him he had also a bundle with him, which was about two feet thick or big when I was peddling I did not read any papers only Sundays, as I am studying the English language.

When I was in Boston last Sunday a friend of mine told me about the Fall River murder. I told him that I was in Fall River and around the neighborhood. I told him about my stranger and my friend said but why did you not report this to the police. I told him I was afraid as they would lock me up as a witness, and another thing, I did not have any license so I was afraid, I told my friend I would write to you or Mr. Jennings. I read last Sunday's Boston *Globe* and thought that I might have seen the murderer. If I should see him in Boston I am sure yes dead sure I should know him again.

He is of medium height dark brown hair reddish whiskers or moustache weighs about 135 pounds gray suit brown derby hat his shoes was what they called Russian leather no blacking on so called summer shoes. He put my blacking on to make them look black and people would not see the blood. It was about 4 o'clock noon that day I only heard about the murder at 6 or 7 o'clock that night. I kept quiet as I have no license and feared to be arrested my stranger was very much afraid he asked me a million times if he looked all right again, and I brushed him off with my shoe brush and told him to wait till dark.

If I come again to Fall River next week I shall call on you if you think it is necessary but all I can swear to is the stranger which I have seen that afternoon this is all but if this man was the murder I can not say, but I shall find him out of 100,000. Will close now will go to Fitchburg tomorrow morning and return to Boston Saturday night. Please do not say anything to the police as I have no license and would be arrested. If I had known about the time I met my stranger it would have been different as I would have followed him up and perhaps got the reward.

I thought it was a poor farm hand so took pity on him as I know as a rule farmers seldom pay their hands during summer.

Hoping that my information will be of some use to you,

I remain very respectfully,
SAMUEL ROBINSKY.

P.S. Please excuse paper and mistakes as I am a foreigner.

Adams released this letter to the press in the attempt to create additional reasonable doubt. The man's description by Robinsky is close to the description of the loiterer that was given by Dr. Handy and all the others, including Lizzie, who reported having seen a mysterious stranger in front of the Borden house on the murder morning. We have already identified him as William L. Bassett.

The letter fooled no one. Jennings sent a telegram to the mayor of Waltham inquiring of a Jewish peddler named Robinsky. The mayor replied that there was no one of that name living in Waltham but that a peddler named Robinsky lived in Boston and came to Waltham on occasion. Although that information would be grounds for additional follow-up, none was made since none was necessary.

It is easy for a foreigner learning English to write a letter that sounds like it was written by a foreigner learning English. It is not easy for a recent college graduate (as was Arthur Phillips) to do so. This letter was written by a recent college graduate who used phrases such as:

"... sending you these few lines ..."
"... when the murder occurred I was only a few miles from Fall River ..."
"... I felt sorry for him and thought only ..."
"... reddish whiskers ..."
"... I shall call on you ..."
"... I know as a rule farmers seldom pay their hands during summer ..."
"... hoping that my information may be of some use to you ..."

This letter was a clear warning to William Bassett to keep silent and not to come forward to give testimony, just as others had warned the murderer to remain silent.

Testimony given at the preliminary hearing has been summarized in the previous three chapters. After the testimonies were over, the attorneys for both sides gave their closing arguments. When a closing argument is made before a jury, it is generally a grandiose oration designed to play on the panel's emotions without regard for the development of truth. When a closing argument is made before a judge, it reinforces the facts proved by testimony and reviews the legal options and procedures available to the court. There was no jury at the preliminary hearing. Jennings (for the defense) and Knowlton (for the prosecution) presented their closing arguments to Judge Blaisdell. The courtroom was crammed elbow to elbow, with priority seating reserved for newspaper reporters. Each attorney offered an emotional oration.

Andrew Jennings spoke first. He began by saying that Andrew Borden had been more than just his client. He had been his friend and a man he had known from his own boyhood. He proclaimed it was "beyond the realm of human credibility" that he should need to defend his friend's youngest daughter from the charge of murdering the father so beloved to her.

"We have had a description of the injuries, and I suggest that even the learned district attorney himself cannot imagine that any person could have committed that crime unless his heart was as black with hatred as hell itself. Blow after blow was showered upon them, cutting through blood, bone, and flesh into the very brain. Not one, not two, but in the case of the woman, eighteen. I know it will be said that the person who did this wanted to make sure. There is an unnecessary brutality about this that suggests nothing but insanity or brutal hatred."

Porter's eyewitness account tells us Lizzie showed emotion at hearing these words: "At this point, for the first time in public since the commission of the crime, Lizzie Borden almost broke down. Her form was convulsed, her lips were trembling, and she shaded her eyes with her hands in order to partically conceal the tears, which were freely flowing" (*The Fall River Tragedy*, page 126).

Jennings continued with words of little significance to anyone hearing them at the time, other than Lizzie and the murderer: "There is another thing. Every blow showed that the person who wielded the hatchet was a person of experience with the instrument. Every blow shows its own line of demarcation and, taken with this fact that the blows were parallel, I venture to say no hand could strike those blows that had not a powerful wrist and experienced in handling a hatchet."

Jennings was not speaking to Judge Blaisdell when he said these words. He was speaking to the murderer and telling him in no uncertain terms to keep still, to keep out of the way, and to enjoy his parole as granted him by Miss Lizzie.

After outlining what actually happened that day, Jennings said, "It becomes the duty of the Commonwealth to investigate an atrocious crime like this one with the greatest care. It is of the utmost importance that the guilty party should be found and not someone simply accused of it." Having no one else to suggest as the killer, Jennings offered up Bridget several times as an excellent alternative, but each time he qualified his charge: "I do not believe that Bridget Sullivan committed murder any more than I believe Lizzie Borden did" and "mind you, I don't say Bridget Sullivan did it. I distinctly state she did not."

Jennings next offered his famed statement that being on the scene physically does not in itself prove Lizzie committed the murder: "Now, to commit a crime there must be opportunity. I submit that unless she alone had an opportunity to commit the crime there is no grounds for holding her." In other words, she was there, but unless you can prove she was the *only* one there, it doesn't mean anything.

He continued, "It is perfectly clear to me why the answers to the questions of her whereabouts at the time of the killing of her mother and later that morning should be inconsistent. I have stated before that I considered the inquisition of the girl an outrage. Here was a girl they had been suspecting for days. She was virtually under arrest, and yet for the purpose of extracting a confession from her to support their theory, they brought her here and put her upon the rack, a thing they knew they would have no right to do if they placed her under arrest. As in the days of the rack and thumbscrews, so she was racked mentally again and again. Day after day the same questions were repeated to her in the hope to elicit some information that would incriminate her. Is it a wonder there are conflicting statements? She irons some handkerchiefs. I don't know but the State is going to say those handkerchiefs were being cleaned of blood. It wouldn't be more presumptuous than several other ideas they have tried. How about that fire? I am surprised the State hasn't taken up that. Perhaps he has not found out that it is hard to start a fire. Now about her whereabouts at the time her father came in. She first says she is upstairs. Then she says she is downstairs, and sticks to that. I submit that, if she was on the stairs when Bridget opened the door to let Mr. Borden in and laughed, as Bridget says she did, she must have been insane, and was insane at the time of the commission of the crime."

It has long been conjectured that Jennings was laying the foundation for an insanity plea here should he find it necessary at some time in the future. Some have gone so far as to say this statement proves Lizzie *was* insane and the family was attempting to hide the fact. As much as the legend loves it, none of this is true.

Jennings then covered the major shortcoming of the case against Lizzie Borden: lack of motive. The prosecution did not provide even a hint of one at the hearing. "Now the government is bound to show that there is a motive for this crime. In the absence of it, unless there is direct evidence, their case has got to fall. What was the motive? The papers all over the country have published it as it was given out to them. Has there been a motive shown here? No, only that five years ago something happened. It was a result of Mr. Borden's giving his wife's stepsister a residence, and the girls said they thought their father ought to have done as much as that for them. After that she called her Mrs. Borden. A man sometimes when pressed for money will commit crime. I beg you to remember if crimes of this sort are committed unless there is a pressing want of money. And yet to get the motive they've got to say that without hatred, bitterness, or previous quarrel, she murders him to get possession of money which, in the natural course of events would be hers within a few years. I say that this is beyond the bounds of human credibility."

Here Jennings was reiterating the contents of his planted newspaper article. He was, after all, the man who knew better than anyone else that "in the natural course of events" Lizzie would receive Andrew's money, although it would be a mere (relatively speaking) $25,000.

He went on to outline the prussic acid testimony of Bence, Kilroy, and Harte, and he successfully planted the seed for the legend's claim that Bence was the only one of the three who could identify Miss Lizzie and that he recognized her by voice only. "One of them, Bence, is taken to her house and he says he recognized her by her voice. She declares that she never left her home Wednesday morning, and by special providence, which seems to have watched over us in parts of this case, her words are corroborated by the dead woman who told John Morse that Lizzie had been sick in her room all day and had not left the house." Having Abby Borden testify for Lizzie took lots of moxie, but Jennings got away with it—and the legend swears by it.

His next statements make brilliantly clear, concise points totally in Lizzie's favor: "This girl has got at the most ten or fifteen minutes to commit the crime and conceal the weapon. Why didn't she wait before she called Bridget Sullivan down-

stairs? What is her condition right afterwards? Is there anything on her when the neighbors come to show that she
committed the crime? If she had time to kill her mother and
clean the bloodstains from her garments, she did not have
time to clear up the evidence of her work downstairs." Jennings then, however, makes a profound blunder: "If she had
on an apron, where is the apron? Where are the blood spots?
Where did she get rid of the weapons? The dress, the shoes
she had on that morning. Are there any shoe buttons found in
the fire? *Is there any smell of burnt clothing? No!*"

Andrew Jennings should have known about Lizzie's burning her dress, which came up later in the grand jury proceeding (see page 241). If he had been told of the dress burning
by one of the four who knew of it, it is difficult to understand
why he said these words. At the grand jury it was the dress
burning that condemned Lizzie.

Jennings' most telling argument was the review of Professor Wood's testimony that none of the two axes and two
hatchets found at the time were murder weapons. "I have no
doubt that every person with a feeling of sympathy for that
girl felt their hearts leap with joy as Professor Wood gave his
testimony. If I could have had my way I would have shouted
for joy."

Jennings finished with an all-out emotional plea: "They
haven't proven that this girl had anything to do with the
murder. They can't find any blood on her dress, on her hair,
on her shoes. They can't find any motive. They can't find the
axes, and so I say, I demand the woman's release. The grand
jury, if they meet more evidence, can indict her. They can't
find a motive, no blood, no poison, and so I say that this
woman shan't be sent to prison on such evidence as this,
shan't be sent to jail, shan't be deprived of her liberty and her
good name. Don't, Your Honor, when they don't show any
incriminating circumstance, don't put the stigma of guilt
upon this woman, reared as she has been and with a past
character beyond reproach. Don't let it go out in the world as
the decision of a just judge that she is probably guilty. God
grant Your Honor wisdom to decide, and, while you do your
duty, do it as God tells you to do it, giving the accused the
benefit of the doubt."

Porter reported there were tears in the eyes of most of those present. Arthur Phillips was weeping unashamedly as was Lizzie who sat hiding her face. "As Mayor Coughlin, Dr. Dolan, and other prominent persons stepped forward to grasp the hand of the attorney, a ripple of applause started, which rapidly swelled into a loud expression of admiration and sympathy, and with the echo of this applause, which there was no attempt to suppress, the court was adjourned until the afternoon" (page 132).

News of Jennings' moving plea for Miss Lizzie's innocence spread rapidly. Those who were unable to get in the morning session doubled their efforts—and their bribes to the bailiffs—to get a seat in the afternoon. The crowd hushed as Hosea Knowlton began with an apology to all who cast him as the villain in the drama: "I can fully appreciate Your Honor's feelings. The crime of murder touches the deepest sensibilities of feelings. There is the deepest feeling of horror about it, and above all is the unnaturalness that brings the thrill of horror to every mind. The man who is accustomed even to conflicts of arms may not be expected to be free from horror at the thought of the assassin. While it was not a pleasant summons that came to me, I should not have been true to duty if I had not undertaken to ferret out the criminal. It was so causeless a crime. The people interested in it were so free from ordinary bickerings or strife that of all cases that transcend the ideas of men, this case was that case. The murdered man's daughter was arrested. I perfectly understood the surprise and indignation that started up. I am sorry that Your Honor was criticized. Does not Your Honor believe my own soul is filled with anguish that I must go on and believe the prisoner guilty, and yet the path of duty is not always the path of pleasure. The straight and narrow path is often full of anguish, and does not have the popular voice behind it."

Knowlton reviewed the case, stating that although he would not try to attribute a motive to Lizzie, he did need to point out that she was "the only person in the world with whom she [Abby] is not in accord." He stressed opportunity by saying that Lizzie was present in the house and that Jennings had failed to tell how anyone else "could have got in there, remained an hour and a half, killed two people and then have gone out without being observed. Here was a house with the front door locked, the windows closed, the cellar door locked, and the screen door closed, with somebody on guard in the kitchen."

Knowlton reviewed the crime: "I'm going to assume Your Honor believes Bridget Sullivan has told the exact truth. What took place, Bridget Sullivan? Mr. Morse went off that morning and left Lizzie in the kitchen alone. Mrs. Borden told her [Bridget] to wash windows and she goes out to do it. In the lower part of the house there was no person left, and Lizzie and her mother went upstairs. Mrs. Churchill saw Mr. Borden go off and then saw Bridget washing windows. Then the hatchet was driven into the brain of Abby Borden. Many a man has been convicted because he alone could have committed the crime. Maggie finishes her work, and then, until Mr. Borden comes in, Lizzie and Mrs. Borden are alone upstairs. Mr. Borden comes to the front door. *I don't care to comment on Lizzie's laughter at Bridget's expression.* Then Lizzie comes downstairs and commences to iron. Bridget leaves her alone with her father. Less than fifteen minutes later the death of Mr. Borden takes place. *She could have but one alibi, she could not be downstairs; she could not be anywhere except where she could not see any person come from the house* (italics added).

Mr. Knowlton has been most perceptive. His clever choice of words and his reconstruction of what actually happened lack only his placing of the murderer into the scene to fill the few gaps he left. His refusal to comment on Lizzie's laugh reveals his full knowledge of whom Bridget had heard, and his pinpointing of Lizzie's self-reasoned need to be some place other than in the back yard is evidence that he knew what actually happened.

Concerning the prussic acid incident, Knowlton argued, "Nobody, Your Honor, has said this family was poisoned with prussic acid. All that the Commonwealth says is that this was the first proposition. . . . The crime was done as a matter of deliberate preparation. Those young men recognized her not by her voice, but recognized her *and* her voice."

He next characterized Miss Lizzie as being coldhearted, an accusation few have ever faulted. "I haven't alluded to and I think I will not comment upon the demeanor of the defendant. It is certainly singular. While everybody is dazed, there is but one person who, throughout the whole business, has not been seen to express emotion."

Knowlton concluded, "It has been a source of great disappointment that we have not been able to find the apron with which she must have covered her dress, and which must contain blood, just as surely as did the shoes. It is a source of regret that we have not been able to find the packet, but she had fifteen minutes in which to conceal it. This was not a crime of the moment. It was concealed in the head of a cunning, cool woman, and well has she concealed these things. If Your Honor yielded to the applause which spontaneously greeted the close of the remarks of my earnest, passionate brother, if Your Honor could but yield to the loyalty of his feelings, we would all be proud of it, and would be pleased to hear him say: 'We will let this woman go.' But that would be but temporary satisfaction. We are constrained to find that she has been dealing in poisonous things, that her story is absurd, and that hers and hers alone has been the opportunity for the commission of the crime. Yielding to clamor is not to be compared to that only, and the greatest satisfaction, that of a duty well done."

In contrast to the applause that greeted Jennings as he took his seat, Knowlton took his to silence. No one moved. Eyes were locked onto Judge Blaisdell who paused, not for effect but for time to gain lost composure. They saw tears; they saw compassion. His first words filled the room because of its eerie tomblike silence.

"The long examination is now concluded, and there remains but for the magistrate to perform what he believes to be his duty. It would be a pleasure for him, and he would doubtless receive much sympathy if he could say, 'Lizzie, I judge you probably not guilty. You may go home.' But upon the character of the evidence presented through the witnesses who have been so closely and thoroughly examined, there is but one thing to be done. Suppose for a single moment a man was standing there. He was found close by the guest chamber which, to Mrs. Borden, was a chamber of death. Suppose a man had been found in the vicinity of Mr.

Borden, was the first to find the body, and the only account he. could give of himself was the unreasonable one that he was out in the barn looking for sinkers; then he was out in the yard; then he was out for something else; would there be any question in the minds of men what should be done with such a man?"

A witness to Judge Blaisdell's decision tells us the judge had to pause here, visibly shaking, tears streaming down his cheeks. When he could continue, he said, "So there is only one thing to do, painful as it may be. The judgment of the court is that you are probably guilty, and you are ordered committed to await the action of the superior court."

Almost everybody in the courtroom who heard this verdict reacted with the emotion the moment commanded. One person alone, with every eye in the courtroom straining to catch her reaction, retained the very composure that had helped to damn her. She sat unmoved. No tears now, no trace of any emotion, no fear, no anger, no resentment, no surprise, no horror, no remorse.

By blood, she was a *Borden*!

The Mellen House agreement was still going according to plan.

# Chapter 13

U nder the laws of Massachusetts in 1892, murder was not a bailable crime. Thus Judge Blaisdell's verdict disqualified Lizzie from bond, and she was returned to the county jail in Taunton where she was held for two and one-half months until the grand jury sat at its session scheduled for mid-November. Had Judge Blaisdell ruled "no probable cause," Lizzie would still have faced the same tribunal, but she would have been eligible for bonded freedom.

The Mellen men did everything possible to prepare for the grand jury. In fact, they took an action never before taken in Massachusetts jurisprudence. A grand jury's function is to hear evidence *against* the accused and determine if the evidence presented is sufficient to send the case to a higher court. A grand jury does not hear defense arguments. For it to hear both sides and determine guilt or innocence is a violation of its chartered restrictions and simply isn't done.

For *this* grand jury hearing, however, it was announced that the prosecution had offered Andrew Jennings the opportunity to present *any defense* he wished. The enormity of this is beyond belief. Never had it been done before, and never has it been done since. Robert Sullivan, a former justice of the Superior Court of Massachusetts, called this action "astonishing." He added, "This was a gesture to my knowledge unheard of in Massachusetts, if not in Anglo-American jurisprudence, before or, for that matter, since the indictment of Lizzie Borden" (*Goodbye Lizzie Borden*, page 54).

The local press reported District Attorney Knowlton's explanation for his having made this improper offer by insisting it was done in the interest of *fairness*. He was anxious for the jury to hear both the evidence for and the evidence against Miss Borden. If after hearing both sides they found her not guilty, he would be completely satisfied.

The real reason for the offer should be obvious. Since the grand jury hearings were secret, it would be relatively easy to tell the press that the defense had come up with a masterful something-or-other that proved, beyond any shadow of a doubt, that Lizzie Andrew Borden had not murdered her stepmother or her father. The legal proceedings against her would end, and the State of Massachusetts could choose whether or not to look for another murderer.

Unbelievably, when this offer took place, it did not raise a single public eyebrow, and no one has commented much about it since, perhaps because Jennings refused the offer. His refusal might have been a reflection on his own integrity, or it might have been that Boston's Colonel Adams or the governor's representative, George Seaver, did not allow it. Even without the defense's arguments, the planned scenario almost developed. Charges against Lizzie were almost dismissed.

The grand jury heard testimony for a week and adjourned without giving its verdict. This delay was a good sign for Lizzie. It would appear that there was reasonable doubt as to her guilt in spite (or maybe because) of the best efforts of the prosecution. However, ten days later the jury reconvened to hear Lizzie's closest friend, Alice Russell, who had asked for the opportunity to give additional testimony. Immediately after hearing her testimony, the jury issued indictments against Lizzie for the murder of Andrew Borden, for the murder of Abby Borden, and for the murder of the two Bordens together.

We know from her testimony at the final trial that Miss Russell's few minutes of testimony concerned the dress Lizzie wore the morning of the murders. Lizzie's own mishandling of evidence and Alice Russell's honesty in telling about it increased considerably the cost of pronouncing Lizzie not guilty. The story is another interesting one.

On Saturday, two days after the murders, Marshal Hilliard received into evidence the clothing Lizzie said she wore on the morning of the murders. At the final trial he answered District Attorney Moody's question: "You referred to a dress which you took away. Will you state all that occurred with reference to that?"

"Yes, sir," Hilliard complied. "I asked Mr. Jennings where the dress was she wore that day. He went, and when he came back he brought the dress."

"Where did he go?"

"I was then in the room where Mrs. Borden was found upstairs. He went out into the hallway, and came back into that room. I don't know where he went after he went into the hallway. He came back into the room with that dress—a dress."

"Did you see the prisoner at that time or about that time?"

"I saw her soon after that in what is called Miss Emma's room just inside the door."

"What had you done with the dress at that time?"

"I had passed the dress to Dr. Dolan after it was handed to me."

That this took place two days after the murders does raise the question of whether the dress Lizzie *said* she was wearing was the one she *was* wearing, but the possibility that Lizzie or Andrew Jennings could switch clothes never seemed to occur to Hilliard. After looking at the dress and Lizzie's petticoat that were given to him, he "rolled them up with what I call a lounge cover that was taken from the dining room" and gave them back to Andrew Jennings to take to the station house. Moody questioned his action: "And you said he [Jennings] gave you the same bundle [of clothes] that you gave him?"

"Yes, sir."

"After you got possession again, what did you do with them?"

"I carried them to my office—passed them over to Dr. Dolan."

Since the dress she said she was wearing on the murder morning was carefully in the control of Lizzie and her defense counsel, it should be no surprise that the dress given as evidence was not blood-spattered at all.

At both the preliminary hearing and the final trial, several days of testimony concerned the blood at the scene of Andrew and Abby's murders. There was one unusual feature of the murders to which all who had viewed the scene testified: while an abundance of blood had drained from each body, there was much less *splattered* blood than the brutality of the attack would lead one to expect. But whether there should have been a lot or only a little, all agreed that the dress Lizzie offered in evidence was not blood-spattered at all.

During the three days and nights after the murders, the Borden household (Lizzie, Emma, Uncle John, and Miss Russell) were allowed free access to all parts of the house, and anyone they wanted could enter the house and come and go. No effort was made to preserve the crime scene. In fact, because no one had told her *not* to do it, on Sunday, three days after the murders, Emma cleaned up all blood splatter and splashes in both murder rooms.

No one who saw Lizzie on the morning of the murders would swear that the dress she gave to the police was the same dress they saw her wearing. Two people swore it was *not* the same one; all the rest claimed not to have noticed or said they could not remember.

On Sunday morning, Lizzie made a serious mistake. While others were watching, she put into the fire in the kitchen stove a dress whose description exactly matched the dress two witnesses said she was wearing the morning of the murders. Lizzie said the dress she put in the fire was stained beyond continued use as a house dress, even beyond the point where she would want to use it as rags—an unusual decision in a household celebrated for its frugality. The stains on the dress were said to be brown paint spots.

Two people witnessed this burning: Emma (who, at the trial, said it was her idea that Lizzie finally get rid of "that old thing") and Alice Russell (who, at the trial said she remarked at the time, "If I were you, I wouldn't let anybody see me do that, Lizzie"). Alice Russell's advice was sound, but Lizzie had already let Alice see the burning dress.

On Monday after the dress burning, Miss Russell was interviewed by O. M. Hanscom, New England's most famous member of the Pinkerton Detective Agency, whom Andrew Jennings had hired within hours of the murders. Having been told by Mr. Jennings to cooperate fully with the famous detective, in this interview Miss Russell told him about the dress spattered with brown paint that Lizzie had burned the previous day.

This information put Detective Hanscom in an awkward position. Because of local police resentment that he had been brought in to protect Borden interests, a statement attributed to him had been planted in the local press: "If the parties are guilty, the agency will drop work at once and not become accessory to a crime. If they are not guilty, the agency will hang on and assist materially." This statement was intended to force the Bordens to pay for the services of a detective who could not legally keep evidence of guilt from the prosecution.

Hanscom could hardly withdraw from the case without impugning Lizzie's innocence, but he could not continue to work on the case without reporting his findings to Marshal Hilliard. Jennings' solution was as much ingenious as it was devious. Hanscom was dispatched to Hastings, Iowa, for the duration of the proceedings to "check up" on Uncle John Morris, a brilliant countermove that allowed Jennings and Hanscom to save face while allowing the detective to remain an asset to Miss Lizzie.

Alice Russell said nothing about the dress burning at the inquest, at the preliminary hearing (although Andrew Jennings, who presumably knew that Lizzie had burned the dress, said that a burning dress would imply Lizzie's guilt: "Is there any smell of burnt clothing? No!"), and in her first testimony before the grand jury. But when it became obvious that Lizzie was not above suspicion and yet the grand jury was on the verge of releasing her, Miss Russell asked for and was granted the chance to amend her previous testimony. The change resulted in Lizzie's indictments. Lizzie would have to stand trial.

Although before the murders Alice Russell was the closest and dearest friend of both Emma and Lizzie, it is no wonder that after the trial, Miss Russell was never a visitor to the home of the Borden sisters nor was she remembered in the will of either. Alice Russell died in 1941 in Fall River's home for the aged, still alone, still reticent, and still a heroine. She had known what was morally right, and neither her friendships nor the availability of money from Andrew Jennings for saying or not saying the right things kept her from doing what she felt was the only righteous thing to do.

*Manuel José Correiro*

After the grand jury indictment, Lizzie Borden waited for more than six months for her trial in New Bedford. On June 5, 1893, 148 of the most upstanding citizens of southeastern Massachusetts were summoned to the district courthouse to participate in jury selection for her trial. Less than a week before that, an entirely unrelated event created reasonable doubt as to Lizzie's guilt.

If the killer of the Bordens was to be described, most upstanding citizens of southeastern Massachusetts would say the murderer would be a male Portuguese. Portuguese were considered the lowest caste at the time.

Manuel José Correiro was not just Portuguese, he was from the Azores, and *everybody* knew that people from the Azores were by far the worst of a bad lot. Correiro was considered sub-intelligent by virtue of the fact that he did not understand any English. A farmhand without any marketable skills, he was reported to be not quite right in the head and to have a wild-eyed stare that fit Dr. Handy's mythical "wild-eyed man." He was a slim, slight boy of just eighteen. In every respect, he was the perfect model of what an axe murderer in Fall River in 1892 should be.

On May 31, 1893, on a farm on the outskirts of Fall River, Manuel José Correiro took a hatchet and brutally hacked to death twenty-two-year-old Miss Bertha Manchester at approximately 9:30 in the morning, the same time as Abby Borden's murder. Bertha Manchester was struck about the head and shoulders in the same locations and the same number of times as Abby Borden, according to the medical examiner, the same Dr. William A. Dolan who had handled the Borden murders. Correiro did not run away after the murder; he waited on the property to kill Bertha's father, too, because he owned Correiro money. Bertha's father was delayed, and Correiro left before he returned.

As with the Bordens, there was no excessive splattering of blood. As with the Bordens, valuables at the Manchester house were untouched, at least according to the early reports the jurors would have read. The press was quick to point out the similarities between the two murders, giving Jennings a clear basis for "reasonable doubt." Before a gathering of reporters, he asked, "Are there any among you who will claim Lizzie Borden did this, too?"

The twelve jurors selected to determine Lizzie's fate listened to the evidence of her case and heard the arguments for and against her, knowing that a savage axe murderer had struck again in the same city, in the same insane manner, and with the same sort of weapon. They knew there had been two very similar crimes. They knew that some Portuguese was accused of one of these crimes and that this girl before them was accused of the other. While they knew Lizzie could not have committed the crime of which the Portuguese stood accused, no one had said that he could not have committed the crime of which she was accused. The prosecution had to prove Lizzie guilty above and beyond what it ordinarily would if it was to erase the doubt Manuel Correiro had generated.

Manuel José Correiro was convicted of killing Bertha Manchester and committed to the state prison. In 1901, a most telling date, he was deemed most violent, capable of doing bodily harm, and moved to another prison facility with "a considerable insane department where he could be closely confined and carefully watched."

At his trial, it was shown that he had been in this country only a few months when the Manchester murder occurred. He was *not* in Massachusetts when the Bordens were murdered. The authorities knew this when he first became a suspect, but Lizzie's trial was over well before this information was released. Releasing it earlier could have erased the reasonable doubt Correiro's action created in the minds of the twelve jurors at the Borden trial.

# Chapter 14

The decision of the grand jury to proceed with Lizzie's trial increased the cost of her defense enormously. Whereas the plan had been to have her acquitted in private and be done with it, there would now have to be a full-blown public performance with the press present. Moreover, the grand jury had shown that in spite of the local defense's best efforts, it *was* possible that Lizzie could be found guilty even though she had not murdered Andrew and Abby Borden. The final trial had to be conducted so that Lizzie definitely would be declared not guilty. That was expensive, especially since the final trial was heard at the state level. Local control was gone.

Once the case had slipped through the hands of local control, the Statehouse Gang in Boston must have looked at Andrew Borden's wealth as a plum ripe for picking. No longer would it be only local authorities plucking away at his bank balance; the big boys now had their opportunity. They took over.

The first step was a change in personnel. Judge Josiah C. Blaisdell was forced to withdraw. He was replaced by a tribunal of three judges, all loyal to the state government. In 1891 a law had been enacted in Massachusetts requiring a panel of three justices to hear all capital cases, with the panel to be named by the chief justice of the commonwealth. The purpose of the law was to provide protection from any miscarriage of justice caused by a local government's influence and bias. In Lizzie's case it did just that by substituting state-controlled influence and bias.

In 1893 the chief justice of Massachusetts was Albert C. Mason. He named Caleb Blodgett and Justin J. Dewey as the first two judges to serve the panel for Lizzie's trial. He named himself as the third.

To ensure Lizzie's acquittal, the defense team was headed by former Massachusetts governor George Dexter Robinson who joined Andrew Jennings and Melvin Adams. Robinson wasn't just in charge of the defense; he was in charge of the entire final trial. A spellbinding orator of impressive presence and beloved by all who knew him from afar, Robinson had almost no experience as a criminal trial lawyer. His true value to Lizzie's defense team was in the appointments he had made as a three-term governor and the I.O.U.s he still held. He had appointed Justice Dewey; Justice Mason and he were old political cronies with a long history of party service together; like Mason, Justice Blodgett had been appointed by Robinson's dear friend and predecessor, Governor Long.

The task of prosecuting Lizzie was the responsibility of Attorney General Albert E. Pillsbury. He declined for "health reasons," and so Hosea Knowlton was again in charge of the prosecution with District Attorney William H. Moody assisting him. As if Robinson's influence on the judiciary were not enough, a year earlier he had entered into a law partnership with none other than William Moody. In fact, the Boston *Globe* reported that it was Moody "who suggested the retaining of ex-Gov. Robinson by the defense and that was long before he expected to have any connection with the case itself." Today having the defense attorney and the prosecutor being part of the same law firm would be considered a serious conflict of interest and highly irregular.

With the influence he had, George Robinson may have been worth the twenty-five thousand dollars (the same amount Andrew Borden had willed to Lizzie!) he was paid for working the thirteen days of the final trial, although Lizzie later complained about it openly. To put Robinson's fee in perspective, Knowlton made two thousand dollars per year as district attorney, and the governor of Massachusetts was paid five thousand dollars per year. Robinson's bill was not Lizzie's only legal expense, however. Both Adams and Jennings had worked for her for almost a full year, and their fee was fifteen

*The Borden jury*

thousand dollars—each.

Hosea Knowlton and William Moody, the prosecution, both went on to illustrious careers after the Borden trial. One year later Knowlton became attorney general of Massachusetts. Moody was elected to the United States House of Representatives for two terms and then became secretary of the navy and later attorney general of the United States under Teddy Roosevelt. In 1906 he was appointed justice of the U.S. Supreme Court.

Relatively speaking, Andrew Jennings was an honorable man who, to keep faith with his client, cast his lot with thieves. His victory in this case was so repugnant to him that he never discussed it with anyone after the trial. In fact, all reports stress that if the subject came up in his presence, it was his practice to turn and leave.

In 1893 jury duty was not taken lightly. In an era of five-cent bread and ten dollars per week for eighty hours of labor, a juror in a capital crime was sequestered in the best hotel with meals furnished (including cigars) and paid three dollars *per day*. One hundred years later, jurors are paid only slightly more, but without the cigars. The twelve chosen for this trial were (in alphabetical order): Frank G. Cole, William F. Dean, John C. Finn, Lewis B. Hodges, George Potter, Charles I. Richards, Augustus Swift, William Westcot, Frederic C. Wilbar, Lemuel K. Wilber, John Wilbur, and Allen H. Wordell. Mr. Richards served as foreman.

The final trial lasted for thirteen days. Much of the 1,930 pages of the trial's transcript is taken up with opening statements and closing arguments. (The two closing arguments and the charge to the jury take 320 pages!) Most of what was important in the content of the testimony has already been presented. More interesting are the actions that so blatantly violated every principle of judicial honesty in an effort to ensure the outcome of the trial.

These actions did not go unnoticed at the time. One newspaper called the trial the "Carnival in New Bedford" while another referred to its "Farcical Proceedings." Frustrated over the court's unwillingness to admit the testimony of Eli Bence and others concerning Lizzie's efforts to buy prussic acid, District Attorney Moody actually said he did not wish to prosecute further because of the "bias" (his word) of the court and that the prosecution should simply request of the court an immediate directed verdict of "not guilty."

The trial of Lizzie Borden was no trial. It was a performance necessary to satisfy the legal and public requirements to arrive at the prearranged determination that Lizzie Borden was not guilty.

## The Prosecution

William Moody made the opening statement for the prosecution. He pointed to Lizzie's dislike of Abby as a strong motive for murder. He also outlined the house plans and claimed that the cellar door had been bolted for two days prior to the murder.

When Moody was finished with his opening, Thomas Kieran introduced his engineer's plots and plans of the house and yard. Then the jury, upon a recommendation made by Mr. Knowlton to which Mr. Robinson agreed, was taken to Fall River to view the actual crime scene. The jury members arrived in the city by train in the early afternoon of the second day of the trial under heavy security and with strict rules governing their every action. The curious gathered with them, and, according to one newspaper, "A large crowd of people assembled in the street, and for a while the appearance of the Borden residence and its surroundings was similar to last August."

When their tour was completed, the jurors had a more-than-two-hour wait for the next train back to New Bedford. In a most ironical move, they were taken to the Mellen House for refreshment and sequestering.

The first meaningful witness for the prosecution was John Morse, one of the few witnesses who had full and complete knowledge of what had actually happened that murder day. However, neither the defense nor the prosecution could be sure that he would not say too much. Therefore his time on the stand was short, his testimony was concise, and the questions asked of him were limited and easy to answer. He said nothing to equal, or even come close to, his testimony at the preliminary hearing. He was asked nothing about any conversations he may have had with Lizzie. He was asked nothing about Andrew's will or of any knowledge he had of it. And he was asked nothing about the cellar door that sometimes was said to be open and sometimes said to be closed, although he *was* asked whether the *barn* door was open or not. From the day he testified until the day he died, nothing more is known about John Morse.

At the inquest, Knowlton had asked Lizzie the penetrating, perceptive question, "How many children has your father?" Mr. Moody asked almost the same question of Mr. Morse: "Of that marriage, how many children were there?" But there is a significant difference between the two questions, which, from all outward appearance, sought the same information. In each case the answer was the same; Morse, unlike Lizzie, was not forced to lie.

What Morse was *not* asked should have been grounds for impeachment of both Moody and Knowlton; in what *was* asked, care was taken to be sure that Morse could easily tell the truth. The cautious steps the prosecution and defense took to ensure his answers would be easy and precise show that he was considered a threat. He was called early and was excused as quickly as possible.

His return to the Borden house the morning of the murders was most questionable. Had he, for instance, returned for dinner as he had claimed earlier? Had Andrew invited him back when he left in the morning? Moody managed to avoid these questions as follows: "Won't you describe what occurred at the door, not stating what anyone stated to you but what occurred at the door as you went out?"

Why was Uncle John ordered not to say what Andrew had said to him? His conversation with the deceased was fully admissible.

Similarly, Moody asked, "Now, without any detail, where were you until you returned again that morning to the Borden house?"

Why *not* go into detail?

Early in the trial, George Robinson showed that he was in charge. Abram Hart, John Burrell, and Everett Cook, all of whom worked in Andrew Borden's various banks, next testified in order to establish his movements on the morning of the murder. After asking Hart whether there was any other bank in the building in which he worked, District Attorney Knowlton began, "It is agreed, if Your Honors please, to save calling a number of witnesses . . ."

He was cut off by Robinson who arrogantly said, "I will state what we agreed to. For the purpose of this trial, Your Honors, it is agreed that the defendant having no knowledge in regard to a will or otherwise, so far as is now ascertained, the deceased was intestate. Also without any further inquiries, that the amount of property in the name of Andrew J. Borden at the time of his death may be taken to be from $250,000 to $300,000."

Mr. Knowlton said, "That is agreeable to us. That saves calling a number of witnesses." Mr. Robinson then continued the proceedings by cross-examining Mr. Hart.

Incredibly, no one in one hundred years has pointed out this beginning of the rape of justice. Robinson's pushing Knowlton aside as he did depicts either unquestioned cooperation or humble kowtowing to the boss. In addition to the style, the content of Robinson's speech is unbelievable. He said the prosecution and the defense had agreed that, in spite of Lizzie's inquest testimony to the contrary, she did not know for certain whether her father did or did not leave a will and since *she* was unsure, they had agreed he did not have one.

Can there be any question as to whether Robinson is in charge when the *defense* says that the *prosecution* has agreed to a statement that covers up the actual motive for the murders, that eliminates any hint of Andrew Jennings' and the Silent Government's complicity in the crime of not probating Andrew Borden's will, and that contradicts the most important sections of John Morse's preliminary hearing testimony and the only legitimately incriminating section of Lizzie's inquest testimony?

Bridget Sullivan was the next witness. The Bridget Sullivan who testified at the final trial was not the Bridget Sullivan of ten months earlier. At the hearing she appeared to be a scared-to-death lass; at the final trial she was self-assured, answered questions firmly, and refused to be cowed. During his cross-examination, for instance, Robinson read excerpts from Bridget's inquest testimony and tried to pick it apart. At one point Bridget told him, "I don't know what I testified. I testified the truth as long as I remember. As far as I know I told the truth and nothing more!"

Robinson apologized, in sorts, by telling her, "I do not imply that you did not."

During the ten months since the murders, Bridget had been employed by Mr. and Mrs. Hunt in New Bedford. Mr. Hunt was the New Bedford jailkeeper, and although Bridget was not in jail, she was under a surety bond pledged by Marshal Hilliard and State Detective Seaver. Her position allowed them to watch after her.

Bridget's testimony revealed little new or different from what she had testified earlier. She was followed by Dr. Bowen, whose testimony has already been described.

Before the trial began, common wisdom said that the prosecution had three pieces of damning evidence, primed and ready for an all-out assault on Lizzie. In order to deliver the not-guilty verdict that Lizzie had paid for, the defense would have to neutralize all three. The first was the "murder weapon" (a fifth hatchet) that had been found; the second was Lizzie's own inquest testimony; and the third was the testimony of Lizzie's attempt to buy prussic acid.

When Assistant City Marshal John Fleet made his first trip to the cellar on the day of the murders, he found officers Mullaly and Devine there. With Bridget's help, Mullaly had gathered two axes and two hatchets. Finding them in the Borden cellar was not unusual. It would be akin to finding two barbecue spits and two steak knives in a suburban kitchen today. Fleet considered one of these more suspicious looking than the others and set it on a shelf by itself. He placed the other three in a neat heap on the cellar floor. All four were left in the house overnight(!), and an officer took them to the station house first thing Friday morning. At the preliminary hearing, Professor Wood had testified that the "blood" was rust or paint and that the hairs had grown on a cow, not a human. By all indications, none of these four was the murder weapon.

After questioning Lizzie on the day of the murder, Fleet went back into the cellar a second time. Officer Mullaly was still there, but this time Dr. Dolan was with him. Fleet asked Mullaly to show him where the first hatchets had been found, and Mullaly took him to "a box in the middle cellar." Fleet took down the box and found in it the head of another hatchet. The head had a portion of a hatchet handle in its eye, broken off close to the eye. The head appeared as if it had been washed and, while still wet, dipped into coal ashes, which were plentiful in the basement. The break, however, was clean, recent, and free of the ashes that covered the metal. The rest of the handle that had been broken off was, according to Fleet, not in the box. Michael Mullaly, however, testified that Fleet saw the handle in the box, took it out, and put it back into the box along with the hatchet head. Mullaly was the only one who ever claimed to have seen the handle.

The handleless hatchet head (and, if you believe Mullaly, the handle) evidently stayed in the box in the Borden cellar over the weekend, although it was *not* found in searches of the same area conducted by different personnel on Friday or Saturday. On Monday morning, the fifth day after the murders, however, Officer William Medley found the same handleless hatchet head in a wooden box in the cellar. He showed it to Acting Captain Desmond. On Desmond's instructions, he wrapped it up in some brown paper he found in the water closet, and, after showing it to another officer, took it to the marshal in the station house. At the trial, Medley demonstrated for the court how he had wrapped the hatchet head.

After Medley gave his testimony, Dennis Desmond took the

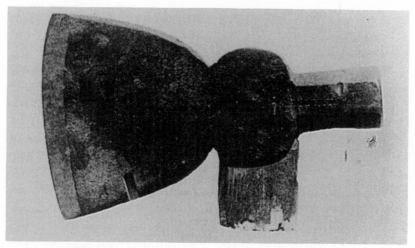

*The handleless hatchet*

stand. He corroborated Medley's testimony, except that Desmond said *he* had wrapped the hatchet head in *newspaper* he took from the water closet. Robinson said nothing, handed Desmond the hatchet head and a piece of newspaper, and asked him to demonstrate for the court just how he had wrapped it.

"I shall have to get a full-sized newspaper to do it in," Desmond explained, "much larger than that, sir (referring to a piece of paper handed witness by counsel)."

"You got a piece out of the water closet?"

"Yes, sir."

"Brown paper?"

"No sir, regular newspaper, but a larger paper than that."

"You wrapped it in a newspaper?"

"Yes, sir."

"You sure about that?"

"Positive."

"A very large newspaper?"

"Yes, quite a big newspaper."

"Larger than that (exhibiting Boston *Globe*)?"

"Yes."

It should be noted here that the Providence *Journal* was a standard fixture in the Borden water closet. It was a full-sized newspaper.

"Well, take that and give us the way you wrapped it up."

Desmond did just that, explaining, "I wrapped it up in some such form as that, and passed it to him."

To make a credible case, the prosecutor had to present something that could have been used as a murder weapon. To deliver an acquittal for Lizzie successfully, the defense had to neutralize the handleless hatchet head, which was said to be the murder weapon. Admittedly, it was found in the cellar of the Borden house, and, unlike the first two hatchets and two axes found, it did fit exactly the cuts in the skulls of both Bordens. However, the confusion surrounding it made it difficult to think of it as the murder weapon. In addition, Assistant Marshal Fleet's testimony indicated that he did not think it was important. At the preliminary hearing, Fleet had testified that other than the first two hatchets and two axes, he had "failed to find anything." At the final trial Robinson asked, "What reason had you for telling the court that you did not find this hatchet head?"

"None other than the hatchet, as I found it in the box—placed it in there again—being all covered with ashes, I didn't take it away," Fleet answered. "The handle having been broken at that time, I didn't think—if it is allowed to go in—that it was used for the purpose of killing."

"Notwithstanding the fresh break in the handle," Robinson said, "the unusual dust on it, notwithstanding all there was about it, being different from the rest, you did not think it was worth talking about?"

"That is the way I looked at it. That is the reason I left it there."

"That is not what I asked you, why you left it, but why you did not testify about it?"

"Because I didn't think it came into play."

The handleless hatchet head exhibited at the trial is now on display in the Lizzie Borden Exhibit at the Fall River Historical Society. It was never proved to be the murder weapon. In fact, it was not, for the murderer took the weapon with him. The defense had defused the prosecution's first weapon against Lizzie.

The second piece of damning evidence the prosecution had against Lizzie was her own inquest testimony. Some of her statements were ambiguous, and some of the things she said were openly contradictory. Almost anything could be suggested or inferred from her words, and while most could be successfully explained away, the explanation would have been an "iffy" undertaking. The defense was being well paid to guarantee the outcome of this trial, and since admitting Lizzie's inquest testimony into the trial record could not be done with guaranteed results, the defense had to ensure that the testimony was not admitted. Then there would be nothing to explain or defend.

After Chief Justice Mason considered the request to include Lizzie's inquest testimony and the arguments against it, he concluded, "The propriety of examining the prisoner at the inquest, and of all that occurred in connection therewith, is entirely distinct from the question of the admissibility of her statements in that examination. It is with the latter question only that this court has to deal.

"The common law regards this species of evidence with distrust. Statements made by one accused of crime are admissible against him only when it is affirmatively established that they were voluntarily made. It has been held that statements of the accused as a witness under oath at an inquest, before he had been arrested as a witness or charged with the crime under investigation, may be voluntary and admissible against him in his subsequent trial, and the mere fact that at the time of his testimony at the inquest he was aware that he was suspected of the crime does not make them otherwise. But we are of the opinion both upon principle and authority that if the accused was at the time of such testimony under arrest, charged with the crime in question, the statements so made are not voluntary and are inadmissible at the trial.

"The common law regards substance more than form. The principle involved cannot be evaded by avoiding the form of arrest if the witness at the time of such testimony is practically in custody. From the agreed facts and the facts otherwise in evidence, it is plain that the prisoner at the time of her testimony was, so far as relates to this question, as effectually in custody as if the formal precept had been served; and, without dwelling on other circumstances which distinguish the facts in this case from those of cases on which the Government relies, we are of the opinion that this consideration is decisive, and the evidence is excluded."

By these few words, the prosecution's second weapon was rendered harmless, dismantled, and scrapped. Lizzie wept.

Robinson had argued that because Lizzie, for all practical purposes, was in custody, her testimony was not voluntary, and since the fifth amendment to the Constitution of the United States does not allow a person to testify against himself if he does not wish to, it would be in violation of the federal Constitution to enter Lizzie's inquest testimony into the final trial as evidence.

Moody argued unsuccessfully against Robinson's first supposition. He said that Lizzie had voluntarily testified when she had every right to refuse. Regardless of the suspicions voiced, regardless of warrants issued but not served, regardless of the around-the-clock posting of police at her home for the purpose of protecting the entire family, she was *not* under arrest at the time she testified. Hence, all she did and said at the inquest was voluntary.

Moody also argued unsuccessfully against Robinson's second supposition. It is the more interesting one because viewed through today's eyes and evaluated by today's standards, Justice Mason's ruling is without fault. Today's legal interpretation would agree with Mason that if Lizzie did not testify voluntarily, the U.S. Constitution prohibits her inquest testimony from being admitted as evidence at her trial. In 1893, however, Moody's understanding of the law, not Mason's interpretation, was correct.

"I am somewhat surprised," said Moody, "that my learned friend should appeal to the Constitution of the United States, or rather to the first amendment to the Constitution of the United States, as a shield to the defendant in this case; because, of course, he must be aware that those amendments, including Article 5, have been held not to regulate the rights between the state and its own citizens, but to regulate the rights between the United States and the citizens of the respective states." In 1893 states' rights had not yet been peeled away from the states by the Warren court.

Robinson had rambled and argued like one totally unprepared, but he did not need to prepare. There was no reason to prepare. He knew what the ruling would be. Judge Mason's decision was not changed.

Two down, one to go.

The prosecution's third piece of damning evidence was the testimony of Eli Bence, Frank Kilroy, and Frederick Harte that the day before the murders Lizzie Borden had attempted to buy some prussic acid, ostensibly to clean her sealskin cape. Even more potentially damaging than the allegation of Lizzie's attempt to buy prussic acid was Mr. Phillips' so-easy-to-misconstrue offer of a face-to-face meeting between Bence and Jennings. While there was no proof that the intent of this suggestion was a payoff to Bence, there was, on the other hand, no proper reason for a *sub rosa* meeting between the counsel for the defense and a major witness for the prosecution.

After Eli Bence was called and sworn, District Attorney Moody asked, "What is your full name?"

"My name is Eli Bence."

"What is your occupation?"

"I am a drug clerk."

"For whom do you work?"

"For D. R. Smith."

"Where is Mr. Smith's shop?"

"On the corner of South Main and Columbia streets in Fall River."

"How long have you been connected with this business?"

"Something between thirteen and fourteen years."

"How long have you been connected with Mr. Smith?"

"Something over four years now."

"And always at this place?"

"For Mr. Smith, yes, sir."

And that is as far as Mr. Bence was allowed to go. Debate about Bence's testimony took all of one afternoon and ran well into the next morning.

Melvin Adams, for the defense, had tried to have the testimony about the attempted purchase of prussic acid thrown out when it was given at the preliminary hearing. Judge Blaisdell refused for the simple reason that dropping it then would have given the prosecution reason to ask for a rehearing if the Mellen House-arranged pronouncement of Lizzie's innocence was made by the grand jury *without* Bence's testimony having been heard. But then the grand jury scenario did not go as planned, and there was a trial. The trial must go the way Lizzie wanted. Bence, Kilroy, Harte, and any others slated to follow them must not be heard.

Robinson interrupted Moody's questioning of Bence. "May it please Your Honors, there is a question here we consider of vital importance, and I believe the Commonwealth also recognizes it as of that character, and we do not want to go into it by piecemeal; and this inquiry, I suggest, ought to stop right here, and the question be discussed with the court alone."

Moody offered to state what he expected to prove by interviewing Bence and the others, but the court nevertheless followed Robinson's request and ordered the jury to withdraw and the witness to return to the witness waiting room.

Moody first argued that since Lizzie's attempted purchase of prussic acid was to clean her sealskins, it had no direct connection with the murders that occurred less than twenty-four hours later. Therefore the testimony ought to be admitted. When he made this concession, Robinson (not the court, mind you) allowed him to present his arguments to the court. Moody had obviously lost before he started.

In several instances earlier in the trial, the court had ruled for the defense by placing a time limit between the time of the murders and when an incident presented by the prosecution had occurred. Things that happened as much as a year earlier were excluded as being "too remote" from the crime for consideration. Unbelievably, Robinson's first argument against the admission of Bence's testimony was based on the remoteness of the event, which had occurred less than one day before the crime. Second, he charged that the testimony should not be heard because Lizzie was charged with murder by axe, not poison.

Moody cited case after case that established precedent in similar incidents and finished by saying, "I can conceive of no more significant act, nothing which tends to show more the purpose of doing mischief to someone than the attempt, under an excuse which was false, to obtain one of the most deadly poisons that is known to humankind at the present time."

Robinson argued that Lizzie had never expressed any intent of murder. He disposed of the possibility of poisoning in Abby Borden's day-before-the-murders complaint of sickness by pointing out the lack of medical evidence of any poison in the stomach of either victim. He concluded, "I must say I have said all the court desires to hear, and I have made my meaning, I trust, plain." There was a touch of threat in this statement, to say nothing of abrasive arrogance.

It appears that the court took its orders directly from Robinson, for at this point, *without a single word being said by anyone*, the court stood and withdrew for private consultation.

When the judges returned, Chief Justice Mason asked the prosecution the purpose of the testimony. Mr. Moody said the testimony was to "bear upon the state of the mind of the defendant prior to the homicide." Mason said, "The court are of the opinion that, provided the preliminary evidence comes up to the proffer, the evidence is competent. Of course, the preliminary evidence must be submitted before the main question can be finally determined." Moody had to present testimony that would show that the testimony of Bence and the others was admissible for the purpose of showing Lizzie's state of mind and what her thoughts were when she sought to purchase the prussic acid.

The next morning, the prosecution called Charles H. Lawton, a druggist in New Bedford. Virtually every question was objected to by Robinson so that nothing was learned. The prosecution next called Henry H. Tillson, a furrier. The court ruled that his more-than-thirty years of experience was not sufficient to qualify him as an expert to state whether prussic acid was a practical agent for use on furs for any reason. The third witness, Nathaniel Hathaway, an analytical chemist with a degree in chemistry from Columbia University, had his testimony harangued by Robinson before he was finally allowed to say that in his opinion prussic acid was unsuitable for any purpose in connection with sealskins, including their cleaning.

During the cross-examination by Robinson, Hathaway did say that prussic acid would kill small insects, but only if it did not kill the person using it first. Robinson's next question is a classic example of absurdity: "Then leave out the effect it may have upon the person using it, or any other person present, there is nothing in prussic acid that makes it an unsuitable article to use to kill moths on furs?"

"No objection under those conditions."

The last witness called by the prosecution was the medical examiner for Bristol County, Dr. William A. Dolan. He was immediately objected to by Robinson. The objection was allowed by the court on the grounds that Dolan *was not qualified and any testimony he gave would be incompetent.*

At this point the jury was again excused. The court and counsel for both sides gathered in a "whispered consultation" that lasted ten minutes and which no one, including the court recorder, was allowed to overhear. After the consultation, no statement was made, no explanation given, no entry inserted in the transcript. The terse ruling was made that Eli Bence's testimony was "finished."

William Moody was angry. He suggested that the court should simply direct a verdict of not guilty and be done with it. Knowlton, however, recalled Henry Tillson and tried to have one more question answered, only to be told by the court, "I think you ought not reopen that question."

The prosecution finally gave up. Its capitulation caught the usually wordy Robinson with nothing to say, and he requested a recess. All three pieces of damning evidence the prosecution had counted on using had been successfully neutralized.

## The Defense

Little needs to be said about the defense offered by Jennings, Adams, and Robinson. It is seldom necessary to prove innocence, just guilt, and Lizzie's guilt had not been proved.

Jennings made the opening argument for the defense. He said:

". . . no matter how much you may want somebody punished for the crime, it is the guilty and not the innocent you want.

". . . A reasonable doubt is a doubt for which you can give a reason. If you can conceive of any other hypothesis that will exclude the guilt of this prisoner and make it possible or probable that someone else might have done this deed, then you have got a reasonable doubt in your mind.

". . . you are not sitting here to answer the question how this deed could have been committed or even who committed it; that is not the issue at all. The Commonwealth here has charged that Lizzie Andrew Borden, in a certain way, at a certain time, killed with malice of forethought. And that, and that alone, is the question you are to answer.

". . . it is not for you to unravel the mystery of how they died, it is not for you to withhold your decision until you have satisfied your mind as to how it was done and just who did it. It is, rather, for you to decide if they have furnished the proof, the proof the law requires, that Lizzie Andrew Borden did it, and that there is absolutely no opportunity for anyone else.

". . . the essential facts from which you are to draw your inference as to her guilt or her innocence are motive, weapon, exclusive opportunity, and conduct and appearance of the defendant."

With reference to the murder weapon, Jennings said, "They have either got to produce the weapon which did the deed and, having produced it, connect it in some way directly with the prisoner, or else they have got to account in some reasonable way for its disappearance." In light of what the prosecution had presented, there was nothing timid about that challenge.

Miss Lizzie's conduct and appearance after the crime were exemplary, with the possible exception of her having burned a paint-spattered dress, a "dress that was soiled and useless, and was burned there right in the broad light of day in the presence of witnesses, with windows open, with the inside door open, with officers on every side of the house." Having set the jury's minds at ease with regard to the one item that was somewhat questionable, Jennings presented the witnesses for the defense.

Martha Chagnon and her stepmother, Marienne Chagnon, heard noises at about 11 o'clock the evening before the murders from the area of the fence between their house and the Borden property.

John W. Grouard testified he had painted the Borden house at a time that coincided with a dressmaking session. Brown paint had been used extensively.

Mary A. Durfee had overheard Mr. Borden having "angry words" with an unknown man who had said, "You have cheated me, and I'll fix you for it." This was excluded by the court because it was too remote since it had occurred more than eight months before the murders.

About 11 o'clock the evening before the murders Charles N. Gifford had found an unknown man asleep on the side steps of his house on Third Street next door to the Chagnons'. He awoke the man and sent him on his way.

Uriah Kirby testified he had seen the same man.

Mark P. Chase, a former policeman and now a hostler—a person who takes care of horses and mules—had seen a stranger with a horse and carriage sitting as if waiting in front of the Borden house for some time just before 11 o'clock on the morning of the murder. Chase said he had never seen the man, the horse, or the carriage before that day.

Hyman Lubinsky, an ice cream salesman, had looked into the Borden side yard on the morning of the murder and "saw a lady come out the way from the barn right to the stairs from the back of the house." Lubinsky did not know Lizzie, but he could testify that the lady he saw was not Bridget, whom he did know.

Everett Brown and Thomas E. Barlow, who became known in the press as "Me and Brownie," were young boys, ne'er-do-wells who claimed they were in the loft of the Bordens' barn only minutes after Sawyer took up his guard post at the side door. If believed, their story made a shambles of Medley's testimony that when he had inspected the barn, no one had been in the loft for some time. Brown and Barlow, however, lost credibility during the course of their testimonies.

Alfred Clarkson and some friendly newspaper reporters repeated their we-were-in-the-loft-too stories.

The most interesting witness for the defense was Joseph Lemay who lived north of Fall River close to where Meridian Street and Wilson Road intersect. Since Lemay spoke only French, all questions were placed through an interpreter, who was also sworn in. Mr. Lemay's testimony was challenged, and so Mr. Jennings submitted the following offer of proof:

"This witness will testify that on the 16th day of August, at his farm, about four miles north of City Hall, while travelling into the woods for the purpose of cutting poles, just before he reached a turn in the road, he heard the words 'poor Mrs. Borden' repeated three times, and immediately saw sitting upon a rock behind a wall and some brushwood a man. He spoke to the man in French twice, but received no answer. On speaking to him the second time the man took up from the ground by his side a hatchet, such as is used in shingling houses, and shook it at him. He stepped back and put his own axe up in an attitude of defense. They remained in that position some few minutes, when the man turned, leaped over a wall, and disappeared in the woods. He said nothing to the witness at any time. The witness noticed upon his shirt spots of blood. He notified the police the same evening of what he had seen and heard."

The challenge to Mr. Lemay's testimony by the prosecution was successful and the court excluded it.

Just who won or lost this round and just what was at stake is not completely discernible. The fact that extensive maneuvering took place gives it importance. Jennings wanted the testimony as a part of the record, and Knowlton wanted full exclusion. In light of later events in the *same* Fall River area in 1901, what the police, who had investigated this incident thoroughly, found may have been beyond the limits of the Mellen House agreement. Containment was necessary.

A host of people testified after Mr. Lemay, most repeating what they had said at the preliminary hearing. Emma Borden, who had not testified before at any of the early hearings, was asked nothing of importance and had nothing revealing to say. This was in spite of pretrial promises and statements that she would testify about the conversations with John Morse, about her father's will, and about her trip to New Bedford. She must have embarrassed Mr. Jennings at one point when she did not allow him to finish his question before she answered.

"And what you have stated . . ." Jennings began.

"Is what you told me," Emma replied.

"Is what you recollect I told you about what he said about it?"

"Yes, sir."

Jennings had ordered Lizzie's silence since the inquest, and so she did not testify as was her right. The defense rested.

# Chapter 15

I n his closing argument, George Robinson made Miss Lizzie the daughter every member of the jury had or wished he had, the daughter to be safely harbored at home as every upright, proper, Christian young lady should be, where the man of the house could afford her protection from the ravages of such dangerous people as the prosecution. The fact that Lizzie was on trial for having killed her "protector" was easily forgotten. Robinson spoke directly to the jury—eye to eye, man to man, father to father. He went on and on. Robinson spoke for more than four hours before the court adjourned for dinner. But Robinson was not finished. After dinner he spoke for more than an hour more.

*Closing Arguments for the Defense*
"Lizzie Andrew Borden, from the day when we opened this trial until this hour, has been in your charge, gentlemen. . . . and the Commonwealth says, 'We entrust her to you.' Now that is your duty. You have her in charge.

"I noticed one day, as we were proceeding with this trial, a little scene that struck me forcibly. She stood here waiting, between the court and the jury, in her quietness and calmness, until it was time for her properly to come forward. It flashed through my mind in a minute: There she stands, protected, watched over, kept in charge by the judges of this court and by the jury who have her in charge. If the little sparrow does not fall unnoticed to the ground, indeed, in God's great providence, this woman has not been alone in this courtroom, but ever shielded by His providence from above, and by the sympathy and watchful care of those who have her to look after."

Robinson did not overlook the horror of the crime, ". . . one of the most dastardly and diabolical crimes that was ever committed in Massachusetts. . . . Who could have done such an act? In the quiet of the home, in the broad daylight of an August day, on the street of a popular city, with houses within a stone's throw, nay, almost touching, who could have done it?

"Inspection of the victims discloses that Mrs. Borden had been slain by the use of some sharp and terrible instrument, inflicting upon her head eighteen blows, thirteen of them crushing through the skull; and below stairs, lying upon the sofa, was Mr. Borden's dead and mutilated body, with eleven strokes upon the head, four of them crushing the skull.

"The terror of those scenes no language can portray. The horrors of that moment we can all fail to describe. And so we are challenged at once, at the outset, to find someone that is equal to the enormity, whose heart is blackened with depravity, whose whole life is a tissue of crime, whose past is a prophecy of the present. A maniac or a friend, we say. Not a man in his senses and with his heart right, but one of those abnormal productions that the Deity creates or suffers, a lunatic or a devil.

"They were well directed blows. They were not the result of blundering. They were aimed steadily and constantly, for a purpose, each one finding its place where it was aimed, and none going amiss on the one side or the other. Surely we are prompted to say at the outset, the perpetrator of that act knew how to handle the instrument, was experienced in its control, had directed it before or others like it, and it was not the careless, sudden, untrained doing of somebody who had been unfamiliar with such implements." Robinson describes what actually happened so accurately that one must conclude he knew the truth.

"I say, then, at the outset, as you begin to contemplate this crime and its possible perpetration by this defendant, you must conclude at the outset that such acts as those are morally and physically impossible for this young woman defendant."

Robinson reviewed the major segments of the prosecution's case that had already been destroyed. He told the jury to realize that the prosecution had said it would prove Lizzie was "preparing a dangerous weapon on August the third" (the prussic acid), but that it was not proved because the court had said it was "not proper to be proved in this case. . . . Whenever another case arises, if these things are pertinent and proper, they shall be heard, but not now." He said that the prosecution had said it would show "the defendent had contradicted herself under oath. . . . Well, there is another question that went to the court, and the court said: That is not proper to this case. You cannot show that. And so there is not anything of the kind. So you will leave those things out, gentlemen. No poison in this case, no prussic acid, no preparation of a weapon by this woman, no statement made by her under oath in this trial or anywhere that you know anything about or have any right to consider, I do not care what you have read."

Robinson then summarized the action of the murder day as he viewed it. He misrepresented and distorted facts by stating things not said in testimony. One peculiar comment was his statement that it was never proved that Lizzie acted with an accomplice. She had never been accused of that either in the final trial or any of the earlier proceedings: ". . . and it is for us to see whether the defendant is connected to them— whether the defendant alone or the defendant with a confederate, if there is any proof about it, did the deed. I am at a loss to know where there is any evidence about any accomplice or anyone else connected with it at all, and so it is only my inquiry to find out if there is any proof as to this defendant. Of course I need only to suggest to you that until there is some sort of evidence that connects somebody with it, it is not well to assume that she must have had somebody because you cannot think of anything else."

Robinson went on at great length about the note Abby Borden was said to have received the morning of the murders. He was either confused or lied. Lizzie's testimony at the inquest and testimonies given at the preliminary hearing and the trial showed that Abby told Lizzie she had received a note and was going out. Lizzie then told Bridget (who had also overheard Lizzie telling Andrew about it) and Mrs. Churchill about the note and that she assumed Abby had left. When Mrs. Churchill also asked Bridget about Abby's whereabouts, Bridget repeated what Lizzie had told her but did not attribute it to Lizzie. Mrs. Churchill assumed Bridget had first-hand knowledge of Abby's having received the note. She did not. Robinson twisted testimony to use Mrs. Churchill's conversation with Bridget to "prove" that Lizzie was not a liar: supposedly, her explanation was independently confirmed by Bridget. He went on about the note: "The note may have been part of the scheme in regard to Mrs. Borden. It may have got there through foul means and with a criminal purpose. We don't know anything about it. But that a note came there on this evidence you cannot question. That Lizzie lied about it is a wrongful aspersion, born out of ignorance of the facts as they were to be developed in this case."

Robinson took Fleet to task for interrogating Lizzie the day of the murder: ". . . plying the grieving woman with questions shortly after her great bereavement. What would you do with a man—I don't care if he had blue on him—that went into your house and was talking to your wife or daughter that way?"

Robinson attempted to prove that Lizzie was in the back yard under a pear tree when her father was killed by pointing out that pear skins had been found in the stomachs of each of the murder victims. Maybe if he went over it quickly, it would seem to make sense; there's no way it does if one thinks about it.

He accounted for Lizzie's wild talk with Miss Russell on the evening before the murders by reminding the gentlemen of the jury that Miss Lizzie was with her "sickness" at that time ". . . and we know from sad experience that there is many a woman at such a time as that is all unbalanced, her disposition disturbed, her mind unsettled for the time being and everything is out of sorts and out of joint and she really is disabled for a period of time."

Mr. Robinson did a laudable job of making the jury see that Lizzie could not have killed two people the way Mr. and Mrs. Borden were slaughtered *without* getting some blood on herself or her clothing, and no one had seen any blood on her or any evidence of recent washing of either her skin or her hair.

He offered a scenario he was sure the prosecution would offer: Lizzie committed both murders "after she had denuded herself." The prosecution did not offer it, and Robinson dismissed it as "foreign and base," but the scenario is deeply entrenched in the legend. It would have made more sense if there had been a shower or a bath tub in the house and if, after killing her father, she had had enough time to use it.

After discussing the prosecution's presentation of the murder weapon, Robinson again came close to the truth of the case. "You may adopt a theory just as well as I. You may find other theories, as I have no doubt you will as you look at the evidence. You will see other ways in which persons could enter that house by which the exclusive opportunity theory is overturned." Robinson all but named William Lewis Bassett, the man waiting outside the house on the murder morning who had been seen and reported by Lizzie, Dr. Handy, Mrs. Manly, and Mrs. Hart. He did outline the man's function: "He was the man that stood outside, and the other man was inside at that same time, and they were looking out for each other."

In a similar manner, Robinson told the jury why a murder weapon had not been found: "We all know very well that men commit these crimes and take away the instruments with them sometimes, and sometimes they fling them aside and leave them on the ground, but oftener, if they used an article found on the premises they would leave it, because it cannot be connected with them, but if they bring an article to a house with which to commit the act, they take it away because it is a clue to their arrest."

After the dinner recess, Robinson spent more than an hour closing his arguments. He reviewed Miss Lizzie's blemish-free life, her selflessness and, most certainly, her innocence. He concluded, "Gentlemen, with great weariness on your part, with abundant patience and intelligence, and care, you have listened to what I have had to offer. So far as you are concerned it is the last word of the defendant to you. Take it; take care of her as you have and give us promptly your verdict 'not guilty' that she may go home and be Lizzie Andrew Borden of Fall River in that bloodstained and wrecked home where she has passed her life so many years."

In fact, after the "not guilty" verdict was handed down,

ew Borden bought a new, larger house on The
t Maplecroft, and became Lizbeth of Maplecroft.

*Closing Arguments for the Commonwealth*

District Attorney Knowlton spoke almost as long as had
Robinson. He spoke eloquently, but it was the closing argument for a lost cause. His heart was not in it.

At the beginning, his argument did not sound like a speech
by an attorney convinced of the guilt of the accused and righ-
teously seeking justice, as closing arguments for the prosecution should be. Rather, it sounded like an apology by a man
who had taken up the jury's time without seeming to know
who committed the crimes.

"My distinguished friend says, 'Who could have done it?'
The answer would have been, 'Nobody could have done it.'

"It is an impossible crime. But it was committed. The difficulty of solving this awful tragedy starts from the very impossibility of the thing itself.

"It is scarcely more credible to believe the *charges* that followed the crime."

Knowlton gave tribute to Lizzie: "The prisoner at the bar is
a woman, and a Christian woman, as the expression is used.
It is no ordinary criminal that we are trying today. It is one of
the rank of lady, the equal of your wife and mine, of your
friends and mine, of whom such things had never been suspected or dreamed before." So far, Knowlton sounded more
like the defense than the prosecution, but he did caution the
panel to step lightly over the label "Christian woman," for
"time and again have we been grieved to learn, pained to find,
that those who are set up to teach us the way of correct life
have been found themselves to be foul as hell inside." He also
warned that "While we revere [women] . . . they are human
like unto us. . . . If they lack in strength and coarseness and
vigor, they make up for it in cunning, in dispatch, in celerity,
in ferocity. If their loves are stronger and more enduring than
those of men, their hates are more undying, more unyielding,
more persistent."

After apologizing for being the one to prosecute Lizzie—
"the saddest duty of my life. . . . If now any word I say, any
evidence I state, any inference I draw, shall be done with any

purpose or intent to do that woman an injustice, may my right hand wither and my tongue cleave to the roof of my mouth," Knowlton apologized for the witnesses—"Men will not tell the truth always"—and for the evidence itself—"*It is scarcely worth while for me to recapitulate the evidence.* I will not do it." In essence, he told the jury that what they had heard was either lies given by perjurers or worthless evidence. The majority of the witnesses had testified for the prosecution.

Knowlton said that the murder of Abby Borden "is the key of the case . . . because the murderer of this man was the murderer of Mrs. Borden." This statement is hard to dispute, but, coupled with another Knowlton made later in his closing argument, it, more than *anything* else said or done during the trial, guaranteed Lizzie Borden's freedom.

Knowlton spent most of the first day outlining how Lizzie had killed Abby. He was even convincing in a few places. Although he first belittled the hatred Lizzie harbored for her stepmother and then ridiculed the animosity the five-year-earlier real estate transaction might have generated, he then, in a peculiar reversal, labored long and hard to show how important each emotion was.

Reviewing the fortresslike nature of the Borden house with its barbed wire, bars, double- and triple-locked doors, he reminded the jury that the enemy was "outside" the household. In his discourse on locked doors, it was only natural for him to stress the cellar door, which "was never unlocked except on the Tuesday before."

Knowlton became gruesomely serious as he outlined in vivid detail just how impossible it would have been for an outsider to have murdered Mrs. Borden without Lizzie Borden having seen or heard him. If any part of his case was solid against Lizzie, it was this. Knowlton went through each minute of the morning, locating all the players in their proper places at the proper times, each doing what he believed he or she was doing at that place and time. With no witnesses, his argument was circumstantial, but nevertheless wholly convincing. An outsider could *not* have murdered Abby Borden. To listen to Hosea Knowlton, one would believe it would have been strikingly impossible. But in every instance where he showed that an outsider could not have murdered Abby Borden without Lizzie's seeing or hearing him, the point could be countered immediately by the assumption that Lizzie Borden was an accomplice. An outsider, acting alone, might not have killed Andrew and Abby, but someone else— someone acting with Lizzie's knowledge and cooperation— did.

Just as Robinson spent an unusual amount of time proving Mrs. Borden had received a note calling her away from the house, Knowlton spent an equal amount proving she did not. Robinson lied; Knowlton used logic; the jury yawned. And the court adjourned for the day.

On the next morning, after another apology to the members of the jury for keeping them separated from their homes and loved ones for another day, Knowlton agreed that no motive had been shown. But that was of no consequence since "motive is not part of the case of the Commonwealth. We are called upon to prove the thing was done, and our duty stops there."

The legend quotes Knowlton as having said in his closing argument that he did not believe Lizzie Borden killed her father. He did *not* say this, but in what must be one of the most inconceivable and ill-chosen statements ever made by a member of the prosecution in a trial, he made it exceedingly easy for this interpretation of what he *did* say to reach the ears of all who heard him.

He said, "There may be that in this case which saves us from the idea that Lizzie Andrew Borden planned to kill her father. I hope she did not. I should be slow to believe she did. I should be slow to ask you to believe that she did." Knowlton did not say he hoped Lizzie did not kill her father. Rather, he was conceding that the murder was not premeditated, that she did not *plan* to kill her father. The ease with which this was misunderstood is shown in that when Robert Sullivan, a former judge, quoted Knowlton in *Goodbye Lizzie Borden*, he misquoted him. "Then came this incredible statement from the prosecutor: 'I should be slow to believe Lizzie Andrew Borden killed her father. I hope she did not'" (page 170).

Earlier the jury had heard Knowlton say, "The murderer of

this man was the murderer of Mrs. Borden." Now they *heard*—unless they were listening very carefully—him say he did not believe Lizzie Borden killed Mr. Borden.

The trial was over.

Earlier Knowlton had told the jury, "If you had read of this account in any tale of fiction, you would have said, 'That will do for a story,' but such things never happen.'" This observation should not be limited to just the actions of the day of the murders. The actions of Knowlton himself were most certainly stranger than fiction would normally allow.

Knowlton defended Officer Medley and his observation of undisturbed dust on the floor of the barn's loft. His most telling point here was Medley's statement that the barn door, when he first entered, was closed and pinned with a spike through the hasp eye. All the other barn visitors had claimed the door was open when they entered.

Knowlton stressed that Lizzie had plenty of time to clean up or conceal any blood spatters she received when she hacked Mrs. Borden. With regard to Mr. Borden, however, he seemed to question whether Lizzie could have killed him. "But as to the second murder," he proclaimed, "the question is one of more difficulty, I cannot answer it. You cannot answer it. You are neither murderers or women. You have neither the craft of the assassin nor the cunning and deftness of the sex."

He reviewed Lizzie's quick-dress-change act with intelligent arguments based on obvious facts. The dress in evidence was not the dress Lizzie had worn when the murders occurred. He pointed out that none of the trained searchers who looked at all her dresses on Thursday, on Friday, and again on Saturday had found a dress stained with paint. On Saturday all had checked the very hook Emma testified held the dress Lizzie burned; no one else had seen it. Knowlton questioned why an avowed Christian woman would choose the hour when bells were chiming to call the devout to services to burn a hitherto-unseen-by-anyone-but-Emma paint-stained dress, a dress Lizzie herself admitted she had worn the morning of the day before the murders. He wondered aloud if the more thorough search announced for the day following the Sabbath, coupled with the announcement Saturday evening that she was a suspect, could have led her to burn her dress.

Discussing Lizzie's dress switch seemed to have triggered a change in Knowlton's attack. He suddenly seemed to be transformed into the fighter he was reputed to be. He conceded nothing; he suggested sensible possibilities; he challenged statements and testimony he had not challenged or questioned when they were made or given. It was, of course, too late. The jury remembered all he had said previously.

Knowlton next speculated on the rolled-up paper ash seen by Harrington and what it was Lizzie could have used to protect herself from the splatters of blood when she killed Abby and Andrew. He pointed out that Emma's and Alice Russell's testimonies were at odds with each other in places and asked the jury, "Which of the two women is worthy of credence?" He praised Miss Alice Russell as "loyal to them, but she was loyal to the God in her soul."

He then discussed the axe and hatchets that had been entered into evidence. "Perhaps it may have impressed some of you—that if this crime was done by someone within the house, although she might burn a dress, although she might conceal the blood spots, although she might do many things to hide perishable articles, a hatchet must be within the walls of the house *unless it was carried out* by some accessory after the fact. And the latter proposition is very difficult to believe. Out of all the interested people in this case, let me say once and for all that I know of no one who is capable of doing it *that has been produced here* as a witness in the case."

Once again, Knowlton went through the step-by-step actions of the murderer to prove that an intruder could not have committed the crimes with Lizzie and Bridget in or around the house. Again, by doing so he demonstrated how easy it would have been for someone who was not a stranger to have committed both murders exactly as they were committed *if* Miss Lizzie was an accomplice, regardless of Bridget's presence outside, in the barn for water, or on the third floor of the house resting.

274

## Charge to the Jury

The last major speech in Lizzie Borden's superior court trial was made by Justice Justin Dewey in the name of the court. It was the charge to the jury, and it was as bizarre as the rest of the case. This was the last pitch made before the carnival tent was folded and moved to some other place in the Commonwealth where other voters could watch their duly elected and properly appointed servants perform feats of magic and sleight of hand, could gape open-mouthed and marvel.

Justice Dewey's charge to the jury was straightforward: He told the jury to find Lizzie innocent. It was the honorable thing to do.

He began by outlining the limitations imposed on him by state law. "The court shall not charge juries with respect to matters of fact. The intention is to prevent the judges presiding at the trial from expressing *any opinion* as to the credibility of the witnesses or the strength of evidence."

The guile of this political veteran beams through with his next words. Knowing what he intended to do to assure Lizzie's freedom, Dewey added a disclaimer. "It will be *your* duty, in considering and deciding the matters of fact necessary to render your verdict, not to allow your judgment to be affected by what you may suppose or believe to be the opinion of the court upon such matters of fact."

Justice Justin Dewey was an "honorable" man. He warned the jury that his personal conviction of Miss Lizzie's innocence was so strong he was going to violate his oath, his office, and the laws of the commonwealth to tell them why he felt that way. However, they, the jury, must not allow this once-in-a-century departure from all that is legal and proper to influence them.

Had he kept still about his criminal action (there is no question but that he broke the letter of the law, not just the spirit of it), Dewey might have escaped the public censure heaped on him in later years. However, in another break with moral behavior, tradition, and good taste, he bragged about his effect on the jury to an interviewer immediately after the trial. "I was satisfied when I made my charge to the jury that the verdict would be 'not guilty,' although one cannot always tell what a jury will do."

Any one of the many statements Justin Dewey made arguing Lizzie's innocence would have been unusual and improper. Taken together, they constitute a new low in Massachusetts jurisprudence.

"I understand the government to concede that the defendant's character has been good; that it has not been merely a negative and neutral one that nobody heard anything against, but one of positive, of active benevolence in religious and charitable work. The question is whether the defendant, *being such as she was*, did the acts charged against her.

"You have the right to take into consideration her character. In some cases it may not be esteemed of much importance. In other cases it may raise a reasonable doubt of a defendant's guilt, *even in the face of strongly incriminating circumstances.*

"Her father left an estate of from $250,000 to $300,000, and that *so far as is known to the defendant, he died without having made a will* [italics added].

This was a clever transition. The restriction of "so far as is now ascertained" that was so necessary several days before is no longer needed. The declaration of "no will" is now solid fact.

"All would admit that the necessity of establishing the presence of the defendant in the house, when, for instance, her father was killed, is a necessary fact. The government could not expect that you would find her guilty of the murder of her father *by her own hand* unless you are satisfied that she was where he was when he was murdered. And, if the evidence left you in reasonable doubt as to that fact so vital, so absolutely essential, the government must fail of its case."

Dewey touched two chords here: first, upon Lizzie's non-charged role as an accomplice and, of greater importance, where she was at the time of the crime. If she were in the barn or under the pear tree enjoying God's bountiful gifts while she rested from her morning's laborious chores of ironing a few handkerchiefs, then she must be innocent. Since the government could not prove she was not doing all these things, it had failed to place her inside the house. Hence, she was not the murderer.

"However numerous may be the facts in the government's process of proof tending to show the defendant's guilt, if there is a fact established which cannot be reasonably reconciled with her guilt, then guilt cannot be said to be established."

Justice Dewey's conscience must have pricked him after that statement, for he added another disclaimer. "Now, gentlemen, you know that I am expressing no opinion as to what was proved. I am only trying to illustrate principles and rules of law and evidence."

Five expert witnesses had testified for the prosecution, and they were in general agreement in all things. Justice Dewey attempted to cancel the testimony of these expert witnesses and of all experts for all time. "Now the government has called as witnesses some gentlemen of scientific and medical knowledge and experience, who are termed experts. Expert testimony constitutes a class of evidence which the law requires you to subject to careful scrutiny. It is a matter of frequent observation to see experts of good standing expressing *conflicting and irreconcilable views* upon questions arising in a trial. They sometimes manifest a strong bias or partisan spirit in favor of the party employing them. They often exhibit a disposition to put forward theories rather than to verify or establish or illustrate facts."

Next on Justice Dewey's agenda was the final rape of justice. Lizzie faced three dangers: conviction as the murderer of Abby and Andrew, conviction as an accomplice to the murderer, and conviction as a conspirator with the murderer. The first of these was no longer a danger; the other two were.

When he suggested a directed verdict, Moody opened a door. Following his suggestion would have placed Lizzie in peril of being tried at a later date on either of the other two charges, of which she was actually guilty. The Mellen House agreement would not permit this to happen. If the agreement would not allow her to be found guilty of murder, it would also not allow her to be tried later as an accomplice to murder or as a conspirator with the murderer.

The situation was most delicate. Although the government's evidence was not good enough to convict Lizzie as the murderer, it was more than good enough to convict her as an accomplice. At Knowlton's request, Dewey swept the whole proposition under the rug without a single tremor disturbing the statue of justice that stood upon it.

"Now, gentlemen, I have been asked by the counsel for the Commonwealth to give you instructions upon another view of this case, a view, so far as I remember, *not suggested in the opening, or in the evidence, or hardly in the closing arguments for the Commonwealth* [italics added]. And yet the evidence is of such a nature that it seems to us that as a matter of law, the government is entitled to have some instruction given you on this point; as a matter of fact, it would be entirely for you to consider whether the claim of the government upon the matter to which I am going to refer is consistent with the claim it has urged on you; whether the government has not put this case to you, practically, upon the idea that the defendant did these acts with her own hands.

"But it is a principle of law that a person may be indicted in just the form in which this defendant is indicted, that is, indicted as if she were charged with doing the act herself, and yet she may be convicted upon the evidence which satisfies a jury beyond a reasonable doubt that the act was done personally by another party, and her relationship to it was that of being present, aiding, abetting, sustaining, encouraging. If she stood in such a relation as that to the act, the act was done by some other person and she aided him, encouraged him, abetted him, was present somewhere, by virtue of an understanding with him, where she could render him assistance, and for the purpose of rendering assistance, then she would be a principal in the act just as much as the other party who might be acting.

". . . If there was another party in this crime, and if she is proved beyond reasonable doubt to have sustained the relation to him in committing that crime which I have expressed to you, then she might be held under this indictment because under such circumstances in the eye of the law, they both being in the sense of the law present, the act of one is the act of both."

Justice Dewey stressed the positive side of this discussion, which told the jury that if they believed Lizzie Borden had acted in concert with some person, totally unknown, totally unnamed, she should be convicted just as if she had acted alone.

What he did *not* say was that if she was found innocent now, under the double jeopardy protection of the Constitution (state or federal) she would be innocent forever, regardless of anything a murderer found later might credit her with having done.

Justice Dewey had just a few loose ends left to clean up. No one had questioned why Lizzie had not testified, and so he volunteered an explanation. He "quoted" her: "She may say, 'I have already told to the officers all that I know about the case, and my statements have been put in evidence: whatever is mysterious to others is also mysterious to me. I have no knowledge more than others have. I have never professed to be able to explain how or by whom these homicides were committed.'"

This "statement," made by any judge just before a jury was set to withdraw to consider a verdict, is beyond credence, even by Massachusetts standards. Dewey followed this with what is a very strange explanation. "If she testifies, she becomes a witness with *less* than the privileges of an ordinary witness. She is subject to cross-examination." This last statement makes no sense. *All* witnesses are subject to cross-examination.

Dewey still had two final rounds in his musket. One was an out-and-out plea for a verdict of not guilty, and the other was to tell the jury not to worry about all the confusing testimony about dresses that were burned or not burned.

"If you are convinced beyond reasonable doubt of the defendant's guilt, it will be your plain duty to declare that conviction by your verdict. If the evidence falls short of producing such conviction, although it may raise a suspicion of guilt or even a strong possibility of guilt, it would be your plain duty to return a verdict of not guilty. If not legally proved to be guilty, the defendant is entitled to a verdict of not guilty.

"Lay aside for the moment the question of the identification of this dress that is presented. Taking the evidence of these several witnesses, considering that evidence carefully, comparing part with part, can you, gentlemen, extract from that testimony such a description of a dress as would enable you from the testimony to identify the dress?"

279

Justice Dewey ran on and on and finally ran down. The jury deliberated for nearly seventy minutes and then declared Lizzie not guilty. After the trial, the New Bedford *Mercury* reported of them, "'We made up our minds on this case when the government finished putting in its evidence,' said one of the jurymen. 'After we reached the jury room we took but one ballot and we were unanimous on this for acquittal.'"

The ballot was voted less than thirty minutes after they began their deliberation. No one examined any of the exhibits. Some of the jurors favored reporting at once, but the foreman advised staying out for an hour. Otherwise, he said, it might appear that they had not been "reasonably deliberative." The remaining time was spent in plans for the future. "We are going to form a permanent association and meet from time to time. Tomorrow we are to have our photograph taken, and we shall send one to Lizzie."

For the first time in almost eleven months, Lizzie Andrew Borden was free to spend her time and her inheritance in any manner she chose. Her first evening of freedom was spent at a dinner party given in her honor by Mr. and Mrs. Charles J. Holmes. During the party, Banker Holmes graciously allowed an interview which the *Globe* reported.

> When the Banker was asked about the verdict he replied, "I expected it. On the ride over Miss Borden spoke of the friends who had clung to her since her trouble began, and said she could never forget them. She spoke also of the very grateful feeling she had for her counsel, and wondered at their zeal and faithfulness."
>
> Mr. Holmes added he had not heard of Miss Borden's intention not to go back to the old house but to build on the hill, the ultra fashionable portion of the city.
>
> News of Miss Borden's whereabouts soon spread, and by 10 o'clock Mr. Holmes's house was a Mecca for the more intimate friends of the now free woman. After the repast, congratulations poured in on Lizzie, the party repaired to the west room and had a merry time.
>
> Lizzie's levee lasted until a very late hour.

Later on there were many gala parties at Maplecroft. Lizbeth was a free and wealthy woman.

# Chapter 16

O n the other side of Fall River, but less than two miles from the murder house, is Maplecroft, now 306 French Street. Its fourteen rooms, four bathrooms, carriage house, spacious gardens, and staff of housekeeper, maid, cook, and coachman became Lizzie's modest home immediately after her acquittal. It has survived the years and stands almost exactly as it did when Lizzie lived there.

When she moved here, Lizzie proclaimed her name henceforth "Lizbeth" and the manor house "Maplecroft." Changing her own name was acceptable, but the second naming was a grave social error, one less forgivable than the mere accusation of murder. The Hill did not serve high tea; they eschewed scones; they did not know golf or polo; they knew nothing of cricket or rugby; they did not ride to the hounds. They never, *never* named their estates.

Lizzie had named hers and, as an added affront to good taste, had the name chiseled into the top stone of the front entrance. All who passed by must see it; all who entered were confronted with it as they climbed the granite steps. The result was predictable: those who were offended made certain they were never in a position to see it. In her new life, "Lizbeth of Maplecroft" had very few guests from Fall River and even fewer who used the front entrance.

The chiseled stone is still in place today. It is still as out of place in this sedate neighborhood as a flashing neon sign proclaiming the availability of inexpensive overnight lodging.

Even today you can look up the street from Maplecroft and

*Maplecroft, date unknown, but while Lizzie was its occupant.*

see the remaining reminder of The House on The Hill. This magnificent property was the Brayton Estate. A wing of a hospital sits on that property now, but most of the low granite wall that girded The House has been spared, perhaps as a memorial.

The Braytons were Fall River in the 1890s. They were preeminent in wealth, power, respect, charity, and every other social category. They took, as Andrew took; but they gave, as Andrew did not.

While The House was a palace, it was not pretentious. The grounds were immaculate and open for all to see. Only a low, open fence separated the formal gardens from the outside world. You could look to your heart's content, and it was magnificent.

The palace faced out onto the beginning of Highland Avenue, which is a full thirty-seven feet wider than Pennsylvania Avenue in Washington, D.C. The message was simple: Pennsylvania Avenue may have been first, but . . .

Andrew Borden could have purchased and lived in any of the other homes in this neighborhood. He chose the house he died in; and when he died, Lizzie chose hers.

*Maplecroft entrance today, with name chiseled in top granite step.* [PHOTO ARNOLD BROWN]

Lizzie's house is correctly situated, just slightly below The House, but about as close to it as she could get. Not that it mattered. Lizzie was never asked to the Brayton House, and the Braytons would never have entered hers. Right after the murders (before Lizzie became suspect), they did drop in at the murder house to pay their respects. That was the proper thing to do, you see. So, quite naturally, they did it.

The Borden sisters made one other change in their new home that raised eyebrows and questions that were never answered. In a neighborhood where doors were not locked in the daytime and, in summer, doors stood open at night to catch any worthwhile cooling breeze—a neighborhood where crime was unknown—the sisters had bars applied to all lower level windows and doors.

Both sisters had an unquestionable need to keep the unwanted from entering the house. The killer was out there. They knew who, and they knew where.

They also knew it could all happen again, and they were afraid.

# Part Three

Part Three

# Chapter 17

*S*eptember 1921

Ellan Eagan was finding it hard to keep up with things. Little Mary had married a man named Henry Hawthorne and soon after had become the mother of the cutest twin girls the world had ever seen (Pete Peterson, my friend in Florida who introduced me to Henry's writings, eventually married Dorothy, one of the twins). What a wonderful time to be alive! How blessed her whole family was! Mary's Henry was a successful salesman now with a brand new, factory fresh Model T Ford that had a centerdoor and a closed body and side windows that went up and down and a windshield that opened to let in a breeze as you went down the road and a speed meter that showed how fast you were going. Henry's sales route covered Taunton, New Bedford, Newport, Providence, and points in between, and he needed the car, he said, to cover more territory. Some days, when he had no more than one tire blowout, he could motor to *two* of the cities and still be home in time for supper.

Every Sunday since Henry had taken delivery of the Model T, Henry, Mary, Ellan, and the twins had been driving to places Ellan had always thought of as being far away. On this Sunday, they were on a picnic and would visit the old farm on which Henry had grown up, several miles north of Fall River. Henry was not sure he wanted to see the old place again because his memories of those early years were not the happiest.

Henry's early life was no secret. When he was a small lad, his parents were poor, and his father had served as a tenant farmer to a man named William Borden who had two hundred acres of farm land, most of it in apples. They gathered the man was strange. From some of the things Henry had told them, both Mary and Ellan guessed that William Borden might even have been "touched." They realized that Henry was just a small boy when his family lived on the farm, and they hoped he had exaggerated some of his stories. In any event, he told them that William Borden had died in 1901 in some horrible way, and Henry referred to him as merely a frightening boyhood memory.

The weather was nice for a drive, and the breeze blowing in the open windshield and passing out the side windows was a marvel. Ellan Eagan had never dreamed that riding in a motorcar could be so pleasant. They traveled the road along the Taunton River, through Assonet, stopped at the Dighton Rock and had a glass of lemonade still cool from Ellan's icebox, and finally arrived in East Taunton. Henry pointed out all the landmarks in the village he had known as a boy, but he seemed to falter as they passed King's Furnace Cemetery and murmured that William Borden was buried there. He finally turned off the main road onto Liberty Street. Here he stopped the car in front of a farmhouse, sat, and just stared, saying nothing to anyone.

They quickly found a quiet spot by the side of the road in full view of the farm and ate the contents of Ellan's basket. After lunch, the twins found some insects worth collecting, and Henry began telling of his early years in the area.

The living was hard. There was always a roof over their heads in the winter and always enough to eat, but there was never a penny for anything not necessary. Henry's first memory of the landlord was one of absolute fright: William Borden had chased him with a hatchet. It was all in fun, of course, Henry's mother told him as she hugged and comforted the scared, sobbing six-year-old. She told the boy that his tormentor might be real scary but certainly was harmless. For as long as the family lived there, Henry was never fully convinced of this. The older Henry grew, the more sure he was that Bill Borden was not harmless.

Just before the turn of the century, Henry's father found a

job in Fall River and the family moved, but the fear stayed with Henry. Finally, in 1901 Bill Borden died, and Henry, not yet a teenager, sighed with a heartfelt relief he could not understand. He still had nightmares.

Both his wife and Ellan Eagan knew most of Henry's story, but here in sight of the scene of his boyhood ordeal, it somehow seemed more alive, more personal. Mrs. Eagan felt Henry wanted to clear the air and that it was her duty to help him. She asked questions she normally would have considered none of her business.

She learned that, on what he considered to be instructions from his mother, Henry forced himself to subdue his fear of William Borden, and they became pals of sorts. About the time he was eight years old, Henry realized that grown-up Bill was mentally about the same age as he was and the games Bill played were boy games played as a grown man would play them. Henry's favorite toys of the moment might include a top, a baseball, and a slingshot; Bill had just one toy, year in and year out: his hatchet, which was always close at hand. Henry played boys' games with his toys; Bill chopped, cut, and killed things with his. Whenever they sat and talked boy talk, Bill produced a whetstone and stroked the blade edge of his hatchet with a sensual rhythm impossible for an eight-year-old to understand.

Bill told Henry strange stories of evil women and evil men, of rich men and rich sisters, of wealth that would some day all be his, of the power and strength and the terror he could generate, of places in which he had been locked up away from everybody, of the marvelous things a hatchet could do and some which no one had ever guessed, like his big secret—his secret so big that no one could ever hear of it because it was too big for human ears. His hatchet knew, but it would never tell. Whenever Bill spoke of his "secret," his eyes came alive and almost glowed.

Henry told Ellan and Mary of one cold winter's day when he went into the cider shed and found Bill intoxicated from "ice cider." Bill practiced the age-old New England art of making a brandy-type product known as applejack, a commodity much in demand in the area where rum had always been considered the Devil's brew. When cider had turned properly, it was casked and frozen in the first New England cold snap. The core was then tapped with a skill handed down from father to son and the applejack drawn off. Bill Borden was not above selling his prize to his psalm-singing Puritan neighbors, but he never offered it for sale before he had sampled it to ensure its quality, which established its price.

Alcohol made Bill Borden into a happy, truly harmless, talkative drunk. After Bill's vision focused on Henry, who had just entered the shed that first time, Bill waxed maudlin about having but two friends in life. He told Henry his hatchet had been his only friend until Henry's family moved there. He told his hatchet he was sorry it could not taste this year's first applejack because it was the best ever and he owed so much to both his friends and he hoped they liked each other and they should all taste his magnificent creation and he wanted to share all that he owned with both his friends so here's a cupful of his first-of-the-season and you and me will drink a toast to our other friend who can't taste it but who has tasted other things unknown to any living person.

Henry had learned to accept Bill's strange rambling and seldom listened to the words, just to the tone of the voice, from which he could sense moods and gauge their sometimes violent changes. This was the happiest state in which he had ever seen Bill Borden. Why applejack should cause this fired Henry's innate curiosity. Bill handed him a cupful.

Predictably, the first sip produced the sensation of filling his mouth with flaming kerosene. Henry's reaction sent Bill into resounding gales of hideous laughter. Henry's second sip was of pure, flaming poison. The third was fire and foul taste. The fourth was still fire, but the taste had improved. The fifth had no fire, and the sixth was damned good.

Henry's mother went looking for him when he didn't appear for supper and found Bill and Henry asleep. Henry remembered being more sick afterward than he had known was possible. Every time he lost his innards, his father forced him to drink some "medicine," and five minutes later he was sick again. It worked. Henry Hawthorne was never again sick from the abuse of hard liquor, not because he shunned it, but because he respected it.

Henry told his wife and his mother-in-law of how Bill had taught him all the secrets of cider making. Bill was married, but his wife Rebecca was sickly and he knew he would never have a son. So Henry was told to pay attention and learn. Henry was scared to death, but he was proud to learn Bill's secrets and did as he was ordered. Henry once asked Bill if his father had taught him all these secret things.

"The deacon taught me a lot; my father didn't teach me nothin'—but I sure taught him," was his reply. Before Henry could ask another question, Bill slipped into one of the funks that Henry recognized as demanding his respectful withdrawal.

After that, Bill told Henry many a wild tale. Although he listened to the words with only half an ear, Henry was able to piece together that Bill's father, Deacon Borden, who lived in Fall River, was not his natural father but had adopted Bill at a very young age. The deacon and Bill both knew who his real father was, but nobody else did; it was a secret, and it didn't matter now. Over and over Henry was told that Bill's real father was dead. Bill's comments meant nothing to him; grown men like Bill didn't need a father! Boys like Henry did.

Henry knew that graduation from his year-long apple knocker's apprenticeship required him to sample the cask set aside with "Henry" chalked on it. Henry was anxious to taste the applejack he had made, but he had no intention of repeating his horrible first year's experience.

On the appointed day and with every deliberate step conducted under Bill's watchful eye, Henry tapped his barrel. Bill smiled proudly at his student but refused Henry's offer of the first sip. Fairly bursting with anticipation, Henry took it himself. It again tasted like a mouthful of flaming kerosene.

Bill laughed almost hysterically. Between gasps for breath, he sampled Henry's private brew and pronounced him a "Master Apple Knocker" with all the rights and privileges of the high office. "You know," Henry said, digressing from his story, "I learned years later that all applejack tastes the same if the cider is good and the casks are cleaned properly. Bill had me hornswoggled. He taught me a trade based on hard labor, and he taught me that hard labor was not for me, so I guess I should be grateful to the b—"

Henry stopped short because the twins were within earshot, but suddenly he realized for the first time in his life that Bill Borden *was* a bastard in the true sense of the word. Why had he never thought of that before? Soon Henry returned to his story.

Henry stuck to his resolve that afternoon and sipped all that Bill offered but spit out most of it when Bill wasn't looking and dumped the rest on the ground. It was an annual ritual for Bill to drink himself senseless on this first tapping day (it was the only time Henry knew him to drink any intoxicants), and Bill expressed his pride in his new graduate's ability to keep pace with him. Henry made a game out of acting silly and giggled enough to match Bill's metamorphosis into the happiest man on earth.

Bill again talked to his ever-present hatchet as if it were a third person in the cider house, as alive as Henry. As Bill sampled more applejack, more and more of what he said was directed to the hatchet, almost as if Henry were not in the shed. He told his hatchet of all the things his other friend, Henry, had learned and how he wished his hatchet could taste the applejack. He was glad they were all friends and, saying that, he turned toward Henry with eyes that were burning but no longer seeing. Henry felt a chill he had never felt before.

Bill told his hatchet that his other friend had asked about his father, and this brought on another fit of loud and frightening laughter that stopped instantly when Bill said: "You knew my father and that fat sow he married when he should have married my mother. Of course you knew them; you were there when they died!"

Henry was instantly as sick as he had been the previous year, but this sick was different. He was sick from outright terror, his terror of Bill Borden's words and his eyes and of his voice and his hatchet. Henry ran as fast as he could to a private place he knew in the middle of the orchard and stayed there until he realized the shivering in his limbs was no longer from fear but from the early winter cold.

Ellan Eagan was shivering too. Henry had finished his story, and Mary was gathering the twins and all the party things for the long trip home. Ellan had felt Henry's terror,

*Ellan Eagan at age 62*
[PHOTO COURTESY LEWIS
"PETE" PETERSON]

and she was quiet all the way home. Mary was sure they had tired poor mother to the point of exhaustion.

Ellan Eagan was not sure what her next step should be. She spent two weeks putting together a picture that was slowly taking form and was almost complete. There were still pieces missing, but she was sure that Henry could supply them when he answered the simple questions she would ask him. She had written down all her old facts as she remembered them from that day so long ago. Her memory of that day was clearer now than ever. Now she could see that man in the Borden yard as just another human being without the supernatural aura she had attributed to him. She could see him in clear, concise detail.

Ellan then made a second list, one that contained all the things Henry had said over the years about Bill Borden, especially those he had told them on the Sunday outing. She had a good picture of him, too. Her third list contained things that had been said at Lizzie Borden's trials about the murderer when somebody assumed it was someone other than Lizzie. She found lots of this in her own collection of newspaper clippings supplemented by what she could find in the local library.

Ellan had been skeptical at first, but she found nothing had been said about the Bordens' murderer that didn't fit her list or Henry's. They weren't always on all three, of course, because her personal list was short, but there was enough agreement to make her feel she knew something no one else knew. Henry was the key to the few items still missing, but before she asked him anything she had to be sure. She went over what she did know one more time, and then another, and another, and then once again.

For a long time Henry had described Bill Borden as a giant of a man—tall and big and menacing. The man she had seen was not tall and not big. For as long as Henry had spoken of Bill Borden, she had absolutely no reason to connect them.

However, on the picnic at the farm that Sunday, Henry had been surprised to see so many of the outbuildings and structures still standing and unchanged. He took Ellan and Mary to a fenced corner of the property to see if his "escape hatch" had survived. He explained that sometimes when Bill chased him brandishing his hatchet, he headed for this corner of the fence and squeezed through a small gap.

When they got to the corner, they found a small, triangular hint of a gap, but Henry guessed it had been fixed. At that instant, one of the twins spotted a butterfly on a flower inside the lot line but out of reach and slipped through the gap as easily as anything. Henry stared in disbelief. "That's right! I was about her size when we lived here. No wonder things look so much smaller! All these years I've remembered Bill Borden as a menacing ogre ten feet tall. But I remember—when he wanted to look over that fence there he had to stand on tiptoe. I can look over it easy. *He was shorter than I am!*"

This had been the first piece of Ellan's puzzle.

The next Friday evening Mary had to attend a meeting of women voters, and Ellan was more than happy to stay with the twins. Henry had spent the day in Boston and had arrived home only ten minutes after Mary had left. At the last minute, the twins had been invited to have supper with a next door playmate, and so Ellan found herself alone with her son-in-law. After preparing him something to eat and while her resolve was at its highest, Ellan placed herself across from Henry, stared directly into his eyes, and without any introduction asked him, "Did Bill Borden ever smell different from anything normal?"

"What the heck!" Henry was startled and amused.

"Just tell me. Did Bill Borden ever stink real bad?" she persisted, almost begging.

"He was a farmer. He killed and gutted chickens and ducks, he slaughtered many a horse, he butchered pigs and cows, and anytime anyone shot a deer he was the one they called upon to butcher it. He mucked his barn twice a day. Of course he stunk. I never knew a farmer who didn't. Why?"

"No," she said sternly. "Was there ever a time when he smelled of stink you can't describe?"

"No," he told her honestly. "But I remember the time he made *me* stink to high heaven, if that answers your question. I'll never forget that awful stench, and I swore I would never smell like that again."

"Well, I hope you never do, too, whatever it was. Tell me about it." They both seemed to relax as Henry returned to his boyhood days with the newfound confidence that he could handle all the frightening memories that had lingered so long in his life.

If there was any secret in the laying in and storing of apple cider, it was to keep the equipment and the final container absolutely clean. Many a lazy householder found he had stored a liquid useless even for vinegar because some unwanted mold or yeast had formed in the cask and had turned the cider bad. Hard oak casks were usually used for cider, but wood is an organic material with pores and cracks where unwanted spores can hide. It was best to clean casks when they were emptied but often they were set aside and were not cleaned until they were ready to be filled the next season. Cleaning them was a hard task. Every snake oil salesman offered commercial cleaners for this purpose, but most apple farmers made their own cask cleaners. Each was convinced his was the best and kept the ingredients and amounts a closely guarded secret. Bill Borden was no exception.

Bill was not above playing pranks on Henry. One memorable practical joke occurred when he told Henry how to clean himself after the last hard day of cleaning the casks. When Henry had finished the cleaning to Bill's satisfaction, Bill handed him a jar of something that looked like axle grease and a cake of lye soap and told him to be sure and rub this secret grease on all the spots of his body where the cider residue and the cleaner had come in contact. Henry did exactly as he was told and, when he got into the waterhole that was a summertime bath tub, every part of his skin he had rubbed with Bill's grease began to burn. When the burning stopped, he noticed the foulest odor he had ever smelled. He sniffed the water, the soap, the rag; they all smelled awful. He dried and dressed and ran from the waterhole, but the stench seemed to follow him.

Henry had to sleep in the barn that night and for the next three nights, too, which was no hardship to a young farm boy. It seemed that the livestock grew restless in his presence though, as if he offended them. He knew he offended any human who came within yards of him. The smell lasted two weeks.

"What did it smell like?" Ellan asked, more serious than Henry had ever seen her.

"Well, you know the sickening sweet smell that boiling horsemeat gives off?" he asked. "Add rotting apples and a rotten egg and just a touch of skunk. *That* smell would be perfume compared to this one. It was awful. And the worst part was that after the first few hours, I didn't smell it myself, but anytime I came near anyone, they sure did. And they were all free with their opinion. Except Bill. You know, I don't think he could smell it either."

Henry added that during his war service he had kidded a veterinarian about the perpetual odor of his boots, and the vet had told him that horse urine had high concentrates of many waste product chemicals in it and that sniffing it was one of the quickest ways to determine imbalances that could point directly to possible health problems in the animal. The vet then delivered an unasked-for lecture on the possible variations in odor that could occur and the ramifications of each.

Henry didn't really listen until the doctor mentioned a fatal

*Henry Hawthorne and Mary Ellan Eagan Hawthorne* [PHOTO COURTESY LEWIS "PETE" PETERSON]

disease called Blister Beetle Poisoning and the related stench always found in the dead horse's bladder. He had laughed when the vet mentioned that the blister beetle is also known as "Spanish Fly," but he stopped laughing when the doctor added that getting any of the dead horse's urine on your own skin was not recommended unless you wanted to be ostracized from the human race until it wore off. When Henry asked if it could be washed off with soap and water, he was told that water would make it worse. Naphtha would be preferred.

"Your Bill Borden acted as a vet or a renderer, didn't he? He removed dead horses, you told me," Ellan stated.

"Oh, I figured it out that Bill had added something to that jar of salve he gave me to use long before the vet explained what it might have been. Tell me, Mother Eagan, what's this all about?"

"No, not yet. Let me make sure first, and then I'll tell you."

Over the next few weeks Ellan went over her lists again and again. She would ask Henry another question now and then, almost always when Mary was not in earshot.

"You told me Bill never left the farm without his hatchet. How did he carry it?"

"He put it in what he called his 'doctor's bag,' which was a coarse homespun schoolboy's bag with drawstrings. First thing he would do was stow that bag under the seat of his buggy, generally before he hitched his team, even."

"Did he have a long duster of the same material?"

"I haven't thought about that coat in years! How did you know about it?"

"Please, Henry. Tell me about it."

"Well, when he worked around the farm, he wore work clothes that were generally filthy. We all did. Bill seemed to enjoy his butchering, but he did not like blood. It was almost like he was afraid of it. He was really a master of neatness. The other farmers marveled when he felled a horse with one blow of that hatchet of his. In almost the same swing he would put the blade through the horse's skull with almost no blood except what drained out. I heard folks say what a real skill that was. Anyway, there was a story all over town of something that happened before we moved there.

"It seems there was this day when he was visiting someplace in his good suit when he heard that a neighbor had a horse that had to be put down. Well, they went to that neighbor's house, and when the fellow saw Bill dressed in his good suit he said, 'Never mind. Come back tomorrow when you're dressed proper.' Bill was never one for people to tell him what to do, and so he said he could do his job dressed like a banker and never worry. You can guess what happened. Bill was showing off, of course, and as sometimes happens when you do, something went wrong. When he delivered the second blow to the horse, blood spurted enough to cover three counties and Bill's suit was a bloody mess. Those who had gathered to watch thought it was the funniest thing to come down the pike in years, but the more they laughed, the madder Bill got. He chopped and chopped and chopped at that poor carcass until the head was mincemeat, and then he turned on those who were laughing. He scared the wits out of them, and something real awful might have happened except the horse's owner was the first one Bill headed for with the bloody hatchet waving over his head. The man happened to have a pistol in his belt because he already had made up his mind to shoot the animal when he learned that Bill was in the neighborhood. Anyway, he showed Bill that pistol, and Bill remembered his manners real quicklike. He lowered the hatchet, asked the man for his dollar fee, was paid, and left.

"After that, he had his wife make him an extra long custom-fitted duster out of homespun, and any time he left the farm in his town clothes, that duster was packed under the seat alongside of his hatchet. And, you know, I never heard tell of his ever causing another blood-spurter after that. He still had that duster when we lived there, and it was as spotless as the day Miss 'Becca made it for him. And now it's my turn. How did you know about it?"

"Not yet," was all Ellan answered. "Not just yet."

Mary and the twins had gone downstreet shopping, and Henry had set out his week's order slips on the dining room table. He had just started summarizing what had to have been his best week ever when his mother-in-law entered the room with a determined air about her. He found his work interesting, but it would be easy to postpone if Ellan was finally ready to share her strange occupation of the past weeks.

"Henry, please listen to me and don't interrupt. When you have heard what no one else has ever heard from me, tell me what you think, agreed?"

"Of course, Mother Eagan," he answered in genuine anticipation.

Ellan relived every moment of that morning of August 4, 1892. The story of her trip down Second Street and the maid washing the windows had been told a thousand times, as had the details of her coming up Second Street and going into Dr. Kelly's yard with an attack of morning sickness. But the story of her few seconds when she was coming up the street and had a clear view into the Bordens' side yard had never been told to any human, saint, or God Himself. She told Henry every step, every sight, every sense, every feeling, every touch of terror she had felt. She told him of a face, a duster coat, of a schoolboy kind of bag, of eyes that burned like fire, of her panic, of police who would not listen, of putting the whole thing out of her mind until now. Then she told him of the unholy smell exactly as she sensed it and could now describe perfectly to him.

She fell silent. She was drained.

Henry Hawthorne said nothing at first. He stared at Ellan as if he were seeing her for the first time. Finally he sat back in his chair, pale, shaken, stunned by what she had said. He, too, had a vision of the past.

Drifting out of the depths of the haze produced by first-tapped applejack, he heard a voice—rambling, ranting, slurring, and slightly insane—speaking in a room containing cider casks, speaking to a most hallowed hatchet. "Of course you knew them. You were there when they died!"

"God help us," he managed to say at last. "He was telling the truth."

# Chapter 18

William Borden lived with his wife, Rebecca, on an apple farm in East Taunton, Massachusetts. It was on this farm that Henry Hawthorne had lived as a boy. William died on April 17, 1901, and his death certificate listed his age as forty-five years (but with no date of birth given), his father as Charles L. Borden, his mother as Phebe Hathaway, and his birthplace as Fall River. With a little investigation, it should be easy to piece together a picture of William Borden. But nothing is easy when it comes to learning about his life or his death.

Although the death certificate tells William's age, place of birth, and parentage, a search for his birth certificate is futile, for there is none on file, even though his death certificate lists Fall River as his birthplace. An extensive page-by-page search of the record books in Fall River showed that what is on file is a certificate of marriage between Charles Borden and Phebe Hathaway dated October 16, 1836. At Taunton, the Bristol County Registry of Deeds lists a request for probate of the will of this same Charles L. Borden who died on August 5, 1883. His widow, however, is not listed as Phebe Borden, but as *Peace* Borden. This request for probate lists Charles's children as Amanda M. Taylor of Fall River, Eliza A. Borden of Fall River, William S. Borden of Taunton, and Joseph H. Borden of Fall River. In addition, three grandsons are listed (Charles, Edward, and Theodore), all said to be children of Charles Borden, deceased, who was presumably a son of Charles L. Borden. Amanda M. Taylor, Eliza A. Borden, Joseph H. Borden, and Peace Borden all signed the request for probate. William S. Borden did not.

There is no death record of Phebe Hathaway, nor is there any marriage record of Charles Borden and Peace. There are, however, birth records for some of the children of Charles Borden:

> Hannah H. Borden—born September 21, 1844; mother's name recorded as Phebe
>
> Eliza A. Borden—born May 21, 1848; mother's name recorded as Phebe
>
> Eliza Borden—born May 23, 1850; mother's name recorded as Phebe
>
> (Male) Borden—born Decemer 27, 1860; mother's name recorded as *Peace*
>
> Joseph H. Borden—born December 27, 1861; mother's named recorded as *Peace*

There are no birth records for William S. or Charles, and there is no explanation for why there are two Elizas.

The available information from the Fall River City Clerk's office is not as complete, nor does it fit together as neatly as we might hope. "Male" Borden is more likely to be Charles than William because William's death certificate gave his age in 1901 as forty-five, which would put his birth in 1856.

It appears that Deacon Borden and Phebe and/or Peace recorded the birth of their children, all except William. Two explanations of why there is no record of William's birth are most possible. First, there is an archaic law in Massachusetts that even today directs birth records of illegitimate persons to be "impounded" and not to be available as public records. In searching for information about Bill Borden's birth, I was denied access to his birth records by this very law. Information about Bill Borden's birth found on his death certificate would have been available to the Fall River City Clerk's office, which issued the certificate, without being a matter of public record then or today if Bill's birth was illegitimate. The other possibility is that someone may simply have removed any record of his birth, not that difficult an act for the magicians who made Andrew Borden's will disappear. This is not as far-fetched as it might seem, for it appears that someone removed other records related to William S. Borden.

The same sleight-of-hand procedure was followed at the State Hospital in Taunton, an insane asylum. One hundred years ago, the Taunton *Daily Gazette* reported the comings and goings at the asylum with the same conscientiousness as it reported local meetings and events. On Sunday, April 20, 1901, the *Gazette* reported the following events in "Taunton and Vicinity":

> Not much promise for a pleasant Sunday.
>
> The Unitarian Sunday school has given $25 to the Children's Mission in Boston.
>
> Henry Taylor, colored, of Fall River, was brought to the Taunton Insane Hospital on Thursday.
>
> Delia Cooney was brought here from North Attleboro and committed to the insane asylum this morning.
>
> At the G.A.R. meeting at Duxbury on Patriots' Day comrade C.S. Anthony of Post 3 made a speech.

The same article noted the death of William, commenting that he "was undoubtedly insane. He spent a period in our asylum some years ago." Based on this report, it would seem that Bill had been committed to the asylum at least once. If so, official records should be available to verify this and tell us more about him. They are not, but there is every indication that they once were.

Three inquiries were made to the Taunton State Hospital. The first was an inquiry about William S. Borden with no indication as to why there was interest. On January 9, 1989, the following answer was received: "In reference to Borden, (William S.) (W.S.) (William I.), we were unable to locate the only file which appeared to be a match." Additional information was received from the same official on February 13, 1989: "A further search of our archives has failed to turn up additional records. However, I did learn that William S. Borden's card lists Amanda Taylor and Eliza Borden as sisters."

This response would confirm that William Borden had been committed at some time to the Taunton Insane Hospital. However, on April 6, 1989, the last of three communications was received—all from the same official—which was most peculiar, short, terse, to the point, and reproduced here in its entirety: "We do not have a record of admission to this facility, at all, ever. If he had been here, we would know."

It appears on the surface that at some time someone had reason to play fast and loose with records on file concerning William S. Borden, on both the city and the state levels.

Although we are not able to find out very much about the life of William Borden, his death is well documented, even if the record is confusing.

On April 17, 1901, the Fall River *Daily Globe* printed the following story:

### MADE SURE WORK.

#### New Boston Woods the Scene of Ghastly Crime

#### Suicide Resorted to Both Hanging and Poisoning

#### His Body Found Suspended from Limb of a Tree

An unknown man committed suicide at an early hour this morning in the woods off New Boston road. His lifeless body was found hanging to a tree. A six ounce bottle which had been drained of its contents—carbolic acid—and the body hanging to the tree with a stake chain used for keeping wood in position, drawn taught about the man's neck, told the story at a glance. The dead man is an utter stranger to the people of the neighborhood, at least to those who viewed the remains and there is nothing about the person which would give the least clue to his identity.

John F. Davis of 846 Meridian street, off New Boston road, is the man who first witnessed the ghastly spectacle. He left his home to do some work in his field nearby and in passing the wooded land some 50 yards or so west of the street, he saw the body hanging from the tree. A cursory examination convinced him that the man was dead and he then hastened to notify the police. He telephoned from Sam Hyde's farm to the Central police station. Inspector Shea received the summons and after notifying Medical Examiner Buck he went to the locality mentioned to make what investigation was deemed necessary on the part of the police.

The medical examiner and the inspector took charge of the body immediately upon their arrival. From their examination of the surroundings, they concluded that the suicide had first taken the dose of carbolic acid, after which he threw the bottle on the ground beside his hat, the only portion of his clothing that he had discarded. Presumably fearing that the carbolic acid might not prove the effective avenue through which he proposed to shuffle off this mortal coil, he adopted a more sure medium. Appearances indicated that he climbed the tree, fastened the stake chain securely about his neck and then let himself down. His feet were some four feet above the ground and the space from his head to the limb about which the chain was fastened was about three feet, so therefore he was virtually suspended in mid-air by his neck, with little danger of slipping the noose.

When Medical Examiner Buck had finished his customary examination Inspector Shea compiled a description of the dead man and his clothing, and by the means of which it is hoped to identify him. The inspector believes the man to be about 50 years of age and in life measured about 5 feet, 9 inches in height. He had a light complexion, with brown hair and moustache slightly mixed with gray, and blue eyes. His clothing was almost new, and had probably not been worn but a few times. A black overcoat covered a brown suit with a small check and he wore a pair of congress shoes. The discarded hat was a brown soft one.

Inspector Shea carefully searched for some papers or articles on his person by means of which identification might be acquired, but there was positively nothing which would give a clue to his family circle. A small canvas bag containing about $6 was found on his person, and that may be taken as an indication that starvation was not the prime reason for self-destruction.

The examiner and inspector agreed after they had completed their investigation that the suicide must have taken his life within a short time, probably not more than 12 hours before the discovery and perhaps but a very few hours before Mr. Davis came upon this unpleasant find. This conclusion was reached because the dead man's clothing was absolutely dry showing that he could not have committed the act until the rain had ceased falling, otherwise there would have been evidence of his exposure in the storm.

305

Another conclusion reached by Inspector Shea is that the man was probably a laborer or one used to hard work as a glance at his hands would show. From these deductions and description which the police will make the best possible use of, it is believed that the identity of the dead man will soon be disclosed.

The body is now at Winward's undertaking rooms, having been taken there at the request of the medical examiner.

The good citizens of Fall River and the surrounding environs had no trouble accepting this crime as suicide because they had no cause to suspect it as anything else. They certainly had no reason to connect it with the Borden murders that had taken place nine years earlier, nor did they have immediate reason to connect it to the Bertha Manchester murder eight years earlier. The *Globe*, the only newspaper to carry the story of the finding of the body, followed up the next day with an article that included its misidentification but did cite the coincidence that this tragedy happened on a site so close to the Manchester farm. Although the second story was close, it included nothing that allowed the public to grasp the significance of what happened.

The Hill's own *Herald* carried the follow-up story with the correct identification of the body; in retrospect, this, too, tells us much. Some details of this "suicide" beg for review.

The man drank from a six-ounce bottle of poison, placed the bottle and his hat side by side on the ground, climbed a tree, and secured a logging chain around his neck and to the limb of a tree in such a manner that he would be suspended with his feet four feet from the ground. There was a three-foot clearance between his head and the limb. Since he did all this in predawn darkness when he must have been more preoccupied with the task of making sure that the chain did not slip, he earns our respect for his athletic prowess. Consider that the poison he had taken before he began this difficult work may have clouded his judgment.

Assuming the distance from his neck to his shoes was five feet, while sitting on a branch twelve feet from the ground (three plus five plus four feet), he adjusted the chain's length to produce the proper distances and made sure it was wrapped properly in two places (not the least of which was his neck) to eliminate slippage. He then either jumped or fell off the limb, breaking his neck most violently, or he let himself down the chain hand over hand until it tightened around his neck choking off his air supply.

The man was dressed in what sounds like his best Sunday-go-to-meeting clothes as if, instead of suicide, he had planned to visit (or already had visited) someone of high status. If nothing else, he was most certainly overdressed for suicide by logging chain. Imagine picking up a heavy logging chain, carrying it to a tree, climbing to a branch twelve feet off the ground while wearing an overcoat and congress boots! What an amazing show of agility and determination for a man whose age was estimated at fifty years. He had gone to a fair amount of trouble to commit this supposed suicide, and yet he left no note or identification. It is difficult to imagine why he needed a good night's sleep before hanging himself, yet because of the weather that night (it rained until then, but his clothes were dry) we learn that he chose 4 o'clock in the morning as the most opportune time. And one cannot help but remember that the victims of the old horse operas of years ago were left hanging about four feet off the ground when the bed of the buckboard or farm wagon was used as the platform for the hanging.

Although they may have been coincidences, some of the names in this report ring a distant bell. The body was found by John F. Davis of Meridian Street; Uncle John was staying at a home owned by a Mr. Davis before the Borden murders. Meridian Street was where the Manchester farm was located where Manuel Correiro supposedly murdered Bertha Manchester. Winward's Undertaking Rooms is the same establishment that Lizzie Borden requested for her parents. It is comforting to know that in 1901 a mere six dollars would guarantee an unknown suicide the services of Fall River's finest "undertaking rooms."

Suicide indeed!

On the next day, April 18, 1901, the dead man was erroneously identified by the *Daily Globe* as George F. Borden:

307

## SUICIDE IDENTIFIED

### George F. Borden of East Taunton Was the Victim

George F. Borden, 38 Liberty street, East Taunton, is the man who committed suicide in the New Boston road woods, yesterday morning. The publication of the description of the dead man in yesterday's paper was a valuable assistant to the police department and early this morning Inspector Shea who figured in the case yesterday, was able to state positively who the dead man was.

Borden was formerly a resident of this city and will be known to many people when it is stated that he was a son of the late Deacon Charles Borden of Ninth street. From acquaintances of the family in this city it is learned that he has a wife living at the above address but no family. Two sisters of the suicide are in a Taunton institution. He has a half brother living in the person of William Lewis Bassett, a farmer of Westport.

An inquiry into Borden's movements previous to his suicidal action reveals the information that he was a lodger at the house of William Michen, Tuesday evening. Michen lives in a farmhouse in the territory about half way between New Boston road and the Manchester estate, where Bertha Manchester was murdered some years ago by José de Correiro.

It is learned that Borden conducted a profitable farm at his home in East Taunton. He would at intervals bring produce into the local market and always found ready buyers. It was his custom when intending to stay a night or two in this vicinity to be the guest of William Michen. From the latter's story it appears that Borden spent the night with him and about 4 o'clock yesterday morning, some time before Michen's usual hour of arising, Borden got up quietly and left the premises. The ice chains with which he hung himself to the tree where he was found by John F. Davis were taken from Michen's barn.

Inspector Shea's theory that Borden had taken a dose of carbolic acid and fearing that it might not prove effectual, then tied himself up to the tree, has been accepted by Borden's acquaintances here as the plan followed.

The police deduction that the suicide had been committed within a few hours, at least, since the rain ceased falling, is borne out by the story Michen tells, and therefore when Mr. Davis discovered the body at 8 o'clock Borden could not have been dead more than four hours.

Mrs. Borden, wife of the suicide, was notified this morning by telegraph of her husband's death and she is expected to arrive here this afternoon and make the necessary arrangements for burial.

This edition of the *Globe* tells us the name of the man found hanged in the woods: George F. Borden of East Taunton. Let's see, a man named William S. Borden lived on Liberty Street in East Taunton (same number, come to think of it, as "George F." Borden). Is it possible that George was related to William? Same address, same father listed (Deacon Charles Borden of Ninth Street in Fall River). George's family is listed; yes, he did have a half brother, but his name is William L. Bassett of Westport. He also had two sisters, who, it says, are locked up.

We were correct on one point—Meridian Street was a true bellringer—"George" committed suicide in woods close to the farm where the hatchet slaying of Bertha Manchester took place about eight years earlier.

Coincidence.

Manuel José de Correiro was convicted of that murder, and he was "institutionalized" after his trial. If you can believe what his interpreter said at the trial, José claimed he was innocent. Poor man was crazy beyond belief: he continued to claim he didn't do it. He actually should have been hanged but there was some reason for doubt, so it was decided to just lock him up where he could do no further harm. Twenty-five years later, this "criminally insane" man was pardoned (yes, *pardoned*!), put on a boat, and deported to the Azores. May it never be said that those in power in Massachusetts could not temper mercy.

About 4 o'clock in the morning (daylight would be hours away at that hour in April), Mr. George F. Borden noiselessly left the house where he was accustomed to stay when he was in the neighborhood, went to his host's barn, found "ice" chains (not "logging" chains as we were told yesterday), swallowed his poison, and hanged himself just as it was outlined for us the day before.

Most of this was Inspector Shea's theory. Alas, a few details important to the truth-seeker were omitted, but, as usual, no one noticed; our suicide was yesterday's news. Did he die from the poison he took, from a broken neck, or from asphyxiation? Was he bringing produce to market as claimed? If so, where was his wagon and why had he dressed to the nines?

Interestingly, The Hill's own Fall River *Daily Herald* does make the correct identification on the same day, April 18:

## SUICIDE IDENTIFIED

### He Was East Taunton Cider
### Merchant, Named Borden

The suicide of yesterday has been identified as William S. Borden of East Taunton. He was a farmer, with a wife and apple orchard which yielded him many barrels of cider yearly which he peddled through the country. It was the errand on which he came to Fall River on Tuesday night. His canvass for customers found him at the home of William Meachim, Meridian street, late that day where he was accommodated with food and lodging. He arose early yesterday, probably at about 4 o'clock, and, taking a chain such as was used to secure the tailboard of a heavy wagon, disappeared into the adjacent lot. The chain in question was taken from Mr. Meachim's wagon. There he hung himself besides drinking carbolic acid. No excuse for the act could be offered until the identification which came this morning at about 7:30 o'clock when the body was viewed by Mr. Meachim, and by W.W. Coolidge, who is a distant relative.

The deceased has two sisters in the Taunton asylum. His age was about 50 years. The late Deacon Charles Borden of Seventh street was his father. William Lewis Bassett, of Westport, is his half brother.

It is established that Mr. Borden was very erratic, though it is not known here that he ever before exhibited suicidal tendencies. Mrs. Borden was notified this forenoon at her home, 38 Liberty street, East Taunton, who signified an intention of setting out at once for this city to look after the disposition of the remains.

While the *Daily Herald* got William's name correct, most of the other information is the same as reported in the *Globe*. The *Daily Herald* does report that a reason for the "act" could be given once the body was identified, but, alas, the reason is not given to us.

As with the life of William S. Borden, many of the aspects of his death are laced with suspicion of cover-up. It is highly unusual that the *Globe* or any newspaper would make such a horrendous error as to misidentify a man found dead by hanging and then not attempt to correct it.

It is doubtful that the error was a deliberate action by the *Herald*; it was reporting what had been given to it. When you think for a moment about Lizbeth of Maplecroft and the high-placed citizens who wanted to ensure absolute separation between her and Bill Borden, the source becomes a bit clearer.

Without the aid of the *Herald*'s contribution, it is likely that people who were acquainted with Bill Borden (such as Henry Hawthorne) might have missed the connection between Lizzie and Bill and *that*—if we might speculate—was the point. It was not an error. The newspapers were reporting what had been given to them, yet their reports differ. The misidentification of the dead man, spiked with just enough truth, created confusion and directed attention away from the details of the death, which was murder, not suicide. I can offer no concrete evidence for this statement. The people that committed the crime were professionals and left no evidence. But this assumption makes sense of the strange coincidences and answers the unanswered questions.

Without preservatives, cider would seldom be available in mid-April; any offered at that time would be well past its prime. Yet, this last article tells us that cider was the reason for William Borden's coming to Fall River to commit suicide. How seriously are we to take the allegation that a cider salesman will dress elegantly to peddle his wares, even if he intends to climb trees in the dark?

William Borden was the killer of Abby and Andrew Borden

and was the probable killer of Bertha Manchester. Quite possibly he was also guilty of more serious crimes, such as making impossible demands of the wrong people. He may have grown greedy. If nothing else, he represented a major threat and a serious danger, not to Lizzie who had been acquitted of the only crime of which she was ever accused, but to certain members of the Mellen House gang who had so much to lose. They had William Borden killed, and the public accepted the murder as suicide.

# Finale

# Chapter 19

Henry Hawthorne died in 1978 at the age of eighty-nine. He had spent more than fifty years trying to determine if the strange man he had known so well and feared so much was the murderer of Andrew and Abby Borden. He had been threatened with bodily harm and arrest, abused, laughed at, and generally labeled a nut. I have followed his trail and cannot disprove him. What follows is supposition. While there may be a minimum of objective evidence to prove it is true, there is no evidence that demonstrates it is *not* true. And it is more consistent with all the testimony and evidence presented at every public hearing and at the trial than any other explanation I know.

For whatever reason, at the age of thirty-three, Andrew J. Borden, whose marriage to his first wife Sarah was not an entirely happy one, had an affair with Phebe Hathaway Borden. Phebe had married Charles L. Borden in 1836 and, it is assumed, was still married to him at the time of the affair. In 1856 a boy, William, was born of this liaison. In the same year Alice Esther Borden was birthed by Andrew's legal wife, Sarah. Marital troubles between Andrew and Sarah were hinted at only in the planted newspaper article that denied Andrew had left a will, but Sarah had been dead for almost thirty years, and it was assumed that their marriage had no direct bearing on the case. John Morse, however, lived in Fall River during this troubled time and knew of William Borden and the circumstances of his birth.

Henry Hawthorne says he spoke with a woman who claimed to be the midwife who delivered Phebe Hathaway of

315

*Henry Hawthorne, age 78* [Photo courtesy Lewis "Pete" Peterson]

Andrew's son and to have full knowledge of the affair. This is certainly possible, but not at all provable.

In 1860, four years after the birth of William, Charles L. Borden fathered a child by his second wife, Peace Borden. What happened to Phebe in the interim is not known. Charles would not have been pleased with her obvious infidelity. Since William S. Borden had been born to Phebe, Charles was declared the father, but he refused to legitimize Bill's birth. His birth is therefore not a matter of public record. Although divorce was not impossible in those days, it was considered a disgrace and never broadcast. It is likely that Andrew supported his son in some manner, although there is no evidence.

One interesting real estate transaction from this period may or may not shed light on the situation. The farm at 38 Liberty Street in East Taunton was deeded to Simon and Catherine Hathaway from 1864 to 1872. Their relationship to Phebe Hathaway is unknown and not determinable; the coincidences in names and dates once again causes pause, especially when in 1872 the *same* property was deeded to Lewis B. Gammons, the father of Rebecca Francis Gammons. Two years later, Rebecca was legally married to William S. Borden. This *may* be just a coincidence, but coincidences keep falling on top of each other as this case unfolds. For twenty-seven years Bill and Rebecca Borden lived and worked on that farm until his death in 1901.

In both of the 1901 accounts of Bill Borden's death, William Lewis Bassett was mentioned as his half brother. How they became half brothers is unknown, but it is likely that William Lewis Bassett was the son of Peace Borden by a previous marriage. They were half brothers through Charles Borden, who was not the biological father of either.

When the Bordens were murdered, a strange man was reported by Dr. Handy, by Officer Hyde, and by several witnesses as hanging about the Borden house. Mark Chase testified to a man waiting in front of the house with a horse and wagon. Officer Mullaly testified that in his early interrogation of Lizzie she told him of a man she had seen that morning outside the house. She never mentioned that man again. Assistant Marshal Fleet testified that in his early questioning of Lizzie she told him of a man who came to the front door the morning of the murder and spoke with her father. She never spoke of this happening again, either. In both instances, the man was William Lewis Bassett.

At the time of the murders, William Borden was making demands of his father. For whatever reason, Uncle John was mediator between Andrew and William, and his presence was required when William insisted on meeting with Andrew. Lizzie, too, was involved in the arrangement as a go-between of some sort. John Morse was on the scene when Andrew, in what may have been an answer or an open warning to both Lizzie and William, killed Lizzie's pigeons by decapitating them. Uncle John was on the scene when Mrs. Borden's watch and jewelry were stolen, which may have been William's answer to Andrew. Lizzie was *not* there when this incident took place, but to divert suspicion from William she went so far as to allow herself to become suspect, just as she did for the murders. And then, on the day Lizzie warned of extreme danger, Uncle John was on the scene again.

Bassett's assignment on the murder morning (we'll never know who told him to do this, but all indicators point to John

Morse) was to deliver a note to Mrs. Borden that would cause her to leave the house, thus providing Andrew and Bill the freedom for open and uninterrupted conversation without fear of Mrs. Borden's negative interjections. It is safe to assume that Abby would have been strongly opposed to Andrew's dealings with his illegitimate son. The reported "agitation" William Bassett exhibited while he waited for Mrs. Borden was caused by her not coming out of the house. He had no way of knowing that William Borden had killed her.

William Lewis Bassett did not know before the fact that a crime was going to be committed, but he had full knowledge of exactly what happened after it had been committed. Threat or payoff let him maintain his silence. Bassett lived in Westport, and it was on the road to Westport that, according to the letter given to the press by Jennings, Samuel Robinsky met a farmhand he described as physically identical to William Bassett. The letter, supposedly written by Robinsky, was a message from Lizzie's defense team to Bassett. When Bill was hanged, William Lewis Bassett's name was stressed in the reporting as an open warning to him to continue his silence, *or else.*

It is documented that William Lewis Bassett had a daughter named Leah Beatrice who died as a young child on December 5, 1892, four months after the murders. Henry Hawthorne stated that Leah Beatrice was in need of medical attention that required money and that William Borden promised his half brother he would speak to a "rich man" and get the financial help needed for Leah. Like Henry's report of a midwife, this is possible, but not provable.

Andrew drew up a will that was unacceptable to two of his children or maybe unacceptable to all three of them. He was giving twenty-five thousand dollars each to Lizzie and Emma. Uncle John said that Andrew was giving away some of his money as philanthropic bequests which he was not allowed to name. William Borden may have been getting some money. But assuming that Andrew was not giving away the majority of his estate, that still left a lot of money unaccounted for. Both Lizzie and Bill would have been upset if the bulk of the estate was going to Abby because she would have had no reason to give them any of it upon her death.

On the day he was murdered, Andrew had an appointment to speak with his son. In one of the planted newspaper articles, it was firmly established that John Morse was in full sympathy with his nieces, and it is doubtful he had any interest in Bill's welfare. Emma had washed her hands of the entire affair, letting others negotiate her inheritance with her father. Doing this, she had uncharacteristically removed herself from Fall River (but close to where John Morse was staying), another coincidence, of course. Uncle John and Andrew were at odds about what Andrew intended to do, and on the eve of the murders, John and Andrew had an argument about it.

After the trial, District Attorney Knowlton gave an interview in which he said that if he could know exactly what subject was discussed in the living room that evening between Andrew and John Morse, he would have no problem gaining a conviction of the party responsible for Andrew's death. He couldn't have meant Lizzie since she was no longer eligible for conviction. If he really thought this was true, one wonders why at the legal proceedings he never asked John Morse a single question about what that subject might have been.

William may have entered the Borden house by the front door, opened by Uncle John (with Lizzie's knowledge) at some time before midnight on August 3, talked with Lizzie and Uncle John, and then slept in the same room as Uncle John or in Emma's empty bedroom. An alternative is that he spent the night in the hayloft of the Borden barn and was admitted to the cellar that morning by Lizzie after Uncle John and her father had left the house. At that time Bridget was outside at the front of the house, and Lizzie, knowing that a note had been delivered to her stepmother, thought Abby had changed her clothes and left the house with William Bassett on some real or imagined errand of mercy.

Lizzie wisely feared Bill. She knew he would be in or close to the house the evening before the murders, and so she told Alice Russell she would sleep "with her eyes half open in fear somebody would do something." Although she had every reason to fear her half brother, she was convinced, perhaps by ego, that she could control him. Her attempt to buy prussic acid was actually a desire for a strong defensive weapon against Bill should one be required, exactly as Arthur Phillips, Jennings' assistant, wrote fifty years later.

William Borden was either already upstairs in one of the bedrooms or in the barn waiting to be admitted to the house when Lizzie went down for breakfast. In either event, he was in the front bedroom when Abby unexpectedly went into the room where she kept some of her clothes. She may have walked in to get a suitable street dress and surprised Bill as he waited there to see his father. She may also have taunted him with the answer Andrew was prepared to give Bill when he returned from downstreet. Why Bill killed Abby is open to speculation, but hate and insanity seldom need a rationale for their actions. In Bill's mind, Abby, as the wife of his father, had usurped the position *his* mother—Phebe Hathaway—should have had after, in all likelihood, she had been divorced by Charles. The triggering of years of harbored hatred is easy to understand in this situation. It has long been suggested that Lizzie killed her stepmother out of hatred. It is far easier to accept hatred as a motive for Bill's action than it is as a motive for a murder by Lizzie.

Whether from surprise, from fear of discovery, from triggered insane hatred, or from some combination of all of these, Bill killed Abby. Lizzie did not know that he had done this until she found her father's body and wondered aloud whether Mrs. Borden might not be in the house after all, in spite of the note that was delivered to her by William Bassett. Abby had told Lizzie she was going out, and Lizzie did not know she had not left the house. Her defense at the inquest that she could not have killed Abby because she did not know Abby was in the house was the simple truth.

Lizzie undoubtedly kept her distance from Bill while he waited upstairs for his father to return that morning. She was in the kitchen when Bridget, fumbling with the front door lock with which she was fully familiar but which Uncle John may have jammed or placed in an unaccustomed position the night before, heard Bill, upstairs, laugh at her expletive. Bridget assumed it was Lizzie she heard since, as far as she knew, only she and Lizzie were in the house.

Andrew entered with his package, exchanged a few normal

pleasantries with Bridget, took his bedroom key from the mantle, and went upstairs to his safe. Whatever Andrew brought home that morning, it was in some way connected to Bill. It was the size and shape of bank notes, but it could have been a deed to an over-the-river Borden property or a copy of the will that included (or excluded) Bill. Andrew may have had it in his hand ready to give or show to Bill, or he may have changed his mind and placed it in the safe. After the murders, when the safe was opened under the watchful eyes of Andrew Jennings and Officer Harrington, its contents were noted as a "large amount of cash and a great many papers," but "nothing incriminating." Just as knowledge about the John Morse-Andrew Borden conversation of the evening before could have led to the conviction of a murderer, a certified listing by unbiased accountants of the contents of Andrew's safe would have embarrassed several highly placed people, including Knowlton, and produced grounds for their indictments.

When Bridget went upstairs for her nap, Andrew ordered Lizzie out of the house—she went into the back yard and ate some pears while he met with his son. After killing his father, Bill left by the open cellar door and looked to the front of the house to see if his half brother and his team might still be there. They were not, but Bill was seen by Ellan Eagan and, sensing from her reaction that he might be in danger, he retreated into the Borden back yard where, before leaving, he may even have talked with Lizzie, although he would not have mentioned what he had just done. He then headed for Uncle Hiram Harrington's shop on Fourth Street where, by arrangement, his half brother should be waiting with his out-of-town horse and buggy.

Uncle John's return to the Borden house that morning was brought about by Lizzie's appeal to him delivered by Dr. Seabury Bowen by telephone or, more probably, in person. Uncle John's walk up the hill from Pleasant Street was not up Second Street but Fourth Street to Hiram Harrington's establishment. He expected to intercept Bill Borden there, and he may have. He then went on to the Borden house and entered the *back* yard, retracing the same steps Bill had used in leaving the yard. This is why Uncle John would not have seen the crowds of people on Second Street. Finding nothing to attract his attention in the back yard, he finally entered the house and asked Lizzie his so terse and telling question, "For God's sake, how did this happen?"

As soon as she had the opportunity, Lizzie enlisted her uncle's aid in contacting via telephone and post her half brother William and his half brother William Bassett and with threats, money, or promises, convinced both of them to keep out of the way. If they did, they were told, everything would be taken care of. In return for his giving up any claim to his father's fortune, Bill was guaranteed that he would not be charged with the dual murder.

Lizzie's concern now was Andrew's fortune. If the will could be kept hidden, her father's fortune would *all* be hers and Emma's, rather than the measly twenty-five thousand dollars Andrew had considered adequate. But Bill Borden's silence was essential. The course of action Lizzie chose seems, at first, drastic and dangerous. But it was foolproof as long as she had the actual murderer as her ace in the hole.

Lizzie Borden had to become the prime suspect. She must be tried and she must be found not guilty. Should anything upset the plan, all that was necessary was her "finding" and handing over to the authorities the actual murderer. At the inquest, Knowlton had paved the way for this by asking Lizzie, "You have not been able to find this man?"

"I have not," she replied. "I don't know if anyone else has."

"Have you caused a search to be made for him?"

"Yes, sir."

In retrospect, this interaction, which seems strange when first read, makes perfect sense.

We do not know who ordered the commitment of William Borden to the Taunton State Hospital or when it was done. Like the contents of Andrew's safe, the hospital records would tell us much, but they are missing.

Whether Bill Borden killed Bertha Manchester is, again, provable only by circumstantial evidence, evidence far more damning to him than that used to convict Manuel José Correiro. Furthermore, Bill Borden's dead body was found close to the Manchester farm in the same woods that Mr. Jennings attempted to introduce through the French-speaking Joseph

Lemay who, several days after the murders, had happened upon a man armed with a hatchet who was lamenting "poor Mrs. Borden" (in French, we assume). On cue, the court allowed the outline of Mr. Lemay's statement to remain on the record but promptly tossed out his actual testimony, accomplishing two purposes: clear messages instructing Bill to continue holding his peace and that in the event an appeal should be required, the testimony could be reintroduced and Bill Borden easily "found" and convicted.

If Bill killed Miss Manchester, the only question is whether it was entirely his own doing or was at the encouragement of others. The timing in relation to Lizzie's trial and the sympathy it created on the jury could force a suspicious mind to assume that someone with an interest in Miss Lizzie's welfare (more directly, her father's fortune) could have "contracted" for the murder. If Bill's file were available at the Taunton State Hospital, it would be a cinch bet (assuming the file had not been "officially" revised) that he was placed in confinement soon after Miss Manchester's murder.

The Bible cautions us not to judge lest we ourselves are willing to face judgment. So for the safety of our souls, we will refrain from judgment. Let us merely accuse together.

In the then male-only world of Massachusetts politics, public officials who deviated from paths ordered for the common man were the norm; they were never accused of wrongdoing, much less anything criminal. Thus, there is nothing new or surprising in the actions of the Mellen House gang, Lizzie's defense team, the prosecution team, or the court that sat at her trials. Their actions were not for Lizzie or for the Bordens. They acted for themselves and for the monetary reward, and they would have done the same for any of "their own."

John V. Morse, Dr. Seabury W. Bowen, and Hiram C. Harrington rushed to the aid of a damsel in distress in the best tradition of knights of old and gentlemen of all ages. They, too, earned their financial rewards.

Emma L. Borden and Bridget Sullivan were innocents caught in the backlash of an event that overtook them. They should have been rewarded for the mental anguish they suffered. Emma died with an estate valued at almost $500,000 in 1927 dollars. At her death, "Lizbeth's" estate was less than half that; somewhere her expenses must have been much greater. Bridget received nothing.

William S. Borden, the unfortunate victim of his misbegotten birth, was rewarded with an early exit from his life of woe.

Manuel José Correiro, symbol of the new American way of life, came to this country a poor, ignorant immigrant. In a matter of months, he surrendered all his freedom and was eating state-provided meals and being housed and clothed at taxpayer expense. This continued for more than twenty-five years before he left the country and returned to Portugal.

Eli Bence, Alice Russell, Henry Hawthorne, and others of their ilk are among us even today. By telling the truth, by refusing to play the game, they are the troublemakers who generate grist for newsmongers and outrageous fees for lawyers.

The final curtain call is for Lizzie Andrew Borden, our heroine. Innocent of murder but guilty of greed, she allowed herself to become the victim and pawn of corrupt political power. We can forgive her transgression. Sapped of all moral fiber by the shock she suffered from the crime and desperate at the thought of losing her wealth and reputation, she was manipulated and used to forward the ambitions of avaricious men who, because they commanded respect, easily won her confidence.

Lizbeth, I stand. I salute you. I raise my cup to you and drink a toast in your honor and to your memory. The only other crime of which you may be successfully accused is that of being years ahead of your time.

I welcome your soul to our generation, the "me first" mentality, and the success-at-any-price world. Time has finally caught up with you. It is a shame you did not live to see it.

# *Appendix*

Inquest Testimony of Lizzie Borden
*Source:* New Bedford *Evening Standard*, June 12, 1893

Q-1  Q. (Mr. Knowlton) Give me your full name.
A. Lizzie Andrew Borden.
Q. Is it Lizzie or Elizabeth?
A. Lizzie.
Q. You were so christened?
A. I was so christened.
Q. What is your age, please?
A. Thirty-two.
Q. Your mother is not living?
A. No sir.
Q. When did she die?
A. She died when I was two and a half years old.
Q. You do not remember her, then?
A. No sir.
Q. What was your father's age?
A. He was seventy next month.
Q. What was his whole name?
A. Andrew Jackson Borden.
Q. And your stepmother, what is her whole name?
A. Abby Durfee Borden.
Q-2  Q. How long had your father been married to your stepmother?
A. I think about twenty-seven years.
Q. How much of that time have they lived in that house on Second street?
A. I think, I am not sure, but I think about twenty years last May.
Q. Always occupied the whole house?
A. Yes sir.

Q. Somebody told me it was once fitted up for two tenements.
A. When we bought it it was for two tenements, and the man we bought it off stayed there a few months until he finished his own house. After he finished his own house and moved into it there was no one else ever moved in; we always had the whole.
Q. Have you any idea how much your father was worth?
A. No sir.
Q. Have you ever heard him say?
A. No sir.
Q. Have you ever formed any opinion?
A. No sir.
Q. Do you know something about his real estate?
A. About what?
Q. His real estate?
A. I know what real estate he owned, part of it; I don't know whether I know it all or not.
Q-3  Q. Tell me what you know of.
A. He owns two farms in Swanzey, the place on Second street and the A. J. Borden building and corner, and the land on South Main street where McMannus is, and then a short time ago he bought some real estate up further south that, formerly, he said belonged to a Mr. Birch.
Q. Did you ever deed him any property?
A. He gave us some years ago, Grandfather Borden's house on Ferry street, and he bought that back from us some weeks ago, I don't know just how many.
Q. As near as you can tell.
A. Well, I should say in June, but I am not sure.
Q. What do you mean by bought it back?
A. He bought it of us, and gave us the money for it.
Q. How much was it?
A. How much money? He gave us $5,000 for it.
Q. Did you pay him anything when you took a deed from him?
A. Pay him anything? No sir.
Q. How long ago was it you took a deed from him?
A. When he gave it to us?
Q. Yes.
A. I can't tell you; I should think five years.
Q. Did you have any other business transactions with him besides that?
A. No sir.
Q. In real estate?
A. No sir.

Q-4   Q. Or in personal property?

       A. No sir.

       Q. Never?

       A. Never.

       Q. No transfer of property one way or the other?

       A. No sir.

       Q. At no time?

       A. No sir.

       Q. And I understand he paid you the cash for this property?

       A. Yes sir.

       Q. You and Emma equally?

       A. Yes sir.

       Q. How many children has your father?

       A. Only two.

       Q. Only you two?

       A. Yes sir.

       Q. Any others ever?

       A. One that died.

       Q. Did you ever know of your father making a will?

       A. No sir, except I heard somebody say once that there was one several years ago; that is all I ever heard.

       Q. Who did you hear say so?

       A. I think it was Mr. Morse.

Q-5   Q. What Morse?

       A. Uncle John V. Morse.

       Q. How long ago?

       A. How long ago I heard him say it? I have not any idea.

       Q. What did he say about it?

       A. Nothing, except just that.

       Q. What?

       A. That Mr. Borden had a will.

       Q. Did you ask your father?

       A. I did not.

       Q. Did he ever mention the subject of will to you?

       A. He did not.

       Q. He never told you that he had made a will, or had not?

       A. No sir.

       Q. Did he have a marriage settlement with your stepmother that you knew of?

       A. I never knew of any.

       Q. Had you heard anything of his proposing to make a will?

       A. No sir.

       Q. Do you know of anybody that your father was on bad terms with?

A. There was a man that came there that he had trouble with, I don't know who the man was.

Q-6 Q. When?

A. I cannot locate the time exactly. It was within two weeks. That is I don't know the date or day of the month.

Q. Tell all you saw and heard.

A. I did not see anything. I heard the bell ring, and father went to the door and let him in. I did not hear anything for some time, except just the voices; then I heard the man say, "I would like to have that place, I would like to have that store. Father says, "I am not willing to let your business go in there." And the man said, "I thought with your reputation for liking money, you would let your store for anything." Father said, "You are mistaken." Then they talked a while, and then their voices were louder, and I heard father order him out, and went to the front door with him.

Q. What did he say?

A. He said that he had stayed long enough, and he would thank him to go.

Q. Did he say anything about coming again?

A. No sir.

Q. Did your father say anything about coming again, or did he?

A. No sir.

Q. Have you any idea who that was?

A. No sir. I think it was a man from out of town, because he said he was going home to see his partner.

Q. Have you had any efforts made to find him?

A. We have had a detective, that is all I know.

Q. You have not found him?

A. Not that I know of.

Q. You can't give us any other idea about it?

A. Nothing but what I have told you.

Q. Beside that do you know of anybody that your father had bad feelings toward, or who had bad feelings toward your father?

A. I know of one man that has not been friendly with him; they have not been friendly for years.

Q-7 Q. Who?

A. Mr. Hiram C. Harrington.

Q. What relation is he to him?

A. He is my father's brother-in-law.

Q. Your mother's brother?

A. My father's only sister married Mr. Harrington.

Q. Anybody else that was on bad terms with your father, or that your father was on bad terms with?

A. Not that I know of.

Q. You have no reason to suppose that man you speak of a week or two ago, had ever seen your father before, or has since?

A. No sir.

Q. Do you know of anybody that was on bad terms with your stepmother?

A. No sir.

Q. Or that your stepmother was on bad terms with?

A. No sir.

Q. Had your stepmother any property?

A. I don't know, only that she had half the house that belonged to her father.

Q. Where was that?

A. On Fourth Street.

Q. Who lives in it?

A. Her half-sister.

Q-8 Q. Any other property beside that that you know of?

A. I don't know.

Q. Did you ever know of any?

A. No sir.

Q. Did you understand that she was worth anything more than that?

A. I never knew.

Q. Did you ever have any trouble with your stepmother?

A. No sir.

Q. Have you, within six months, had any words with her?

A. No sir.

Q. Within a year?

A. No sir.

Q. Within two years?

A. I think not.

Q. When last that you know of?

A. About five years ago.

Q. What about?

A. Her stepsister, half-sister.

Q. What name?

A. Her name now is Mrs. George W. Whitehead.

Q-9 Q. Nothing more than hard words?

A. No sir, they were not hard words; it was simply a difference of opinion.

Q. You have been on pleasant terms with your stepmother since then?

A. Yes sir.

Q. Cordial?

A. It depends upon one's idea of cordiality, perhaps.

Q. According to your idea of cordiality?

A. Quite so.

Q. What do you mean by "quite so"?

A. Quite cordial. I do not mean the dearest of friends in the world, but very kindly feelings, and pleasant. I do not know how to answer you any better than that.

Q. You did not regard her as your mother?

A. Not exactly, no; although she came here when I was very young.

Q. Were your relations towards her that of daughter and mother?

A. In some ways it was, and in some it was not.

Q. In what ways was it?

A. I decline to answer.

Q. Why?

A. Because I don't know how to answer it.

Q. In what ways was it not?

A. I did not call her mother.

Q-10   Q. What name did she go by?

A. Mrs. Borden.

Q. When did you begin to call her Mrs. Borden?

A. I should think five or six years ago.

Q. Before that time you had called her mother?

A. Yes sir.

Q. What led to the change?

A. The affair with her stepsister.

Q. So that the affair was serious enough to have you change from calling her mother, do you mean?

A. I did not choose to call her mother.

Q. Have you ever called her mother since?

A. Yes, occasionally.

Q. To her face, I mean?

A. Yes.

Q. Often?

A. No sir.

Q. Seldom?

A. Seldom.

Q. Your usual address was Mrs. Borden?

A. Yes sir.

Q-11   Q. Did your sister Emma call her mother?

A. She always called her Abby from the time she came into the family.

Q. Is your sister Emma older than you?

A. Yes sir.

Q. What is her age?

A. She is ten years older than I am. She was somewhere about fourteen when she came there.

Q. What was your stepmother's age?

A. I don't know. I asked her sister Saturday, and she said sixty-four. I told them sixty-seven; I did not know. I told as nearly as I knew. I did not know there was so much difference between she and father.

Q. Why did you leave off calling her mother?

A. Because I wanted to.

Q. Is that all the reason you have to give me?

A. I have not any other answer.

Q. Can't you give me any better reason than that?

A. I have not any reason to give, except that I did not want to.

Q. In what other respect were the relations between you and her not that of mother and daughter, besides not calling her mother?

A. I don't know that any of the relations were changed. I had never been to her as a mother in many things. I always went to my sister, because she was older and had the care of me after my mother died.

Q. In what respects were the relations between you and her that of mother and daughter?

A. That is the same question you asked before; I can't answer you any better now than I did before.

Q. You did not say before you could not answer, but that you declined to answer.

A. I decline to answer because I do not know what to say.

Q-12 Q. That is the only reason?

A. Yes sir.

Q. You called your father father?

A. Always.

Q. Were your father and mother happily united?
(PAUSE)

A. Why, I don't know but that they were.

Q. Why do you hesitate?

A. Because I don't know but that they were, and I am telling the truth as nearly as I know it.

Q. Do you mean me to understand that they were happy entirely, or not?

A. So far as I know they were.

Q. Why did you hesitate then?

A. Because I did not know how to answer you any better than what came into my mind. I was trying to think if I was telling it as I should; that is all.

Q. Do you have any difficulty in telling it as you should, any difficulty in answering my questions?

A. Some of your questions I have difficulty in answering because I don't know just how you mean them.

Q. Did you ever know of any difficulty between her and your father?

A. No sir.

Q. Did he seem to be affectionate?

A. I think so.

Q. As man and woman who are married ought to be?

A. So far as I have ever had any chance of judging.

Q-13 Q. They were?

A. Yes.

Q. What dress did you wear the day they were killed?

A. I had on a navy blue, sort of a bengaline; or India silk skirt, with a navy blue blouse. In the afternoon they thought I had better change it. I put on a pink wrapper.

Q. Did you change your clothing before the afternoon?

A. No sir.

Q. You dressed in the morning, as you have described, and kept that clothing on until afternoon?

A. Yes, sir.

Q. When did Morse come there first, I don't mean this visit, I mean as a visitor, John V. Morse?

A. Do you mean this day that he came and stayed all night?

Q. No. Was this visit his first to your house?

A. He has been in the east a year or more.

Q. Since he has been in the east has he been in the habit of coming to your house?

A. Yes; came in any time he wanted to.

Q. Before that had he been at your house, before he came east?

A. Yes, he has been here, if you remember the winter that the river was frozen over and they went across, he was here that winter, some 14 years ago, was it not?

Q. I am not answering questions, but asking them.

A. I don't remember the date. He was here that winter.

Q. Has he been here since?

A. He has been here once since, I don't know whether he has or not since.

Q-14 Q. How many times this last year has he been at your house?

A. None at all to speak of, nothing more than a night or two at a time.

Q. How often did he come to spend a night or two?

A. Really I don't know; I am away so much myself.

Q. Your last answer is that you don't know how much he had been here, because you had been away yourself so much?

A. Yes.

Q. That is true the last year, or since he has been east?

A. I have not been away the last year so much, but other times I have been away when he has been here.

Q. Do I understand you to say that his last visit before this one was 14 years ago?

A. No, he has been here once between the two.

Q. How long did he stay then?

A. I don't know.

Q. How long ago was that?

A. I don't know.

Q. Give me your best remembrance.

A. Five or six years, perhaps six.

Q. How long has he been east this time?

A. I think over a year; I am not sure.

Q. During the last year how much of the time has he been at your house?

A. Very little that I know of.

Q-15    Q. Your answer to that question before was, I don't know because I have been away so much myself.

A. I did not mean I had been away very much myself the last year.

Q. How much have you been away the last year?

A. I have been away a great deal in the daytime, occasionally at night.

Q. Where in the daytime, any particular place?

A. No, around town.

Q. When you go off nights, where?

A. Never unless I have been off on a visit.

Q. When was the last time when you have been away for more than a night or two before this affair?

A. I don't think I have been away to stay more than a night or two since I came from abroad, except about three or four weeks ago I was in New Bedford for three or four days.

Q. Where at New Bedford?

A. At 20 Madison street.

Q. How long ago were you abroad?

A. I was abroad in 1890.

Q. When did he come to the house the last time before your father and mother were killed?

A. He stayed there all night Wednesday night.

333

Q. My question is when he came there.

A. I don't know; I was not at home when he came; I was out.

Q. When did you first see him there?

A. I did not see him at all.

Q-16 Q. How did you know he was there?

A. I heard his voice.

Q. You did not see him Wednesday evening?

A. I did not; I was out Wednesday evening.

Q. You did not see him Thursday morning?

A. I did not; he was out when I came down stairs.

Q. When was the first time you saw him?

A. Thursday noon.

Q. You had never seen him before that?

A. No sir.

Q. Where were you Wednesday evening?

A. I spent the evening with Miss Russell.

Q. As near as you can remember, when did you return?

A. About nine o'clock at night.

Q. The family had then retired?

A. I don't know whether they had or not. I went right to my room; I don't remember.

Q. You did not look to see?

A. No sir.

Q. Which door did you come in at?

A. The front door.

Q-17 Q. Did you lock it?

A. Yes sir.

Q. For the night?

A. Yes sir.

Q. And went right up stairs to your room?

A. Yes sir.

Q. When was it that you heard the voice of Mr. Morse?

A. I heard him down there about supper time—no, it was earlier than that. I heard him down there somewhere about three o'clock, I think, I was in my room Wednesday, not feeling well, all day.

Q. Did you eat supper at home Wednesday night?

A. I was at home; I did not eat any supper, because I did not feel able to eat supper; I had been sick.

Q. You did not come down to supper?

A. No sir.

Q. Did you hear him eating supper?

A. No sir. I did not know whether he was there or not.

Q. You heard him in the afternoon?

A. Yes sir.

Q. Did you hear him go away?

A. I did not.

Q. You did not go down to see him?

A. No sir.

Q-18    Q. Was you in bed?

A. No sir. I was on the lounge.

Q. Why did you not go down?

A. I did not care to go down, and I was not feeling well, and kept my room all day.

Q. You felt better in the evening?

A. Not very much better. I thought I would go out, and see if the air would make me feel any better.

Q. When you came back at nine o'clock, you did not look in to see if the family were up?

A. No sir.

Q. Why not?

A. I very rarely do when I come in.

Q. You go right to your room?

A. Yes sir.

Q. Did you have a night key?

A. Yes sir.

Q. How did you know it was right to lock the front door?

A. That was always my business.

Q. How many locks did you fasten?

A. The spring locks itself, and there is a key to turn, and you manipulate the bolt.

Q. You manipulated all those?

A. I used them all.

Q-19    Q. Then you went to bed?

A. Yes, directly.

Q. When you got up the next morning, did you see Mr. Morse?

A. I did not.

Q. Had the family breakfasted when you came down?

A. Yes sir.

Q. What time did you come down stairs?

A. As near as I can remember, it was a few minutes before nine.

Q. Who did you find down stairs when you came down?

A. Maggie and Mrs. Borden.

Q. Did you inquire for Mr. Morse?

A. No sir.

Q. Did you suppose he had gone?

A. I did not know whether he had or not; he was not there.

Q. Your father was there?

A. Yes sir.

Q. Then you found him?

A. Yes sir.

Q. Did you speak to either your father or Mrs. Borden?

A. I spoke to them all.

Q. About Mr. Morse?

A. I did not mention him.

Q-20  Q. Did not inquire anything about him?

A. No sir.

Q. How long before that time had he been at the house?

A. I don't know.

Q. As near as you can tell?

A. I don't know. He was there in June sometime, I don't know whether he was there after that or not.

Q. Why did you not go to Marion with the party that went?

A. Because they went sooner than I could, and I was going Monday.

Q. Why did they go sooner than you could; what was there to keep you?

A. I had taken the secretaryship and treasurer of our C. E. society, had the charge, and the roll call was the first Sunday in August, and I felt I must be there and attend to that part of the business.

Q. Where was your sister Emma that day?

A. What day?

Q. The day your father and Mrs. Borden were killed?

A. She had been in Fairhaven.

Q. Had you written to her?

A. Yes sir.

Q. When was the last time you wrote to her?

A. Thursday morning, and my father mailed the letter for me.

Q-21  Q. Did she get it at Fairhaven?

A. No sir, it was sent back. She did not get it at Fairhaven, for we telegraphed for her, and she got home here Thursday afternoon, and the letter was sent back to this post office.

Q. How long had she been in Fairhaven?

A. Just two weeks to a day.

Q. You did not visit in Fairhaven?

A. No sir.

Q. Had there been anybody else around the house that week, or premises?

A. No one that I knew of, except the man that called to see him on this business about the store.

Q. Was that that week?

A. Yes sir.

Q. I misunderstood you probably, I thought you said a week or two before.

A. No, I said that week. There was a man came the week before and gave up some keys, and I took them.

Q. Do you remember of anybody else being then around the premises that week?

A. Nobody that I know of or saw.

Q. Nobody at work there?

A. No sir.

Q. Nobody doing any chores there?

A. No sir, not that I know of.

Q. Nobody had access to the house, so far as you know, during that time?

A. No sir.

Q-22  Q. I ask you once more how it happened that, knowing Mr. Morse was at your house, you did not step in and greet him before you retired?

A. I have no reason, except that I was not feeling well Wednesday, and so did not come down.

Q. No, you were down. When you came in from out.

A. Do you mean Wednesday night?

Q. Yes.

A. Because I hardly ever do go in. I generally went right up to my room, and I did that night.

Q. Could you then get to your room from the back hall?

A. No sir.

Q. From the back stairs?

A. No sir.

Q. Why not? What would hinder?

A. Father's bedroom door was kept locked, and his door into my room was locked and hooked, I think, and I had no keys.

Q. That was the custom of the establishment?

A. It had always been so.

Q. It was so Wednesday, and so Thursday?

A. It was so Wednesday, but Thursday they broke the door open.

Q. That was after the crowd came; before the crowd came?

A. It was so.

Q. There was no access, except one had a key, and one would have to have two keys?

A. They would have to have two keys if they went up the back way to get into my room. If they were in my room; they would have to have a key to get into his room, and another to get into the back stairs.

Q-23  Q. Where did Mr. Morse sleep?

A. In the next room over the parlor in front of the stairs.

Q. Right up the same stairs that your room was?

A. Yes sir.

Q. How far from your room?

A. A door opened into it.

Q. The two rooms connected directly?

A. By one door, that is all.

Q. Not through the hall?

A. No sir.

Q. Was the door locked?

A. It has been locked and bolted, and a large writing desk in my room kept up against it.

Q. Then it was not a practical opening?

A. No sir.

Q. How otherwise do you get from your room to the next room?

A. I have to go into the front hall.

Q. How far apart are the two doors?

A. Very near, I don't think more than so far (measuring).

Q. Was it your habit when you were in your room to keep your door shut?

A. Yes sir.

Q-24  Q. That time, that Wednesday afternoon?

A. My door was open part of the time, and part of the time I tried to get a nap and their voices annoyed me, and I closed it. I kept it open in summer more or less, and closed in winter.

Q. Then, unless for some special reason, you kept your door open in the summer?

A. Yes sir, if it was a warm day. If it was a cool day, I should have closed it.

Q. Where was your father when you came down Thursday morning?

A. Sitting in the sitting room in his large chair, reading the Providence Journal.

Q. Where was your mother? Do you prefer me to call her Mrs. Borden?

A. I had as soon you called her mother. She was in the dining room with a feather duster dusting.

Q. When she dusted did she wear something over her head?

A. Sometimes when she swept, but not when dusting.

Q. Where was Maggie?

A. Just come in the back door with the long pole, brush, and put the brush on the handle, and getting her pail of water; she was going to wash the windows around the house. She said Mrs. Borden wanted her to.

Q. Did you get your breakfast that morning?

A. I did not eat any breakfast; I did not feel as though I wanted any.

Q. Did you get any breakfast that morning?

A. I don't know whether I ate half a banana; I don't think I did.

Q. You drank no tea or coffee that morning?

A. No sir.

Q. And ate no cookies?

A. I don't know whether I did or not. We had some molasses cookies; I don't know whether I ate any that morning or not.

Q-25    Q. Were the breakfast things put away when you got down?

A. Everything except the coffee pot; I am not sure whether that was on the stove or not.

Q. You said nothing about Mr. Morse to your father or mother?

A. No sir.

Q. What was the next thing that happened after you got down?

A. Maggie went out of doors to wash the windows and father came out into the kitchen and said he did not know whether he would go down to the post office or not. And then I sprinkled some handkerchiefs to iron.

Q. Tell me again what time you came down stairs.

A. It was a little before nine, I should say about quarter; I don't know sure.

Q. Did your father go down town?

A. He went down later.

Q. What time did he start away?

A. I don't know.

Q. What were you doing when he started away?

A. I was in the dining room I think; yes, I had just commenced; I think, to iron.

Q. It may seem a foolish question. How much of an ironing did you have?

A. I only had about eight or ten of my best handkerchiefs.

Q. Did you let your father out?

A. No sir, he went out himself.

Q. Did you fasten the door after him?

A. No sir.

Q-26    Q. Did Maggie?

A. I don't know. When she went up stairs she always locked the door, she had charge of the back door.

Q. Did she go out after a brush before your father went away?

A. I think so.

Q. Did you say anything to Maggie?

A. I did not.

339

Q. Did you say anything about washing the windows?

A. No sir.

Q. Did you speak to her?

A. I think I told her I did not want any breakfast.

Q. You do not remember of talking about washing the windows?

A. I don't remember whether I did or not; I don't remember it. Yes, I remember; yes, I asked her to shut the parlor blinds when she got through, because the sun was so hot.

Q. About what time do you think your father went down town?

A. I don't know, it must have been after nine o'clock. I don't know what time it was.

Q. You think at that time you had begun to iron your hand-kerchiefs?

A. Yes sir.

Q. How long a job was that?

A. I did not finish them; my flats were not hot enough.

Q. How long a job would it have been if the flats had been right?

A. If they had been hot, not more than 20 minutes, perhaps.

Q-27    Q. How long did you work on the job?

A. I don't know, sir.

Q. How long was your father gone?

A. I don't know that.

Q. Where were you when he returned?

A. I was down in the kitchen.

Q. What doing?

A. Reading an old magazine that had been left in the cupboard, an old Harper's Magazine.

Q. Had you got through ironing?

A. No sir.

Q. Had you stopped ironing?

A. Stopped for the flats.

Q. Were you waiting for them to be hot?

A. Yes sir.

Q. Was there a fire in the stove?

A. Yes sir.

Q. When your father went away, you were ironing them?

A. I had not commenced, but I was getting the little ironing board and the flats.

Q. Are you sure you were in the kitchen when your father returned?

A. I am not sure whether I was there or in the dining room.

Q-28    Q. Did you go back to your room before your father returned?

A. I think I did carry up some clean clothes.

Q. Did you stay there?

A. No sir.

Q. Did you spend any time up the front stairs before your father returned?

A. No sir.

Q. Or after he returned?

A. No, sir. I did stay in my room long enough when I went up to sew a little piece of tape on a garment.

Q. What was the time when your father came home?

A. He came home after I came down stairs.

Q. You were not up stairs when he came home?

A. I was not up stairs when he came home; no, sir.

Q. What was Maggie doing when your father came home?

A. I don't know whether she was there or whether she had gone up stairs; I can't remember.

Q. Who let your father in?

A. I think he came to the front door and rang the bell, and I think Maggie let him in, and he said he had forgotten his key; so I think she must have been down stairs.

Q. His key would have done him no good if the locks were left as you left them?

A. But they were always unbolted in the morning.

Q. Who unbolted them that morning?

A. I don't think they had been unbolted; Maggie can tell you.

Q-29  Q. If he had not forgotten his key it would have been no good?

A. No, he had his key and could not get in. I understood Maggie to say he said he had forgotten his key.

Q. You did not hear him say anything about it?

A. I heard his voice, but I don't know what he said.

Q. I understood you to say he said he had forgotten his key?

A. No, it was Maggie said he said he had forgotten the key.

Q. Where was Maggie when the bell rang?

A. I don't know, sir.

Q. Where were you when the bell rang?

A. I think in my room up stairs.

Q. Then you were up stairs when you father came home?

A. I don't know sure, but I think I was.

Q. What were you doing?

A. As I say, I took up these clean clothes, and stopped and basted a little piece of tape on a garment.

Q. Did you come down before your father was let in?

A. I was on the stairs coming down when she let him in.

Q. Then you were up stairs when your father came to the house on his return?

A. I think I was.

Q. How long had you been there?

A. I had only been upstairs just long enough to take the clothes up and baste the little loop on the sleeve. I don't think I had been up there over five minutes.

Q-30   Q. Was Maggie still engaged in washing windows when your father got back?

A. I don't know.

Q. You remember, Miss Borden, I will call your attention to it so as to see if I have any misunderstanding, not for the purpose of confusing you; you remember, that you told me several times that you were down stairs, and not up stairs when your father came home? You have forgotten, perhaps?

A. I don't know what I have said. I have answered so many questions and I am so confused I don't know one thing from another. I am telling you just as nearly as I know.

Q. Calling your attention to what you said about that a few minutes ago, and now again to the circumstance you have said you were up stairs when the bell rang, and were on the stairs when Maggie let your father in; which now is your recollection of the true statement, of the matter, that you were down stairs when the bell rang and your father came?

A. I think I was down stairs in the kitchen.

Q. And then you were not up stairs?

A. I think I was not; because I went up almost immediately, as soon as I went down, and then came down again and stayed down.

Q. What had you in your mind when you said you were on the stairs as Maggie let your father in?

A. The other day somebody came there and she let them in and I was on the stairs; I don't know whether the morning before or when it was.

Q. You understood I was asking you exactly and explicitly about this fatal day?

A. Yes, sir.

Q. I now call your attention to the fact that you had specifically told me you had gone up stairs, and had been there about five minutes when the bell rang, and were on your way down, and were on the stairs when Maggie let your father in that day—.

A. Yes, I said that, and then I said I did not know whether I was on the stairs or in the kitchen.

Q. Now how will you have it?

A. I think, as nearly as I know, I think I was in the kitchen.

Q. How long was your father gone?

A. I don't know, sir, not very long.

Q. An hour?

A. I should not think so.

Q-31  Q. Will you give me the best story you can, so far as your recollection serves you, of your time while he was gone?

A. I sprinkled my handkerchiefs, and got my ironing board and took them in the dining room. I took the ironing board in the dining room and left the handkerchiefs in the kitchen on the table and whether I ate any cookies or not I don't remember. Then I sat down looking at the magazine waiting for the flats to heat. Then I went in the sitting room and got the Providence *Journal*, and took that into the kitchen. I don't recollect of doing anything else.

Q. Which did you read first, the *Journal* or the magazine?

A. The magazine.

Q. You told me you were reading the magazine when your father came back?

A. I said in the kitchen, yes.

Q. Was that so?

A. Yes, I took the Journal out to read, and had not read it. I had it near me.

Q. You said a minute or two ago you read the magazine awhile, and then went and got the *Journal* and took it out to read?

A. I did, but I did not read it; I tried my flats then.

Q. And went back to reading the magazine?

A. I took the magazine up again, yes.

Q. When did you last see your mother?

A. I did not see her after when I went down in the morning and she was dusting the dining room.

Q. Where did you or she go then?

A. I don't know where she went. I know where I was.

Q. Did you or she leave the dining room first?

A. I think I did. I left her in the dining room.

Q. You never saw her or heard her afterwards?

A. No sir.

Q-32  Q. Did she say anything about making the bed?

A. She said she had been up and made the bed up fresh, and had dusted the room and left it all in order. She was going to put some fresh pillow slips on the small pillows at the foot of the bed, and was going to close the room, because she was going to have company Monday and she wanted everything in order.

Q. How long would it take to put on the pillow slips?

A. About two minutes.

Q. How long to do the rest of the things?

A. She had done that when I came down.

Q. All that was left was what?

A. To put on the pillow slips.

Q. Can you give me any suggestions as to what occupied her when she was up there, when she was struck dead?

A. I don't know of anything except she had some cotton cloth pillow cases up there, and she said she was going to commence to work on them. That is all I know. And the sewing machine was up there.

Q. Whereabouts was the sewing machine?

A. In the corner between the north and west side.

Q. Did you hear the sewing machine going?

A. I did not.

Q. Did you see anything to indicate that the sewing machine had been used that morning?

A. I had not. I did not go in there until after everybody had been in there, and the room had been overhauled.

Q. If she had remained down stairs, you would undoubtedly have seen her?

A. If she had remained down stairs, I should have, if she had remained in her room, I should not have.

Q. Where was that?

A. Over the kitchen.

Q-33  Q. To get to that room she would have to go through the kitchen?

A. To get up the back stairs.

Q. That is the way she was in the habit of going?

A. Yes, sir, because the other doors were locked.

Q. If she had remained down stairs, or had gone to her own room, you undoubtedly would have seen her?

A. I should have seen her if she had stayed downstairs; if she had gone to her room, I would not have seen her.

Q. She was found a little after 11 in the spare room, if she had gone to her own room she must have gone through the kitchen and up the back stairs, and subsequently have gone down and gone back again?

A. Yes sir.

Q. Have you any reason to suppose you would not have seen her if she had spent any portion of the time in her own room, or down stairs?

A. There is no reason why I should not have seen her if she had been down there, except when I first came down stairs, for two or three minutes I went down cellar to the water closet.

Q. After that you were where you practically commanded the view of the first story the rest of the time?

A. I think so.

344

Q. When you went up stairs for a short time, as you say you did, you then went in sight of the sewing machine?

A. No, I did not see the sewing machine, because she had shut that room up.

Q. What do you mean?

A. I mean the door was closed. She said she wanted it kept closed to keep the dust and everything out.

Q. Was it a room with a window?

A. It has three windows.

Q. A large room?

A. The size of the parlor; a pretty fair sized room.

Q-34    Q. It is the guest room?

A. Yes, the spare room.

Q. Where the sewing machine was was the guest room?

A. Yes, sir.

Q. I ask again, perhaps you have answered all you care to, what explanation can you give, can you suggest, as to what she was doing from the time she said she had got the work all done in the spare room until 11 o'clock?

A. I suppose she went up and made her own bed.

Q. That would be in the back part?

A. Yes sir.

Q. She would have to go by you twice to do that?

A. Unless she went when I was in my room that few minutes.

Q. That would not be time enough for her to go and make her own bed and come back again?

A. Sometimes she stayed up longer and sometimes shorter; I don't know.

Q. Otherwise than that, she would have to go in your sight?

A. I should have to have seen her once; I don't know that I need to have seen her more than once.

Q. You did not see her at all?

A. No sir, not after the dining room.

Q. What explanation can you suggest as to the whereabouts of your mother from the time you saw her in the dining room, and she said her work in the spare room was all done, until 11 o'clock?

A. I don't know. I think she went back into the spare room, and whether she came back again or not, I don't know; that has always been a mystery.

Q. Can you think of anything she could be doing in the spare room?

A. Yes sir. I know what she used to do sometimes. She kept her best cape she wore on the street in there, and she used occasionally to go up there to get it and to take it into her room. She kept a great deal in the guest room drawers; she used to go up there and get things and put things; she used those drawers for her own use.

Q-35   Q. That connects her with her own room again, to reach which she had to go down stairs and come up again?

A. Yes.

Q. Assuming that she did not go into her own room, I understand you to say she could not have gone to her own room without your seeing her?

A. She could while I was down cellar.

Q. You went down immediately you came down, within a few minutes, and you did not see her when you came back?

A. No sir.

Q. After that time she must have remained in the guest chamber?

A. I don't know.

Q. So far as you can judge?

A. So far as I can judge she might have been out of the house, or in the house.

Q. Had you any knowledge of her going out of the house?

A. No sir.

Q. Had you any knowledge of her going out of the house?

A. She told me she had had a note, somebody was sick, and said "I am going to get the dinner on the way," and asked me what I wanted for dinner.

Q. Did you tell her?

A. Yes, I told her I did not want anything.

Q. Then why did you not suppose she had gone?

A. I supposed she had gone.

Q. Did you hear her come back?

A. I did not hear her go or come back, but I supposed she went.

Q-36   Q. When you found your father dead you supposed your mother had gone?

A. I did not know. I said to the people who came in "I don't know whether Mrs. Borden is out or in; I wish you would see if she is in her room."

Q. You supposed she was out at the time?

A. I understood so; I did not suppose anything about it.

Q. Did she tell you where she was going?

A. No sir.

Q. Did she tell you who the note was from?

A. No sir.

Q. Did you ever see the note?

A. No sir.

Q. Do you know where it is now?

A. No sir.

Q. She said she was going out that morning?

A. Yes sir.

## Wednesday, August 10, 1892

Mr. Knowlton asks:

Q. I shall have to ask you once more about that morning. Do you know what the family ate for breakfast?

A. No sir.

Q. Had the breakfast all been cleared away when you got down?

A. Yes sir.

Q. I want you to tell me just where you found the people when you got down that you did find there?

A. I found Mrs. Borden in the dining room. I found my father in the sitting room.

Q-37 Q. And Maggie?

A. Maggie was coming in the back door with her pail and brush.

Q. Tell me what talk you had with your mother at that time?

A. She asked me how I felt. I said I felt better than I did Tuesday, but I did not want any breakfa. She asked me what I wanted for dinner, I told her nothing. I told her I did not want anything. She said she was going out, and would get the dinner. That is the last I saw her, or said anything to her.

Q. Where did you go then?

A. Into the kitchen.

Q. Where then?

A. Down cellar.

Q. Gone perhaps five minutes?

A. Perhaps. Not more than that; possibly a little bit more.

Q. When you came back did you see your mother?

A. I did not; I supposed she had gone out.

Q. She did not tell you where she was going?

A. No sir.

Q. When you came back was your father there?

A. Yes sir.

Q. What was he doing?

A. Reading the paper.

Q. Did you eat any breakfast?

A. No sir, I don't remember whether I ate a molasses cookie or not. I did not eat any regularly prepared breakfast.

Q-38   Q. Was it usual for your mother to go out?

A. Yes sir, she went out every morning nearly, and did the marketing.

Q. Was it usual for her to be gone away from dinner?

A. Yes sir, sometimes, not very often.

Q. How often, say?

A. O, I should not think more than—well I don't know, more than once in three months, perhaps.

Q. Now I call your attention to the fact that twice yesterday you told me, with some explicitness, that when your father came in you were just coming down stairs?

A. No, I did not, I beg your pardon.

Q. That you were on the stairs at the time your father was let in, you said with some explicitness. Do you now say you did not say so?

A. I said I thought first I was on the stairs; then I remembered I was in the kitchen when he came in.

Q. First you thought you were in the kitchen; afterwards you remembered you were on the stairs?

A. I said I thought I was on the stairs; then I said I knew I was in the kitchen. I still say that now. I was in the kitchen.

Q. Did you go into the front part of the house after your father came in?

A. After he came in from down street I was in the sitting room with him.

Q. Did you go into the front hall afterwards?

A. No sir.

Q. At no time?

A. No sir.

Q. Excepting the two or three minutes you were down cellar, were you away from the house until your father came in?

A. No sir.

Q-39   Q. You were always in the kitchen or dining room, excepting when you went up stairs?

A. I went up stairs before he went out.

Q. You mean you went up there to sew a button on?

A. I basted a piece of tape on.

Q. Do you remember you did not say that yesterday?

A. I don't think you asked me. I told you yesterday I went up stairs directly after I came up from down cellar, with the clean clothes.

Q. You now say after your father went out, you did not go up stairs at all?

A. No sir, I did not.

Q. When Maggie came in there washing the windows, you did not appear from the front part of the house?

A. No sir.

Q. When your father was let in, you did not appear from up stairs?

A. No sir. I was in the kitchen.

Q. That is so?

A. Yes sir, to the best of my knowledge.

Q. After your father went out, you remained there either in the kitchen or dining room all the time?

A. I went in the sitting room long enough to direct some paper wrappers.

Q. One of the three rooms?

A. Yes sir.

Q. So it would have been extremely difficult for anybody to have gone through the kitchen and dining room and front hall, without your seeing them?

A. They could have gone from the kitchen into the sitting room while I was in the dining room, if there was anybody to go.

Q-40 Q. Then into the front hall?

A. Yes sir.

Q. You were in the dining room ironing?

A. Yes sir, part of the time.

Q. You were in all of the three rooms?

A. Yes sir.

Q. A large portion of that time, the girl was out of doors?

A. I don't know where she was, I did not see her. I supposed she was out of doors, as she had the pail and brush.

Q. You know she was washing windows?

A. She told me she was going to, did not see her do it.

Q. For a large portion of the time, you did not see the girl?

A. No sir.

Q. So far as you know you were alone in the lower part of the house a large portion of the time, after your father went away, and before he came back?

A. My father did not go away, I think until somewhere about 10, as near as I can remember, he was with me down stairs.

Q. A large portion of the time after your father went away, and before he came back, so far as you know, you were alone in the house?

A. Maggie had come in and gone up stairs.

Q. After he went out, and before he came back; a large portion of the time after your father went out, and before he came back, so far as you know, you were the only person in the house?

A. So far as I know, I was.

349

Q. And during that time, so far as you know, the front door was locked?

A. So far as I know.

Q-41 Q. And never was unlocked at all?

A. I don't think it was.

Q. Even after your father came home, it was locked up again?

A. I don't know whether she locked it up again after that or not.

Q. It locks itself?

A. The spring lock opens.

Q. It fastens it so it cannot be opened from the outside?

A. Sometimes you can press it open.

Q. Have you any reason to suppose the spring lock was left so it could be pressed open from the outside?

A. I have no reason to suppose so.

Q. Nothing about the lock was changed before the people came?

A. Nothing that I know of.

Q. What were you doing in the kitchen when your father came home?

A. I think I was eating a pear when he came in.

Q. What had you been doing before that?

A. Been reading a magazine.

Q. Were you making preparations to iron again?

A. I had sprinkled my clothes, and was waiting for the flat. I sprinkled the clothes before he went out.

Q. Had you built up the fire again?

A. I put in a stick of wood. There was a few sparks. I put in a stick of wood to try to heat the flat.

Q-42 Q. You had then started the fire?

A. Yes sir.

Q. The fire was burning when he came in?

A. No sir, but it was smoldering and smoking as though it would come up.

Q. Did it come up after he came in?

A. No sir.

Q. Did you do any more ironing?

A. I did not. I went in with him, and did not finish.

Q. You did not iron any more after your father came in?

A. No sir.

Q. Was the ironing board put away?

A. No sir, it was on the dining room table.

Q. When was it put away?

A. I don't know. Somebody put it away after the affair happened.

Q. You did not put it away?

A. No sir.

Q. Was it on the dining room table when you found your father killed?

A. I suppose so.

Q. You had not put it away then?

A. I had not touched it.

Q-43 Q. How soon after your father came in, before Maggie went up stairs?

A. I don't know. I did not see her.

Q. Did you see her after your father came in?

A. Not after she let him in.

Q. How long was your father in the houe before you found him killed?

A. I don't know exactly, because I went out to the barn. I don't know what time he came home. I don't think he had been home more than fifteen or twenty minutes; I am not sure.

Q. When you went out to the barn, where did you leave your father?

A. He had laid down on the sitting room lounge, taken off his shoes, and put on his slippers, and taken off his coat and put on the reefer. I asked him if he wanted the window left that way.

Q. Where did you leave him?

A. On the sofa.

Q. Was he asleep?

A. No sir.

Q. Was he reading?

A. No sir.

Q. What was the last thing you said to him?

A. I asked him if he wanted the window left that way. Then I went into the kitchen, and from there to the barn.

Q. Whereabouts in the barn did you go?

A. Up stairs.

Q. To the second story of the barn?

A. Yes sir.

Q-44 Q. How long did you remain there?

A. I don't know, fifteen or twenty minutes.

Q. What doing?

A. Trying to find lead for a sinker.

Q. What made you think there would be lead for a sinker up there?

A. Because there was some there.

Q. Was there not some by the door?

A. Some pieces of lead by the open door, but there was a box full of old things up stairs.

Q. Did you bring any sinker back from the barn?

A. I found no sinker.

Q. Did you bring any sinker back from the barn?

A. Nothing but a piece of a chip I picked up on the floor.

Q. Where was that box you say was up stairs, containing lead?

A. There was a kind of a workbench.

Q. Is it there now?

A. I don't know, sir.

Q. How long since have you seen it there?

A. I have not been out there since that day.

Q. Had you been in the barn before?

A. That day, no sir.

Q-45 Q. How long since you had been in the barn before?

A. I don't think I had been into it. I don't know as I had in three months.

Q. When you went out did you unfasten the screen door?

A. I unhooked it to get out.

Q. It was hooked until you went out?

A. Yes sir.

Q. It had been left hooked by Bridget if she was the last one in?

A. I suppose so; I don't know.

Q. Do you know when she did get through washing the outside?

A. I don't know.

Q. Did you know she washed the windows inside?

A. I don't know.

Q. Did you see her washing the windows inside?

A. I don't know.

Q. You don't know whether she washed the dining room and sitting room windows inside?

A. I did not see her.

Q. If she did, would you not have seen her?

A. I don't know. She might be in one room and I in another.

Q. Do you think she might have gone to work and washed all the windows in the dining room and sitting room and you not know it?

A. I don't know. I am sure, whether I should or not, I might have seen her, and not know it.

Q-46 Q. Miss Borden, I am trying in good faith to get all the doings that morning of yourself and Miss Sullivan, and I have not succeeded in doing it. Do you desire to give me any information or not?

A. I don't know it—I don't know what your name is.

Q. It is certain beyond reasonable doubt she was engaged in washing the windows in the dining room or sitting room when your father came home. Do you mean to say you know nothing of either of those operations?

352

A. I knew she washed the windows outside; that is, she told me so. She did not wash the windows in the kitchen, because I was in the kitchen most of the time.

Q. The dining room and sitting room; I said.

A. I don't know.

Q. It is reasonably certain she washed the windows in the dining room and sitting room, inside while your father was out, and was engaged in this operation when your father came home; do you mean to say you know nothing of it?

A. I don't know whether she washed the windows in the sitting room and dining room or not.

Q. Can you give me any information how it happened at that particular time you should go into the chamber of the barn to find a sinker to go to Marion with to fish the next Monday?

A. I was going to finish my ironing; my flats were not hot; I said to myself "I will go and try and find that sinker; perhaps by the time I get back the flats will be hot." That is the only reason.

Q. How long had you been reading an old magazine before you went to the barn at all?

A. Perhaps half an hour.

Q. Had you got a fish line?

A. Not here; we had some at the farm.

Q. Had you got a fish hook?

A. No sir.

Q. Had you any apparatus for fishing at all?

A. Yes, over there.

Q. Had you any sinkers over there?

A. I think there were some. It is so long since I have been there; I think there were some.

Q-47  Q. You had no reason to suppose you were lacking sinkers?

A. I don't think there were any on my lines.

Q. Where were your lines?

A. My fishlines were at the farm here.

Q. What made you think there were no sinkers at the farm on your lines?

A. Because some time ago when I was there I had none.

Q. How long since you used the fishlines?

A. Five years, perhaps.

Q. You left them at the farm then?

A. Yes sir.

Q. And you have not seen them since?

A. Yes sir.

Q. It occurred to you after your father came in it would be a good time to go to the barn after sinkers, and you had no reason to suppose there was not abundance of sinkers at the farm and abundance of lines?

A. The last time I was there there were some lines.

Q. Did you not say before you presumed there were sinkers at the farm?

A. I don't think I said so.

Q. You did say so exactly. Do you now say you presume there were not sinkers at the farm?

A. I don't think there were any fishlines suitable to use at the farm; I don't think there were any sinkers on any line that had been mine.

Q. Do you remember telling me you presumed there were lines, and sinkers and hooks at the farm?

A. I said there were lines I thought, and perhaps hooks. I did not say I thought there were sinkers on my lines. There was another box of lines over there beside mine.

Q-48  Q. You thought there were not sinkers?

A. Not on my lines.

Q. Not sinkers at the farm?

A. I don't think there were any sinkers at the farm. I don't know whether there were or not.

Q. Did you then think there were no sinkers at the farm?

A. I thought there were no sinkers anywhere, or I should not have been trying to find some.

Q. You thought there were no sinkers at the farm to be had?

A. I thought there were no sinkers at the farm to be had.

Q. That is the reason you went into the second story of the barn to look for a sinker?

A. Yes sir.

Q. What made you think you would find sinkers there?

A. I heard Father say, and I knew there was lead there.

Q. You thought there might be lead there made into sinkers?

A. I thought there might be lead there with a hole in it.

Q. Did you examine the lead that was down stairs near the door?

A. No sir.

Q. Why not?

A. I don't know.

Q. You went straight to the upper story of the barn?

A. No, I went under the pear tree and got some pears first.

Q-49  Q. Then went to the second story of the barn to look for sinkers for lines you had at the farm, as you supposed, as you had seen them there five years before that time?

A. I went up to get some sinkers, if I could find them. I did not intend to go to the farm for lines; I was going to buy some lines here.

Q. You then had no intention of using your own line and hooks at Marion?

A. I could not get them.

Q. What was the use of telling me a little while ago you had no sinkers on your line at the farm?

A. I thought I made you understand that those lines at the farm were no good to use.

Q. Did you not mean for me to understand one of the reasons you were searching for sinkers was that the lines you had at the farm, as you remembered them, had no sinkers on them?

A. I said the lines at the farm had no sinkers on them.

Q. I did not ask you what you said. Did you not mean for me to understand that?

A. I meant for you to understand I wanted the sinkers, and was going to have new lines.

Q. You had not then bought your lines?

A. No sir, I was going out Thursday noon.

Q. You had not bought any apparatus for fishing?

A. No hooks.

Q. Had bought nothing connected with your fishing trip?

A. No sir.

Q. Going to go fishing the next Monday, were you?

A. I don't know that we should go fishing Monday.

Q. Going to the place to go fishing Monday?

A. Yes sir.

Q-50   Q. This was Thursday and you had no idea of using any fishing apparatus before the next Monday?

A. No sir.

Q. You had no fishing apparatus you were proposing to use the next Monday until then?

A. No sir, not until I bought it.

Q. You had not bought anything?

A. No sir.

Q. Had not started to buy anything?

A. No sir.

Q. The first thing in preparation for your fishing trip the next Monday was to go to the loft of that barn to find some old sinkers to put on some hooks and lines that you had not then bought?

A. I thought if I found no sinkers I would have to buy the sinkers when I bought the lines.

Q. You thought you would be saving some thing by hunting in the loft of the barn before you went to see whether you should need lines or not?

A. I thought I would find out whether there were any sinkers before I bought the lines; and if there was, I should not have to buy any sinkers. If there were some, I should only have to buy the lines and the hooks.

Q. You began the collection of your fishing apparatus by searching for the sinkers in the barn?

A. Yes sir.

Q. You were searching in a box of old stuff in the loft of the barn?

A. Yes sir, up stairs.

Q. That you had never looked at before?

A. I had seen them.

Q. Never examined them before?

A. No sir.

Q-51   Q. All the reason you supposed there was sinkers there was your father had told you there was lead in the barn?

A. Yes, lead; and one day I wanted some old nails; he said there was some in the barn.

Q. All the reason that gave you to think there was sinkers was your father said there was old lead in the barn?

A. Yes sir.

Q. Did he mention the place in the barn?

A. I think he said up stairs; I am not sure.

Q. Where did you look up stairs?

A. On that workbench, like.

Q. In anything?

A. Yes, it was a box, sort of a box, and then some things lying right on the side that was not in the box.

Q. How large a box was it?

A. I could not tell you. It was probably covered up with lumber, I think.

Q. Give me the best idea of the size of the box you can.

A. Well, I should say, I don't know, I have not any idea.

Q. Give me the best idea you have.

A. I have given you the best idea I have.

Q. What is the best idea you have?

A. About that large (measuring with hands).

Q. That long?

A. Yes.

Q-52   Q. How wide?

A. I don't know.

Q. Give me the best idea you have.

A. Perhaps about as wide as it was long.

Q. How high?

A. It was not very high.

Q. About how high?
(Witness measures with her hands.)
Q. About twice the length of your forefinger?
A. I should think so. Not quite.
Q. What was in the box?
A. Nails, and some old locks, and I don't know but there was a door knob.
Q. Anything else?
A. I don't remember anything else.
Q. Any lead?
A. Yes, some pieces of tea lead, like.
Q. Foil, what we call tin foil, the same as you use on tea chests?
A. I don't remember seeing any tin foil; not as thin as that.
Q. Tea chest lead?
A. No sir.

Q-53  Q. What did you see in shape of lead?
A. Flat pieces of lead, a little bigger than that; some of them were doubled together.
Q. How many?
A. I could not tell you.
Q. Where else did you look beside in the box?
A. I did not look anywhere for lead except on the workbench.
Q. How full was the box?
A. It was nearly as full as it could have been.
Q. You looked on the bench, beside that, where else?
A. Nowhere except on the bench.
Q. Did you look for anything else beside lead?
A. No sir.
Q. When you got through looking for lead did you come down?
A. No, sir. I went to the west window over the hay, to the west window, and the curtain was slanted a little. I pulled it down.
Q. What else?
A. Nothing.
Q. That is all you did?
A. Yes sir.
Q. That is the second story of the barn?
A. Yes sir.
Q. Was the window open?
A. I think not.
Q. Hot?
A. Very hot.
Q. How long do you think you were up there?
A. Not more than fifteen or twenty minutes, I should not think.
Q. Should you think what you have told me would occupy four

minutes?

A. Yes, because I ate some pears up there.

Q. Do you think all you have told me would take you four minutes?

A. I ate some pears up there.

Q. I asked you to tell me all you did.

A. I told you all I did.

Q. Do you mean to say you stopped your work, and then, additional to that, sat still and ate some pears?

A. While I was looking out of the window, yes sir.

Q. Will you tell me all you did in the second story of the barn?

A. I think I told you all I did that I can remember.

Q. Is there anything else?

A. I told you. I took some pears up from the ground when I went up; I stopped under the pear tree and took some pears up when I went up.

Q. Have you now told me everything you did up in the second story of the barn?

A. Yes sir.

Q-55 Q. I now call your attention, and ask you to say whether all you have told me—I don't suppose you stayed there any longer than necessary?

A. No sir, because it was very close.

Q. I suppose that was the hottest place there was on the premises?

A. I should think so.

Q. Can you give me any explanation why all you have told me would occupy more than three minutes?

A. Yes, it would take me more than three minutes.

Q. To look in that box that you have described the size of on the bench and put down the curtain and then get out as soon as you conveniently could; would you say you were occupied in that business twenty minutes?

A. I think so, because I did not look at the box when I first went up.

Q. What did you do?

A. I ate my pears.

Q. Stood there eating the pears, doing nothing?

A. I was looking out of the window.

Q. Stood there, looking out of the window eating the pears?

A. I should think so.

Q. How many did you eat?

A. Three, I think.

Q. You were feeling better than you did in the morning?

A. Better than I did the night before.

Q. You were feeling better than you were in the morning?

A. I felt better in the morning than I did the night before.

Q-56 Q. That is not what I asked you. You were then, when you were in that hot loft, looking out of the window and eating three pears, feeling better, were you not, than you were in the morning when you could not eat any breakfast?

A. I never eat any breakfast.

Q. You did not answer my question, and you will, if I have to put it all day. Were you, then when you were eating those three pears in that hot loft, looking out of that closed window, feeling better than you were in the morning when you ate no breakfast?

A. I was feeling well enough to eat the pears.

Q. Were you feeling better than you were in the morning?

A. I don't think I felt very sick in the morning, only—Yes, I don't know but I did feel better. As I say, I don't know whether I ate any breakfast or not, or whether I ate a cookie.

Q. Were you then feeling better than you did in the morning?

A. I don't know how to answer you, because I told you I felt better in the morning anyway.

Q. Do you understand my question? My question is whether, when you were in the loft of that barn, you were feeling better than you were in the morning when you got up?

A. No, I felt about the same.

Q. Were you feeling better than you were when you told your mother you did not care for any dinner?

A. No sir, I felt about the same.

Q. Well enough to eat pears, but not well enough to eat anything for dinner?

A. She asked me if I wanted any meat.

Q. I ask you why you should select that place, which was the only place which would put you out of sight of the house, to eat those three pears in?

A. I cannot tell you any reason.

Q. You observe that fact, do you not? You have put yourself in the only place perhaps, where it would be impossible, for you to see a person going into the house?

A. Yes sir, I should have seen them from the front window.

Q. From anywhere in the yard?

A. No sir, not unless from the end of the barn.

Q-57 Q. Ordinarily in the yard you could see them, and in the kitchen where you had been, you could have seen them?

A. I don't think I understand.

Q. When you were in the kitchen, you could see persons who came in at the back door?

A. Yes sir.

Q. When you were in the yard, unless you were around the corner of the house, you could see them come in at the back door?

A. No sir, not unless I was at the corner of the barn; the minute I turned I could not.

Q. What was there?

A. A little jog like, the walk turns.

Q. I ask you again to explain to me why you took those pears from the pear tree?

A. I did not take them from the pear tree.

Q. From the ground, wherever you took them from. I thank you for correcting me, going into the barn, going up stairs into the hottest place in the barn, in the rear of the barn, the hottest place, and there standing and eating those pears that morning?

A. I beg your pardon, I was not in the rear of the barn. I was in the other end of the barn that faced the street.

Q. Where you could see anybody coming into the house?

A. Yes sir.

Q. Did you not tell me you could not?

A. Before I went into the barn, at the jog on the outside.

Q. You now say when you were eating the pears, you could see the back door?

A. Yes sir.

Q. So nobody could come in at that time without your seeing them?

A. I don't see how they could.

Q-58 Q. After you got through eating your pears you began your search?

A. Yes sir.

Q. Then you did not see into the house?

A. No sir, because the bench is at the other end.

Q. Now I have asked you over and over again, and will continue the inquiry, whether anything you did at the bench would occupy more than three minutes?

A. Yes, I think it would, because I pulled over quite a lot of boards in looking.

Q. To get at the box?

A. Yes sir.

Q. Taking all that, what is the amount of time you think you occupied in looking for that piece of lead which you did not find?

A. Well, I should think perhaps I was ten minutes.

Q. Looking over those old things?

A. Yes sir, on the bench.

Q. Now can you explain why you were ten minutes doing it?

A. No, only that I can't do anything in a minute.

Q. When you came down from the barn, what did you do then?

A. Came into the kitchen.

Q-59 Q. What did you do then?

A. I went into the dining room and laid down my hat.

Q. What did you do then?

A. Opened the sitting room door, and went into the sitting room, or pushed it open; it was not latched.

Q. What did you do then?

A. I found my father, and rushed to the foot of the stairs.

Q. What were you going into the sitting room for?

A. To go up stairs.

Q. What for?

A. To sit down.

Q. What had become of the ironing?

A. The fire had gone out.

Q. I thought you went out because the fire was not hot enough to heat the flats.

A. I thought it would burn, but the fire had not caught from the few sparks.

Q. So you gave up the ironing and was going up stairs?

A. Yes, sir, I thought I would wait till Maggie got dinner and heat the flats again.

Q. When you saw your father where was he?

A. On the sofa.

Q. What was his position?

A. Lying down.

Q. Describe anything else you noticed at that time.

A. I did not notice anything else, I was so frightened and horrified. I ran to the foot of the stairs and called Maggie.

Q. Did you notice that he had been cut?

A. Yes; that is what made me afraid.

Q-60 Q. Did you notice that he was dead?

A. I did not know whether he was or not.

Q. Did you make any search for your mother?

A. No sir.

Q. Why not?

A. I thought she was out of the house; I thought she had gone out. I called Maggie to go to Dr. Bowen's. When they came I said, "I don't know where Mrs. Borden is." I thought she had gone out.

Q. Did you tell Maggie you thought your mother had come in?

A. No sir.

Q. That you thought you heard her come in?

A. No, sir.

Q. Did you say to anybody that you thought she was killed up stairs?

A. No sir.

Q. To anybody?

A. No sir.

Q. You made no effort to find your mother at all?

A. No sir.

Q. Who did you send Maggie for?

A. Dr. Bowen. She came back and said Dr. Bowen was not there.

Q. What did you tell Maggie?

A. I told her he was hurt.

Q-61   Q. When you first told her?

A. I says "Go for Dr. Bowen as soon as you can. I think father is hurt."

Q. Did you then know that he was dead?

A. No sir.

Q. You saw him?

A. Yes sir.

Q. You went into the room?

A. No sir.

Q. Looked in at the door?

A. I opened the door and rushed back.

Q. Saw his face?

A. No, I did not see his face, because he was all covered with blood.

Q. You saw where the face was bleeding?

A. Yes sir.

Q. Did you see the blood on the floor?

A. No sir.

Q. You saw his face covered with blood?

A. Yes sir.

Q. Did you see his eyeball hanging out?

A. No sir.

Q-62   Q. See the gashes where his face was laid open?

A. No sir.

Q. Nothing of that kind?

A. No sir. (Witness covers her face with her hand for a minute or two; then examination is resumed.)

Q. Do you know of any employment that would occupy your mother for the two hours between nine and eleven in the front room?

A. Not unless she was sewing.

Q. If she had been sewing you would have heard the machine?

A. She did not always use the machine.

Q. Did you see, or were there found, anything to indicate that she was sewing up there?

A. I don't know. She had given me a few weeks before some pillow cases to make.

Q. My question is not that. Did you see, or were there found, anything to indicate that she had done any sewing in that room that morning?

A. I don't know. I was not allowed in that room; I did not see it.

Q. Was that the room where she usually sewed?

A. No sir.

Q. Did you ever know her to use that room for sewing?

A. Yes sir.

Q. When?

A. Whenever she wanted to use the machine.

Q. When she did not want to use the machine, did you know she used that room for sewing?

A. Not unless she went up to sew a button on; or something.

Q-63  Q. She did not use it as a sitting room?

A. No sir.

Q. Leaving out the sewing, do you know of anything else that would occupy her for two hours in that room?

A. No, not if she had made the bed up, and she said she had when I went down.

Q. Assuming the bed was made?

A. I don't know anything.

Q. Did she say she had done the work?

A. She said she had made the bed, and was going to put on the pillow cases, about 9 o'clock.

Q. I ask you now again, remembering that—

A. I told you that yesterday.

Q. Never mind about yesterday. Tell me all the talk you had with your mother when you came down in the morning?

A. She asked me how I felt. I said I felt better, but did not want any breakfast. She said what kind of meat did I want for dinner. I said I did not want any. She said she was going out, somebody was sick, and she would get the dinner, get the meat, order the meat. And, I think she said something about the weather being hotter, or something; and I don't remember that she said anything else. I said to her, "Won't you change your dress before you go out." She had on an old one. She said, "No, this is good enough." That is all I can remember.

Q. In this narrative you have not again said anything about her having said that she had made the bed?

A. I told you that she said she made the bed.

Q. In this time saying, you did not put that in. I want that conversation that you had with her that morning. I beg your pardon

363

again, in this time of telling me, you did not say anything about her having received a note.

A. I told you that before.

Q. Miss Borden, I want you now to tell me all the talk you had with your mother, when you came down, and all the talk she had with you. Please begin again.

A. She asked me how I felt. I told her. She asked me what I wanted for dinner. I told her not anything, what kind of meat I wanted for dinner. I told her not any. She said she had been up and made the spare bed, and was going to take up some linen pillow cases for the small pillows at the foot, and then the room was done. She says: "I have had a note from somebody that is sick, and I am going out, and I will get the dinner at the same time." I think she said something about the weather. I don't know. She also asked me if I would direct some paper wrappers for her, which I did.

Q. She said she had had a note?

A. Yes sir.

2-64 Q. You told me yesterday you never saw the note?

A. No sir, I never did.

Q. You looked for it?

A. No sir, but the rest have.

Q. She did not say where she was going?

A. No sir.

Q. Does she usually tell you where she is going?

A. She does not generally tell me.

Q. Did she say when she was coming back?

A. No sir.

Q. Did you know that Mr. Morse was coming to dinner?

A. No sir, I knew nothing about him.

Q. Was he at dinner the day before?

A. Wednesday noon? I don't know. I had not seen him; I don't think he was.

Q. Were you at dinner?

A. I was in the house. I don't know whether I went down to dinner or not. I was not feeling well.

Q. Whether you ate dinner or not?

A. I don't remember.

Q. Do you remember who was at dinner the day before?

A. No sir. I don't remember, because I don't know whether I was down myself or not.

2-65 Q. Were you at tea Wednesday night?

A. I went down, but I think, I don't know, whether I had any tea or not.

Q. Did you sit down with the family?

A. I think I did, but I am not sure.

Q. Was Mr. Morse there?

A. No sir, I did not see him.

Q. Who were there to tea?

A. Nobody.

Q. The family were there, I suppose?

A. Yes, sir; I mean nobody but the family.

Q. Did you have an apron on Thursday?

A. Did I what?

Q. Have an apron on Thursday?

A. No sir, I don't think I did.

Q. Do you remember whether you did or not?

A. I don't remember sure, but I don't think I did.

Q. You had aprons, of course?

A. I had aprons, yes sir.

Q. Will you try and think whether you did or not?

A. I don't think I did.

Q-66   Q. Will you try and remember?

A. I had no occasion for an apron on that morning.

Q. If you can remember, I wish you would.

A. I don't remember.

Q. That is all the answer you can give me about that?

A. Yes sir.

Q. Did you have any occasion to use the axe or hatchet?

A. No sir.

Q. Did you know where they were?

A. I knew there was an old axe down cellar; that is all I knew.

Q. Did you know anything about a hatchet down cellar?

A. No sir.

Q. Where was the old axe down cellar?

A. The last time I saw it it was stuck in the old chopping block.

Q. Was that the only axe or hatchet down cellar?

A. It was all I knew about.

Q. When was the last you knew of it?

A. When our farmer came to chop wood.

Q. When was that?

A. I think a year ago last winter; I think there was so much wood on hand he did not come last winter.

Q-67   Q. Do you know of anything that would occasion the use of an axe or hatchet?

A. No sir.

Q. Do you know of anything that would occasion the getting of blood on an axe or hatchet down cellar?

A. No sir.

Q. I do not say there was, but assuming an axe or hatchet was found down cellar with blood on it?

A. No sir.

Q. Do you know whether there was a hatchet down there before the murder?

A. I don't know.

Q. You are not able to say your father did not own a hatchet?

A. I don't know whether he did or not.

Q. Did you know there was found at the foot of the stairs a hatchet and axe?

A. No sir, I did not.

Q. Assume that is so, can you give me any explanation of how they came there?

A. No sir.

Q. Assume they had blood on them, can you give any occasion for there being blood on them?

A. No sir.

Q. Can you tell of any killing of an animal? or any other operation that would lead to their being cast there, with blood on them?

A. No sir, he killed some pigeons in the barn last May or June.

Q. What with?

A. I don't know, but I thought he wrung their necks.

Q-68 Q. What made you think so?

A. I think he said so.

Q. Did anything else make you think so?

A. All but three or four had their heads on, that is what made me think so.

Q. Did all of them come into the house?

A. I think so.

Q. Those that came into the house were all headless?

A. Two or three had them on.

Q. Were any with their heads off?

A. Yes sir.

Q. Cut off or twisted off?

A. I don't know which.

Q. How did they look?

A. I don't know, their heads were gone, that is all.

Q. Did you tell anybody they looked as though they were twisted off?

A. I don't remember whether I did or not. The skin I think was very tender, I said why are these heads off? I think I remember of telling somebody that he said they twisted off.

Q. Did they look as if they were cut off?

A: I don't know, I did not look at that particularly.

Q. Is there anything else besides that that would lead, in your opinion so far as you can remember, to the finding of instruments in the cellar with blood on them?

A. I know of nothing else that was done.
(Judge Blaisdell)—Was there any effort made by the witness to notify Mrs. Borden of the fact that Mr. Borden was found?

Q-69    Q. Did you make any effort to notify Mrs. Borden of your father being killed?

A. No sir, when I found him I rushed right to the foot of the stairs for Maggie. I supposed Mrs. Borden was out. I did not think anything about her at the time, I was so—

Q. At any time did you say anything about her to anybody?

A. No sir.

Q. To the effect that she was out?

A. I told father when he came in.

Q. After your father was killed?

A. No sir.

Q. Did you say you thought she was up stairs?

A. No sir.

Q. Did you ask them to look up stairs?

A. No sir.

Q. Did you suggest to anybody to search up stairs?

A. I said, "I don't know where Mrs. Borden is;" that is all I said.

Q. You did not suggest that any search be made for her?

A. No sir.

Q. You did not make any yourself?

A. No sir.

Q. I want you to give me all that you did, by way of word or deed, to see whether your mother was dead or not, when you found your father was dead.

A. I did not do anything, except what I said to Mrs. Churchill. I said to her: "I don't know where Mrs. Borden is. I think she is out, but I wish you would look."

Q-70    Q. You did ask her to look?

A. I said that to Mrs. Churchill.

Q. Where did you intend for her to look?

A. In Mrs. Borden's room.

Q. When you went out to the barn did you leave the door shut, the screen door?

A. I left it shut.

Q. When you came back did you find it shut or open?

A. No, sir; I found it open.

Q. Can you tell me anything else that you did, that you have not told me, during your absence from the house?

A. No, sir.

Q. Can you tell me when it was that you came back from the barn, what time it was?

A. I don't know what time it was.

Q. Have you any idea when it was that your father came home?

A. I am not sure, but I think it must have been after 10, because I think he told me he did not think he should go out until about 10. When he went out I did not look at the clock to see what time it was. I think he did not go out until 10, or a little after. He was not gone so very long.

Q. Will you give me the best judgment you can as to the time your father got back? If you have not any, it is sufficient to say so.

A. No, sir, I have not any.

Q. Can you give me any judgment as to the length of time that elapsed after he came back, and before you went to the barn?

A. I went right out to the barn.

Q. How soon after he came back?

A. I should think not less than five minutes; I saw him taking off his shoes and lying down; it only took him two or three minutes to do it. I went right out.

Q-71 Q. When he came into the house did he not go into the dining room first?

A. I don't know.

Q. And there sit down?

A. I don't know.

Q. Why don't you know?

A. Because I was in the kitchen.

Q. It might have happened, and you not have known it?

A. Yes sir.

Q. You heard the bell ring?

A. Yes sir.

Q. And you knew when he came in?

A. Yes sir.

Q. You did not see him?

A. No sir.

Q. When did you first see him?

A. I went into the sitting room, and he was there; I don't know whether he had been in the dining room before or not.

Q. What made you go into the sitting room?

A. Because I wanted to ask him a question.

Q. What question?

A. Whether there was any mail for me.

Q-72 Q. Did you not ask him that question in the dining room?

A. No sir, I think not.

Q. Was he not in the dining room sitting down?

A. I don't remember his being in the dining room sitting down.

Q. At that time was not Maggie washing the windows in the sitting room?

A. I thought I asked him for the mail in the sitting room; I am not sure.

Q. Was not the reason he went in the dining room because she was in the sitting room washing windows?

A. I don't know.

Q. Did he not go upstairs to his own room before he sat down in the sitting room?

A. I did not see him go.

Q. He had the key to his room down there?

A. I don't know whether he had it; it was kept on the shelf.

Q. When you did go into the sitting room to ask him a question, if it was the sitting room, what took place then?

A. I asked him he had any mail. He said, "None for you." He had a letter in his hand. I supposed it was for himself. I asked him how he felt. He said he should lie down. I asked him if he thought he should have a nap. He said he would try to. I asked him if he wanted the window left the way it was or if he felt a draught. He said, "No." That is all.

Q. Did you help him about lying down?

A. No sir.

Q. Fix his pillows or head?

A. No sir; I did not touch the sofa.

Q. Did he lie down before you left the room?

A. Yes sir.

Q-73  Q. Did anything else take place?

A. Not that I remember of.

Q. Was he then under medical treatment?

A. No sir.

Q. The doctor had not given him any medicine that you know of?

A. No, sir; he took some medicine; it was not doctor's medicine; it was what we gave him.

Q. What was it?

A. We gave him castor oil first and then Garfield tea.

Q. When was that?

A. He took the castor oil some time Wednesday. I think some time Wednesday noon, and I think the tea Wednesday night; Mrs. Borden gave it to him. She went over to see the doctor.

Q. When did you first consult Mr. Jennings?

A. I can't tell you that; I think my sister sent for him; I don't know.

Q. Was it you or your sister?

A. My sister.

Q. You did not send for him?

A. I did not send for him. She said did we think we ought to have him. I said do as she thought best. I don't know when he came first.

Q. Now, tell me once more, if you please, the particulars of that trouble that you had with your mother four or five years ago.

A. Her father's house on Fourth street was for sale—

Q. Whose father's house?

A. Mrs. Borden's father's house. She had a stepmother and a half sister, Mrs. Borden did, and this house was left to the step-mother and a half sister, if I understood it right, and the house was for sale. The stepmother, Mrs. Oliver Gray, wanted to sell it, and my father bought out the Widow Gray's share. She did not tell me and he did not tell me, but some outsiders said that he gave it to her. Put it in her name. I said if he gave that to her, he ought to give us something. Told Mrs. Borden so. She did not care anything about the house herself. She wanted it so this half sister could have a home, because she had married a man that was not doing the best he could, and she thought her sister was having a very hard time and wanted her to have a home. And we always thought she persuaded father to buy it. At any rate, he did buy it, and I am quite sure she did persuade him. I said what he did for her people, he ought to do for his own children. So he gave us Grandfather's house. That was all the trouble we ever had.

Q-74 Q. You have not stated any trouble yet between you and her?

A. I said there was feeling four or five years ago when I stopped calling her mother. I told you that yesterday.

Q. That is all there is to it then?

A. Yes, sir.

Q. You had no words with your stepmother then?

A. I talked with her about it and said what he did for her he ought to do for us; that is all the words we had.

Q. That is the occasion of his giving you the house that you sold back to him?

A. Yes, sir.

Q. Did your mother leave any property?

A. I don't know.

Q. Your own mother?

A. No, sir; not that I ever knew of.

Q. Did you ever see that thing? (Wooden club.)

A. Yes, sir, I think I have.

Q. What is it?

A. My father used to keep something similar to this, that looked very much like it under his bed. He whittled it out himself at the farm one time.

Q. How long since you have seen it?

A. I have not seen it in years.

Q. How many years?

A. I could not tell you. I should think ten to fifteen years; not since I was quite a little girl, if that is the one. I can't swear that it is the one; it was about that size.

Q-75 Q. How many years, ten or fifteen?

A. I was a little girl, it must be as much as that.

Q. When was the last time the windows were washed before that day?

A. I don't know.

Q. Why don't you know?

A. Because I had nothing to do with the work down stairs.

Q. When was the last time that you ate with the family, that you can swear to, before your mother was killed?

A. Well, I ate with them all day Tuesday, that is, what little we ate, we sat down to the table; and I think I sat down to the table with them Wednesday night, but I am not sure.

Q. All day Tuesday?

A. I was down at the table.

Q. I understand you to say you did not come down to breakfast?

A. That was Wednesday morning.

Q. I understood you to say that you did not come down to breakfast?

A. I came down, but I did not eat breakfast with them. I did not eat any breakfast. Frequently I would go into the dining room and sit down to the table with them and not eat any breakfast.

Q. Did you give to the officer the same skirt you had on the day of the tragedy?

A. Yes, sir.

Q-76 Q. Do you know whether there was any blood on the skirt?

A. No, sir.

Q. Assume that there was, do you know how it came there?

A. No, sir.

Q. Have you any explanation of how it might come there?

A. No, sir.

Q. Did you know there was any blood on the skirt you gave them?

A. No, sir.

Q. Assume that there was, can you give any explanation of how it came there, on the dress skirt?

371

A. No, sir.

Q. Assume that there was, can you suggest any reason how it came there?

A. No, sir.

Q. Have you offered any?

A. No, sir.

Q. Have you ever offered any?

A. No, sir.

Q. Have you said it came from flea bites?

A. On the petticoats I said there was a flea bite. I said it might have been. You said you meant the dress skirt.

Q. I did. Have you offered any explanation how that came there?

A. I told those men that were at the house that I had had fleas; that is all.

Q-77 Q. Did you offer that as an explanation?

A. I said that was the only explanation that I knew of.

Q. Assuming that the blood came from the outside, can you give any explanation of how it came there?

A. No, sir.

Q. You cannot now?

A. No, sir.

Q. What shoes did you have on that day?

A. A pair of ties.

Q. What color?

A. Black.

Q. Will you give them to the officer?

A. Yes.

Q. Where are they?

A. At home.

Q. What stockings did you have on that day?

A. Black.

Q. Where are they?

A. At home.

Q. Have they been washed?

A. I don't know.

Q-78 Q. Will you give them to the officer?

A. Yes, sir.

Q. The window you was at is the window that is nearest the street in the barn?

A. Yes, sir; the west window.

Q. The pears you ate, you got from under the tree in the yard?

A. Yes, sir.

Q. How long were you under the pear tree?

A. I think I was under there very nearly four or five minutes. I stood looking around. I looked up at the pigeon house that they have closed up. It was no more than five minutes, perhaps not as long. I can't say sure.

Q. (Judge Blaisdell) Was this witness on Thursday morning in the front hall or front stairs or front chamber, any part of the front part of the house at all?

Q. What do you say to that?

A. I had to come down the front stairs to get into the kitchen.

Q. When you came down first?

A. Yes, sir.

Q. Were you afterwards?

A. No, sir.

Q. Not at all?

A. Except the few minutes I went up with the clean clothes, and I had to come back again.

Q. That you now say was before Mr. Borden went away?

A. Yes, sir.


## Thursday, August 11, 1892

Q-79 Q. Is there anything you would like to correct in your previous testimony?

A. No, sir.

Q. Did you buy a dress pattern in New Bedford?

A. A dress pattern?

Q. Yes, a dress pattern.

A. I think I did.

Q. Where is it?

A. It is at home.

Q. Where?

A. Where at home?

Q. Please.

A. It is in a trunk.

Q. In your room?

A. No, sir; in the attic.

Q. Not made up?

A. O, no, sir.

Q. Where did you buy it?

A. I don't know the name of the store.

Q. On the principal street there?

A. I think it was on the street that Hutchinson's book store is on. I am not positive.

Q-80 Q. What kind of a one was it, please?

A. It was a pink stripe and a white stripe, and a blue stripe corded gingham.

Q. Your attention has already been called to the circumstance of going into the drug store of Smith's, on the corner of Columbia and Main streets, by some officer, has it not, on the day before the tragedy?

A. I don't know whether some officer has asked me, somebody has spoke of it to me; I don't know who it was.

Q. Did that take place?

A. It did not.

Q. Do you know where the drug store is?

A. I don't.

Q. Did you go into any drug store and inquire for prussic acid?

A. I did not.

Q. Where were you on Wednesday morning that you remember?

A. At home.

Q. All the time?

A. All day, until Wednesday night.

Q. Nobody there but your parents and yourself and the servant?

A. Why, Mr. Morse came sometime in the afternoon, or at noon time, I suppose, I did not see him.

Q. He did not come so to see you?

A. No, sir, I did not see him.

Q. He did not come until afternoon anyway, did he?

A. I don't think he did; I am not sure.

Q-81  Q. Did you dine with the family that day?

A. I was down stairs, yes, sir. I did not eat any breakfast with them.

Q. Did you go into the drug store for any purpose whatever?

A. I did not.

Q. I think you said yesterday that you did not go into the room where your father lay, after he was killed, on the sofa, but only looked in at the door?

A. I looked in; I did not go in.

Q. You did not step into the room at all?

A. I did not.

Q. Did you ever, after your mother was found killed, go into that room?

A. No, sir.

Q. Did you afterwards go into the room where your father was found killed, any more than to go through it to go up stairs?

A. When they took me up stairs they took me through that room.

Q. Otherwise than that did you go into it?

A. No, sir.

Q. Let me refresh your memory. You came down in the night to get some water with Miss Russell, along towards night, or in the evening, to get some water with Miss Russell?

A. Thursday night? I don't remember it.

Q. Don't you remember coming down sometime to get some toilet water?

A. No, sir, there was no toilet water down stairs.

Q. Or to empty the slops?

A. I don't know whether I did Thursday evening or not. I am not sure.

Q-82 Q. You think it may have been some other evening?

A. I don't remember coming down with her to do such a thing. I may have, I can't tell whether it was Thursday evening or any other evening.

Q. Other than that, if that did take place, you don't recollect going into that room for any purpose at any time?

A. No, sir.

Q. Was the dress that was given to the officers the same dress that you wore that morning?

A. Yes, sir.

Q. The India silk?

A. No, it is not an India silk. It is silk and linen; some call it bengaline silk.

Q. Something like that dress there? (Pongee.)

A. No, it was not like that.

Q. Did you give to the officer the same shoes and stockings that you wore?

A. I did, sir.

Q. Do you remember where you took them off?

A. I wore the shoes even after that, all around the house Friday, and Saturday until I put on my shoes for the street.

Q. That is to say you wore them all that day, Thursday, until you took them off for the night?

A. Yes, sir.

Q. Did you tell us yesterday all the errand that you had at the barn?

A. Yes, sir.

Q. You have nothing to add to what you said?

A. No, sir.

Q-83 Q. You had no other errand than when you have spoken of?

A. No, sir.

Q. Miss Borden, of course you appreciate the anxiety that everybody has to find the author of this tragedy, and the questions that I put to you have been in that direction; I now ask you if you can furnish any other fact, or give any other, even suspicion, that will assist the officers in any way in this matter?

A. About two weeks ago—

Q. Was you going to tell the occurrence about the man that called at the house?

A. No, sir. It was after my sister went away. I came home from Miss Russell's one night, and as I came up, I always glanced towards the side door as I came along by the carriage way, I saw a shadow on the side steps. I did not stop walking, but I walked slower. Somebody ran down the steps, around the east end of the house. I thought it was a man, because I saw no skirts, and I was frightened, and of course I did not go around to see. I hurried to the front door as fast as I could and locked it.

Q. What time of night was that?

A. I think about quarter of 9; it was not after 9 o'clock, anyway.

Q. Do you remember what night that was?

A. No, sir; I don't. I saw somebody run around the house once before last winter.

Q. One thing at a time. Do you recollect about how long ago that last occurrence was?

A. It was after my sister went away. She has been away two weeks today, so it must have been within two weeks.

Q. Two weeks today? Or two weeks at the time of the murder?

A. Is not today Thursday?

Q. Yes, but I thought you said she was gone two weeks the day of the murder?

A. Is not today Thursday?

Q. Yes, but that would be three weeks; I thought you said the day your father was murdered she had been away just two weeks?

A. Yes, she had.

Q. Then it would be three weeks today—your sister went away, a week has elapsed?

A. Yes, I had forgotten that a whole week had passed since the affair.

Q-84 Q. Different from that you cannot state?

A. No, sir; I don't know what the date was.

Q. This form when you first saw it was on the steps of the back-door?

A. Yes, sir.

Q. Went down the rear steps?

A. Went down towards the barn.

Q. Around the back side of the house?

A. Disappeared in the dark; I don't know where they went.

Q. Have you ever mentioned that before?

A. Yes, sir; I told Mr. Jennings.

Q. To any officer?

A. I don't think I have, unless I told Mr. Hanscom.

Q. What was you going to say about last winter?

A. Last winter when I was coming home from church one Thursday evening, I saw somebody run around the house again. I told my father of that.

Q. Did you tell your father of this last one?

A. No, sir.

Q. Of course you could not identify who it was either time?

A. No, I could not identify who it was, but it was not a very tall person.

Q. Have you sealskin sacks?

A. Yes, sir.

Q-85  Q. Where are they?

A. Hanging in a large white bag in the attic, each one separate.

Q. Put away for the summer?

A. Yes, sir.

Q. Do you ever use prussic acid on your sacks?

A. Acid? No, sir; I don't use anything on them.

Q. Is there anything else that you can suggest that even amounts to anything whatever?

A. I know of nothing else, except the man who came, and father ordered him out, that is all I know.

Q. That you told about the other day?

A. I think I did; yes, sir.

Q. You have not been able to find that man?

A. I have not; I don't know whether anybody else has or not.

Q. Have you caused search to be made for him?

A. Yes, sir.

Q. When was the offer of reward made for the detection of the criminals?

A. I think it was made Friday.

Q. Who suggested that?

A. We suggested it ourselves, and asked Mr. Buck if he did not think it was a good plan.

Q. Whose suggestion was it, yours on Emma's?

A. I don't remember. I think it was mine.

# Bibliography

Lincoln, Victoria. *A Private Disgrace*. New York: G. P. Putnam's Sons, 1967.

Lyons, Louis M. *One Hundred Years of the Boston Globe*. Cambridge, Massachusetts: Belknap Press of Harvard University, 1971.

Pearson, Edmund. *Trial of Lizzie Borden*. New York: Doubleday, 1937.

Phillips, Arthur S. *The Phillips History of Fall River*. Fascicles I, III. Fall River, Massachusetts: Dover Press, 1944–1946.

Porter, Edwin H. *The Fall River Tragedy*. Fall River, Massachusetts: J. D. Munroe, 1893.

Sullivan, Robert. *Goodbye Lizzie Borden*. Brattleboro, Vermont: The Stephen Greene Press, 1974.

Williams, Smithburn, and Peterson. *Lizzie Borden: A Case Book of Family and Crime in the 1890s*. Bloomington, Indiana: T. I. S. Publications Division, Indiana University, 1980.

# Index

In the following index, not every reference to certain key figures in the Borden case is cited. Miss Lizzie Borden, for instance, is the subject of almost every page and could fill an index of her own. Others also appear on most pages, yet others just once. What follows, therefore, is a listing of all the minor players as they appear and the major characters when what they said or did was of paramount or measurable importance to the case. Major contributions made by each are in *italics*. Photos and sketches are in **bold** type and set at the end of their entries.

# LIZZIE BORDEN

Botas Valley State Bank, Hastings, Iowa, 58
Bowen, Dr. Seabury W., 14, 42, 62, 70, 85, 104, 126, 149–51, 159, *163–74*, 215, 323; **86, 165**
Bowen, Phoebe (Mrs. Dr. Seabury), 138, 149, 165, 173, 196
Bowles, Tom, 157, 165
Brayton, Mr. and Mrs. Hezekiah, 282–83
Brigham, Mary (Mrs. George), 67
Brigham, Mrs. Florence Cook, 95, 106
Bristol County, Massachusetts, 108, 140, 260
Bristol County Registry of Deeds, 301
Brown, Everett, 262
Brownell's, 42, 167
Buck, Dr., 304–05
Buffington, Mrs. E. P. (widow of former mayor), 157, 192
Burrels, John T., 75, 250
Burroughs, Frank, 104–05

Central Congregational Church, 54, 121
Chagnon, Dr., 35, 72–3, 200, 262
Chagnon, Marienne, 72, 223, 261
Chagnon, Martha, 72, 223, 261
Chase, Mark P., 262, 317
Churchill Adelaide, 35–7, 74, 126, 150, 154, *157–61*, 199, 223, 268
Clarkson, Alfred, 224, 262
Cleeg, Jonathan, 75–6
Cook, Charles C., 114, 116
Cook, Everett, 75, 250
Coolidge, W. W., 310
Cooney, Delia, 303
Correiro, Manuel Jośe, *243–44*, 307–08, 324
Coughlin, Honorable Dr. John W., 92, 108, 109, 234
Crystal Spring Bleachery, 120
Cunningham, John, 159, 192–93

Dartmouth, Massachusetts, 112, 115–17
Davidson, Mr. and Mrs., 57
Davis, John F., 304–05, 308
Davis, William, 114, 117
Department of Mental Health, Commonwealth of Massachusetts (Taunton Insane Asylum), 303, 308, 310, 322
Desmond, Captain Dennis, 63, 252
Devine, Officer John, 251
Dewey, Honorable Justin, 246, *275–80*
Dighton Rock, 288
Doherty, Officer Patrick H. (later Captain), 63, 90–1, 157, 192, 200, *204*
Dolan, Dr. William A., 104, 108, 181, 197–98, 211–12, 234, 240, 243, 252, 260

Donnelly, John, *221*
Durfee, Colonel Joseph, 30, 31
Durfee, Mary A., 262

Eagan, Ellan, *19–25, 84–92, 287–300,* 321; **293, 297**
Eagan, Mary, 19, *287–300*
East Taunton, Massachusetts, 288, 308–09
Eddy, Mr., 204
Emery, Annie, 180
Emery, Mr. and Mrs. Daniel, 178–81

Fairhaven, Massachusetts, 41, 112
Fall River *Daily Globe*, 31, 34, 105, 140, 190
Fall River *Herald-News*, 34, 73, 310–11
Fall River Historical Society Museum, 95, 97, 106, 254
Fall River, Massachusetts, 11, *29–35,* 107, 301; **28, 77**
First National Bank, 75
Fleet, Assistant Marshal John, 63, 208–11, 251–54, 268
Flint, Samuel, 167, 169
Flint Village, 83
Flynn, Robert (Flynn Books), 106

Gammons, Lewis B., 316
Gammons, Rebecca Frances (see Borden, Mrs. William), 316
Gerung, Honorable L. G., 57
Gifford, Charles N., 262
grand jury, 98–9, 238–39
Gray, Oliver, 46
Greeley, Horace, 55
Green, Minnie, 153
Grouard, John W., 261

Hall's Stable, 159
Handy, Dr. Benjamin, 83, 86, 87, 91, 222, 228, 243, 317
Hanscom, Pinkerton Detective Superintendent O. M., 56, 241–42
Harrington, Hiram C., 117–22, 126, 130, 182, 321, 323
Harrington, Lauanna (or Laurana) (Mrs. Hiram C.), 117
Harrington, Officer Phillip (later Captain), 63, 66, 89, 90, *213–18*, 321
Hart, Abram G., 75, 116, 250
Hart, Sarah, 223
Harte, Frederick B., 66–8, 126, 232, 258
Harvard University, 211–12
Hastings, Iowa, 56, 242
hatchet, the handleless, 251–54; **253**
Hathaway, Inspector Frank, 114, 115, 117
Hathaway, Nathaniel, 259

380